DATE DUE			

WEST CAMPUS

GAYLORD

Tiananmen Moon

Tiananmen Moon

Inside the Chinese Student Uprising of 1989

Philip J Cunningham

ROWMAN & LITTLEFIELD PUBLISHERS, INC.

Lanham • Boulder • New York • Toronto • Plymouth, UK

ROWMAN & LITTLEFIELD PUBLISHERS, INC.

Published in the United States of America
by Rowman & Littlefield Publishers, Inc.
A wholly owned subsidiary of The Rowman & Littlefield Publishing Group, Inc.
4501 Forbes Boulevard, Suite 200, Lanham, Maryland 20706
www.rowmanlittlefield.com

Estover Road, Plymouth PL6 7PY, United Kingdom

British Library Cataloguing in Publication Information Available

Library of Congress Cataloging-in-Publication Data

Cunningham, Philip J
  Tiananmen moon : inside the Chinese student uprising of 1989 /
Philip J Cunningham.
      p. cm. — (Asian voices)
  Includes index.
  ISBN 978-0-7425-6672-9 (cloth) — ISBN 978-0-7425-6674-3 (electronic)
  1. China—History—Tiananmen Square Incident, 1989. 2. College students—
China—Beijing—Biography. 3. Student movements—China—Beijing—History—20th
century. 4. Beijing (China)—Biography. 5. Tian'an Men (Beijing, China)—History—
20th century. 6. Beijing (China)—Social life and customs—20th century. 7. Foreign
correspondents—China—Beijing—History—20th century. 8. China—History—
Tiananmen Square Incident, 1989—Press coverage. I. Title.
  DS779.32.C867 2009
  951.05'8—dc22

                              2009005168

Printed in the United States of America

∞™ The paper used in this publication meets the minimum requirements of American
National Standard for Information Sciences—Permanence of Paper for Printed Library
Materials, ANSI/NISO Z39.48-1992.

Contents

Part III   Waning Moon

Part IV   No Moon

Preface

If getting caught up in a popular uprising in China has taught me anything, it is that the past, present, and future flow together as one with ferocious intensity. Looking back now at the eventful uprising at Tiananmen Square in Beijing in 1989 makes it all the more clear that what happened there was shaped by things that came before. Today's China, basking in a post-Olympic glow and newfound national strength, is still profoundly haunted by the seminal events of 1989, though the topic is strictly taboo in the media and still feared by influential people in the leadership.

I initially got involved in the demonstrations because of my interest in Chinese history, the abstract study of which I had pursued at college and in graduate school. Then I moved to China. Trying to be a little more Chinese and a little less foreign, I immersed myself in Beijing campus life and cultural activities, mostly with Chinese friends. In the time it takes for a new moon to grow full and then wane back into blackness again, I was pulled so deeply into the vortex of living, breathing history in the making that my life would never be the same.

More than any history book I ever read, or any period film I ever worked on, being on the streets of Beijing as history was being made was the most profoundly moving and eye-opening experience of all.

The Tiananmen demonstrations were crushed, cruelly, breaking the implicit pact that the People's Liberation Army would never turn its guns on the people and burying student activism for many years to come, but not before inspiring millions in China and around the world to push for reform and change, heralding the fall of Communism in Eastern Europe and the Soviet Union. The uprising at Tiananmen, though highly controversial in China to this day, would shape many of the choices of the Chinese leadership and has been an unacknowledged inspiration for much of the change that has swept China ever since.

While residing on a Beijing campus in the late 1980s, I found myself up against the rigid social rules, regulations, and racial exclusions that dampened the joy of living in an otherwise cordial and engaging environment. In times of stress, I found cycling to Beijing's most central location a great way to get away from it all. Especially memorable was a bitterly cold winter night in early 1987 when I discovered the beauty of Tiananmen in the moonlight.

The evening started at a local dance hall. I had bicycled there in the company of someone I was fond of but didn't get to see often. She and I happily danced the night away, sipping nothing more potent than orange soda pop, every fast dance followed by a slow one, as mandated by the cultural commissars of the time, until 11:00 p.m., when we raced back to campus to beat curfew. We got through the side gate of the Shida campus without trouble, but by the time we reached our respective dorms they were closed for the night, padlocked shut.

Afraid that waking up the guards would bring unwanted attention to our late night tryst, we got back on our bikes and plunged back into the inky blackness of Beijing. We cycled up and down empty windswept streets, breathing steamy breaths, working up a sweat despite the winter chill. Hotels, which had convoluted rules about who qualified to register for a room, were not a serious option. The cold night air, cold as it was, was far more welcoming.

Gliding down quiet boulevards in the quiet of the night proved unexpectedly invigorating. Having nowhere to go gave us a vicarious sensation of freedom, the feeling that by keeping on the move, we could avoid the inevitable walls and guarded gateways. When the cold got unbearable, we huddled at a makeshift noodle stand that was throwing up clouds of steam into the frigid night sky. We did our best to be unobtrusive, quietly slurping on noodles on a bench in the company of burly, chain-smoking truck drivers whose view of an exotic interracial coupling was probably not too different from that of a hotel clerk, except they seemed to be cheering us on. There was no heat in the noodle shack to speak of, other than vats of boiling liquid, but the hot air and general merriment of the earthy drivers helped warm things up a bit.

From there we ventured back out into the cold to cycle up and down Beijing's main east-west thoroughfare of Chang'an Boulevard under a brilliant full moon. It was so cold and clear and bright that the moonlight could be mistaken for a thin coat of snow on the pavement.

Beijing was a city of few lights, so the great glowing lamp in the frozen sky was our only guide. We followed the moon the length of Chang'an Boulevard, or perhaps I should say it followed us. When we got to Tiananmen Square there was not a person in sight, just a sea of flagstones reflecting an ethereal glow. The monumental buildings that surround the square were monochrome monoliths, squat tombstones boxing in the luminous diamond-studded sky.

We parked our bikes and lay down in the middle of the square, staring at the moon straight above. It was so quiet and isolated we could have been in the middle of the Gobi Desert. Huddling close for warmth, we whispered, joked, and told stories. It was the most intimate moment we had ever had. Inspired by the impossibility of our togetherness, I made up a song, which went like this:

> Midnight moon of Tiananmen,
> When will I see you again?
> Looking for you everywhere,
> Going in circles around the square . . .
> Riding with you down Chang'an Jie,
> Memories I'd like to share . . .
> Shadows dancing in the dark,
> Lovers talking in the park . . .
> Follow you here,
> Follow you there,
> Bathing in you
> Sweet moonlight everywhere . . .
> Midnight moon of Tiananmen,
> When will I see you again?

Our midnight reverie ended abruptly when a team of policemen patrolling on bicycle spotted two unauthorized bodies napping on the ground near the central monument and ordered us to leave. We did so reluctantly, going in a big sweeping circle around the square to demonstrate our attachment to the location. The memory lingers, the two of us huddled together on a bitterly cold night under a towering sky so vast that it brought to mind a boundless universe.

A few months after our midnight ride, I was a guest on *English on Sunday*, a national radio program produced at the massive Soviet-style headquarters of China Central Broadcasting. The bilingual host of the program, Shen Baoqing, graciously asked me if she could use the lyrics of my song in one of her English publications. We got in a discussion about Tiananmen and we went over the words I had written in English and Chinese. She invited her boss, the branch secretary of the Communist Party, to discuss it with us.

"Well, it's very nice," he said, pausing to grimace. "But, tell me, why do you use such dark images, the moon, night?" he asked. "We Chinese associate Tiananmen with brightness, with the sun!"

"My gracious, he couldn't very well use the sun," Shen Baoqing offered helpfully. "The sun over Tiananmen might be mistaken for Mao."

Not surprisingly, the branch secretary got the last word. "The song should be more positive," he said. "For example, why not change it to 'Under the blue skies of Tiananmen'? It's a much better line."

Not long after that, I rode my bike back to Beijing Normal University under an intensely gray, overcast sky, which I took note of because it accorded so well with my cloudy mood on that particular day. When I watched the evening news that night on China Central Television (CCTV), I heard the announcer repeat a familiar line: "And today there was glorious celebration in the Great Hall of the People," the voice intoned earnestly, "under the blue skies of Tiananmen."

The Chinese belief in the incantatory power of words is such that saying something often enough is almost enough to make it seem almost true. This has to be one of the motivations for all the lies that have been told about Tiananmen since 1989. Much of what the Beijing authorities have repeatedly said about the "counterrevolutionary riots at Tiananmen" is not true, and they do not believe it, even though they must pretend to. Perhaps worse yet, worse than the devious sloganeering that became so counterproductive it was quietly abandoned, was the subsequent silence, a soul-chilling silence that only gets louder with each passing year.

I have written this book to challenge that silence. It is a personal account, at once subjective and idiosyncratic, partial and incomplete, but it aspires to elucidate what modest truth might reside in subjectivity. It is the story of a serendipitous traveler finding himself on the inside of a major uprising, marching shoulder to shoulder with young Beijing rebels and sleeping on Tiananmen Square under the open sky. It is the story of the friendship between a foreign student and his local friends at a time of great upheaval. There are shocking discoveries and humorous asides, journalistic scoops and partisan advocacy, resulting in police troubles and political intrigue. It is also a love story, the chronicle of an affection that speaks to the love of a people, and also a tragedy, for that love ends in heartbreak when the people's dream is destroyed.

Looking back on the one-month period covered by this memoir, it is striking how often the mood on the ground corresponded to the movements of the moon in the sky, though few of us were fully conscious of it at the time.

The full moon over Tiananmen marked the lyrical and literal apogee of the peaceful protests in May 1989, when the citizens of Beijing flocked to Tiananmen Square a million strong to celebrate what was hoped would be a brilliant new chapter of Chinese history. The demonstrations faltered and stalled out as the moon began to withdraw its protective nighttime illumination, while the army delayed its crackdown till the darkest night of the month, the night of no moon. *Tiananmen Moon* is divided into four sections reflecting the ebb and flow of the lunar illumination that fateful month.

The narrative that follows is a testament to the beauty and wonder of a popular uprising that went better than anyone had a right to expect before tragically going awry. It is a commemoration of all who ever marched in peaceful protest, engaged in civil disobedience, or waved the banner of rebellion and sang songs evoking the eternal hope of building a better tomorrow.

The story starts out at Tiananmen under skies that were truly blue, skies that eventually clouded up and turned to gray. More startling, though, is the transformation of Tiananmen, which in the course of a few weeks went from being the grandiose place that deserved nothing less than an arching blue sky to a synonym for cruelty, from a talismanic word to a search engine taboo, from a monument dedicated to remembering past glory to a memory-draining black hole in the heart of Beijing.

This book is dedicated to the wonderful things that once were, and to all the residents of Beijing who took part in the protests of 1989, most especially to those martyred souls who didn't live to see the fruits of their great sacrifice.

Introduction

Looking for the Real China

Blame it on studying Chinese history. On May 3, 1989, I find myself wandering Tiananmen Square wondering why May Fourth—an iconic date in the Communist calendar commemorating the bold student demonstrations of May 4, 1919—is being celebrated a day early.

Today the skies over Tiananmen are not just blue, but cobalt blue, although a few clouds dot the western horizon. There are scattered groups of sightseers on the square, most of whom, judging from the padded clothes, the antiquated box cameras, and the trails of watermelon seeds, have just arrived by train from the provinces and are in town to see one of the must-see sights of a lifetime.

There is also some hustle and bustle near the front of the Great Hall of the People, where a number of spotless chauffeur-driven cars are parked. Neatly dressed young men and women come streaming out of the Great Hall, descending the front steps in groups of two and three, beaming happily like model workers from a propaganda magazine about the good life in socialist China.

Is this the so-called May Fourth celebration? I know there is a meeting of the Asian Development Bank slated for May 4, so perhaps the Great Hall will not be available for young Communists and Communists-to-be to gather in celebration of their bold predecessors, even though tomorrow marks the seventieth anniversary. Maybe it is a sign of the times that a bank meeting outranks one of China's most treasured political anniversaries. Still, there is ample reason to believe the Communist authorities are not looking for a boisterous, well-attended May Fourth commemoration on the square, officially sanctioned or otherwise.

"*Ni hao!* Could someone tell me what's going on?" I try to get the attention of the first cluster of well-groomed socialist poster boys and girls coming my way, but they walk right by without a blink.

No answer, huh? That happens to foreigners speaking Chinese sometimes; it does not compute. Oh, did I say something? Did they not hear me, see me? Had I been rendered invisible by the blue skies of Tiananmen in their mind? Did my faltering, accented speech lack all resonance compared to the soaring rhetoric of the paeans to nationalism just heard inside the Great Hall?

Maybe I ought to smile and speak louder.

"Hi! Hello there! *Ni hao!*" I shout. "Oh, hello! Where are you all going?"

"Home!" mutters one young person in passing.

"Where are you all coming from?" I am fumbling for words; it's my fault, really. Stupid questions beg for stupid answers.

"Bye!" says a pert flower of the official May Fourth youth contingent. Then they are gone.

I try to restore my battered confidence by feigning ignorance to the next group of socialist dream builders exiting the Great Hall.

"Excuse me! What was the meeting about?" I venture.

"Communist Youth League," the first one answers. "The May Fourth celebration!" cheerfully exclaims the second.

"Party Secretary Zhao Ziyang. We saw him, the party secretary!" the first girl adds, beaming with pride. "It's May Fourth."

"But today is May third," I point out, at the risk of dashing what tenuous rapport had been established. "The real May Fourth is tomorrow, is it not? Isn't there going to be a march or something?"

"Tomorrow? There's no rally tomorrow!"

"Yes there is," counters one of them, conspiratorially eyeing her comrade before finishing her line of thought. "But, that doesn't count. That's the illegal rally."

"Today might only be the third," concludes her friend, as if anxious to move on. "But it's the real Fourth." And with that bit of inspired logic, the two of them look at each other, giggle, and then walk away, leaving me standing on the steps alone.

I took a bus back to Beijing Normal University, which everyone called Shida in the interest of brevity. While rummaging around for my bicycle, which some overly conscientious guard, responding to new regulations in response to the stirrings of "chaos," had put into a locked pen near the foreign student dorm, I ran into Ling Shuying, a friend from Japan who had first arrived at Shida about the same time I did in 1986. We shared the distinction, or should I say the stigma, of being fellow residents of the Beijing Normal University Insider Guest House, an "internal" residence hall that was something of a cross between a Chinese-only dorm and a foreigner-only dorm.

My fellow "insider" Ling Shuying was a case in point. She wasn't permitted to stay in the foreign student dorm for "real" foreign students, even though she was born and brought up in Tokyo, because she was technically a Chinese passport holder, a peculiar bureaucratic disposition not uncommon among ethnic Chinese long resident in Japan. By the same token, she wasn't Chinese enough to stay in the dorm for "real" Chinese students.

Then there was the crusty, gray-bearded Russian researcher who university authorities couldn't figure out where to place. He was foreign in a way that was alien from the American and Japanese kids who dominated the foreign dorm, so he too was assigned a room in the Insider Guest House. And then there was my guitar-playing, instant coffee–swilling buddy Nokura Kuniyoshi, a slightly contrary young Japanese businessman who held a foreign passport, but had a guarantor at the university and a special arrangement like I did, permitting him to reside in limbo, despite not being Chinese and not being a registered student. Everyone else was Chinese, but not from Shida, mostly visiting researchers. And of course the facilities were Chinese-grade, meaning no hot water and no bathing facilities.

As Ling and I strolled across campus on our way to the Insider Guest House, we got talking about May Fourth—whether or not the real Fourth could be on the third—and wondering about the Autonomous Federation of Students who had recently formed as an alternative to the party-controlled student groups, like the happy campers I saw at the Great Hall. We ended up gravitating to one of the informal "democracy walls" that had recently sprouted up on campus to view the latest screeds.

LET'S ORGANIZE DEMOCRACY SALONS!

IT IS MY HOPE THE AUTONOMOUS FEDERATION WILL LISTEN TO US

I SAY THE MOST IMPORTANT THING IS TO DEVELOP DEMOCRACY ON CAMPUS

LET'S SPEAK OUR MINDS FREELY

Until recently, most of the student posters that could be found on campus, pasted onto walls with or without permission, were handbills and flyers about upcoming dances, drama productions, and club activities. Then there were the official bulletin boards erected and maintained by school authorities, authorized messages stamped and approved and locked behind glass cases, mostly unremarkable news items laced with rote propaganda. Newspapers like the *People's Daily* were exhibited in a similar fashion.

The biggest of the informal democracy walls was right across from the Insider Guest House. Given the central location and the ceaseless foot traffic in an area which boasted the campus shop, the post office, a tiny branch of the Xinhua bookstore, three food halls, the hot water shack, and the campus baths, the long unadorned wall which ran along the side of the girls' dorm was a great place to post messages.

SUPPORT THE AUTONOMOUS FEDERATION SO AS TO PROPAGATE DEMOCRACY AND FREEDOM

DON'T LISTEN TO THE AUTONOMOUS FEDERATION, WHO DO THEY THINK THEY ARE?

The footpath saw considerable traffic on regular days but today it was all a tangle. The gray brick walls of the girls' dorm were covered from top to bottom with hand-written posters, the day's bulletins freshly pasted on top of the tattered remnants of yesterday's news.

"HOW MUCH LONGER CAN WE GO ON LIKE THIS?" entreated a poster citing corruption as the key. The ink-brushed illustration showed a mop-haired scholar in tattered clothes bearing the weight of a fat bald official on his back, loaded down with a TV set, a sexy female, loose cash, and a club.

A short distance away there was a similar profusion of political manifestos pasted on the wall of the hot water shack, the campus equivalent of the village well.

Every student visited this condensation-soaked, steam-blowing shack at least once a day to fill a thermos with scalding hot water. It was more than a place to replenish a day's supply of drinking water, which bubbled out of the tap hot enough to make tea, but also a place to find out the latest news and gossip. Like the dorm wall, the outside wall of the hot water shack was so aggressively plastered with posters, original poetry, and strident pronouncements that one would have to visit several times a day to keep up.

Ling and I skirted the crush to scan the latest posters, closing in on a promising stretch of wall to study. Reading was difficult enough for us foreigners, given the diverse styles of calligraphy, but getting a clear line of sight was thwarted by the determination of students in front not to budge until they had jotted down, word for word, a personal copy of the inspiring poems and provocative messages, all the more precious for their papery transience. Some of them riffed on the contrast of the original May Fourth and this year's anniversary.

ANOTHER 70 YEARS?

DEMOCRACY AND SCIENCE

I knew about the once fervid hopes invested in "Mr. Science" and "Mr. Democracy" from my study of republican China, but there was stuff about princelings too, not of the Qing Dynasty but of the Communist Party. There was a vicarious thrill in seeing critiques alleging nepotism and corruption in high places, veiled criticisms of the Communists in power if not the system itself. Then there'd be a poster calling for a student strike, partially covered up by another poster saying the activist students were fools, which in turn was covered up by an even more strident call to strike.

Certain repetitive buzzwords started to emerge from the mass of messily written polemics.

WE DEMAND DIALOGUE

REVERSE THE VERDICT OF THE APRIL 26 EDITORIAL

EXPOSE THE SECRET PRIVILEGES OF HIGH LEADERS

I stepped back a bit to remove myself from the scrum of earnest scribes when I sensed someone was watching me. I turned around and there she was, a beautiful someone, a someone I wanted to see. Someone I would like to have seen more often, and would have seen more often had she not imposed strict limits on the terms of our interaction with the words, "I can't. This is China."

"Jin Peili!" she called me by my Chinese name, beaming.

"Bright," I answered, using her nickname. We looked at each other and couldn't stop smiling. She was so willowy and graceful, I felt like hugging her.

But then I thought better of it. Now that things on campus were more politicized than ever, I realized that the need to keep a polite distance, or at least the appearance of such, would be greater than ever.

I looked around to see if we were being observed. In accordance with the low-key paranoia common at the time, I even wondered if there might not be informants and undercover agents in the gathering immediately around us.

Bright's alert eyes required only a quick glance in my direction to understand what I was feeling.

"Don't worry," she said in a reassuring voice, her eyes now smiling. "No problem. It's safe. Things are different now."

"Are you not afraid of being seen with me?"

"Why do you say that?" she said, tugging on my arm playfully.

"Well, you know, the April 27 demo . . . "

"Oh that? It was really exciting. The police pushed and shoved but we broke through, and it was hot, in the sun all day and by the time we got back . . . "

"You what? You, Little Conservative, were in that demo? You?" I asked in disbelief. "That was illegal, wasn't it?"

"Things are really different now. The students, we have more power, China is changing . . . "

So it was, apparently. Bright was changing too. Here was the young woman who had once asked me to pretend not to know her in public places because she didn't want her teachers to know she had a foreign friend. Here was the woman who could effortlessly join the party and become an elite bureaucrat due to her family's top connections.

Just then, Jenny came running over.

"*Aiyo!* It is good to see you," she exclaimed.

"Win any medals lately?" I asked. She loved sports.

"Remember that sandstorm in '87, when the sky turned all yellow and thick with dust?"

"Only Jin Peili would think of bringing the guitar and having a picnic in the middle of a violent dust storm!" laughed Jenny.

We all exchanged some small talk. A foreign student had been killed in a traffic accident; there was a tightening of regulations that put limits on interracial fraternization. Foreign students had been told by their teachers to stay away from the protests or risk expulsion. The bans on fraternization were just the sort of thing that got under my skin and had been the bane of my existence in China. After a burst of student unrest in late 1986 and early 1987, which involved demonstrations in provincial capitals such as Hefei in the central China province of Anhui and in the metropolis of Shanghai, there was a crackdown on interracial relations in the highfalutin name of combating "spiritual pollution" and "bourgeois liberalization," which translated, in simple terms, into police messing with people's personal lives, a sense of which I tried to convey in a film script called *Chinabeat*. A few of my friends read it and liked it; even filmmaker Chen Kaige found it intriguing, especially the irony of family members spying on one another, but all agreed it was too touchy for the moment.

A posse of foreign journalists turned the corner by the hot water shack and came traipsing past us, loaded down with TV cameras, boom microphones, aluminum ladders, and boxes of other gear. I knew a few foreign journalists but a quick glance was enough to tell me I didn't know any of them.

Suddenly I was faced with an old conundrum. Should I say hello to the other foreigners?

In China, especially in settings where foreigners were rare, I often found myself curious about whom the other foreigner might be, but did it really make sense to be friendly to a stranger just because they weren't Chinese? If I saw a white person walking down the street in New York, it is unlikely I would be prompted to say hello, so why here? Why? Just because they're also white?

However, to eschew contact with other foreigners out of "sensitivity" to the feelings of Chinese friends made no sense either, especially since so many Chinese seemed to assume it only natural that the handful of white people resident in Beijing should want to know each other, if they didn't know each other already. After all, isn't that what friendship stores and friendship hotels were all about, creating a habitat where foreign "friends" could be with their own kind?

Bright, Jenny, and Ling Shuying were overly familiar with my misgivings on the topic and immediately started teasing.

"Look, they're your compatriots."

"Why don't you talk to them?"

"Say hi to the *laowai* for me!"

I turned my attention to the retreating journalists, trying to decipher the logos on their gear, wondering what bureau they were from, but by the time I had made up my mind to "talk to my own kind," most of them had passed by, too tired or absorbed in their own thoughts to even notice me. Then on an impulse, to amuse the girls as much as anything else, I decided to approach one of the stragglers in a show of inter-Caucasian solidarity.

"Oh, hi. Hey, how's it goin'?" I offered. "So, what brings you to campus?"

"Eh? Vat you say? I no understand, you see?" The man, evidently European, responded brusquely in an undecipherable accent.

"Never mind," I said, nodding good-bye.

It took Jenny only a brief exchange of whispers with some passing dormmates to get the information I had failed to obtain.

"There was a student press conference for foreign journalists," she explained. "It was in Southwest Dorm, you know, near my old room."

"A press conference in that dorm?" It sounded incongruous, even absurd, given the rundown condition of that particular boys' dorm, where puddles and garbage in the hallways were not an uncommon sight.

"That's where Wuerkaixi lives. You know Wuerkaixi, don't you?" Bright and Jenny smiled knowingly. I'd heard of his reputation as a playboy, but the name drew a blank for our friend from Japan.

"He's just a freshman. He's from Xinjiang, he's a Muslim, from the Uygur minority," Bright explained. "Do you know, he actually has an accent in his Chinese!" Bright looked at me, for she often teased me about my accent. She was trying to make me feel better, or at least less alone.

And she had a point. Foreigners often find common ground with China's minority peoples because they share a common distaste for, and are often victims of, Han Chinese chauvinism. Minority group members, like foreigners, are sometimes given special privileges, but it doesn't begin to make up for the systemic racism that they endure, and unlike foreigners, China is their only home, the People's Republic passport the only traveling papers they can ever hope to acquire.

Wuerkaixi piqued my curiosity. There was something appealingly impudent about him; why, he didn't even go by a Chinese name! I had already surmised he was a master at playing the minority card. He had earned a campus reputation for being outspoken, but sometimes it's easier to be outspoken when you lack normal status and have nothing to lose. He could afford to be different because he was different. In a political culture where the majority group tends to straitjacket itself with a kind of groupthink, there were subtle advantages in being a minority out of the loop.

"There was an article about him in a foreign newspaper," I recalled. "How many students at Shida can say that? And he's got a father in a high position, doesn't he?"

"I don't know," Bright continued, "but he likes to talk big even though he's just a freshman. You know he's in the education department. He has a girlfriend; she always goes with him."

Somehow it made me annoyed and a little jealous to hear Bright talking about someone who spoke Chinese with an accent and who was "always" with his girlfriend on this supposedly puritanical campus. How many times did she make herself scarce with the words "this is China"?

"Let's get something to eat!" I suggested. "How about the Happy Masses?"

The Happy Masses Canteen was a food hall slightly more upscale than the student cafeteria, if only very slightly so. Not only was the food a bit better, but Bright and Jenny would be free from the gaze of fellow students. Happy Masses was luxurious in the sense that it provided dishware and chopsticks, unlike the spartan food hall assembly lines that required one to carry one's own utensils and a metallic bowl into which the servers would slop out generous portions of hot food. On our way there, we passed the hot water shack, which was already jam-packed; the evening rush hour for hot water and the latest round of gossip and hot air had begun.

Beautiful calligraphy was displayed on all four walls of the boxy dining room, but it was hard to appreciate due to the harsh reflection of the overhead fluorescent lights on the glass-covered picture frames. In keeping with the price differential, you only had to stand on line three times—first to purchase your meal coupons, then to order your dishes, and finally to order your drinks—but the lines were short and you didn't have to bring your own utensils and there were usually more than enough seats for everyone to sit down. This was one of the cafeterias frequented by the campus elite, those who had perhaps only pennies more in pocket money, mainly teachers, lowly officials, and graduate students.

One distinctive feature of this eatery was the wooden furniture. Perhaps due to the work of an exuberant or drunken carpenter, the round wooden tables were oversized, rising about a foot higher than usual, well above comfortable elbow height, with the comical result that diners looked like a bunch of kids sitting at a table built for adults. White plastic tablecloths graced the altarlike tables, signaling not only that this was a class institution, but also that one could eat with abandon because the mess was easy to clean up. Beer and orange soda, mostly imbibed from bowls rather than glasses, left puddles and spills all over tables dotted with chicken bones, gristle, and heaps of the other unwanted food matter, a lapse of decorum you wouldn't easily get away with in the student canteen. Was it acceptable to leave a mess because one paid more or was it the other way around?

For the luxury of thoughtful food in this cheerful but thoughtless environment one had to pay twice the price of the student canteen, but even so, a meal could be had for less than a dollar. Like elsewhere on campus, food was purchased with meal coupons rather than cash, but the Happy Masses meal tickets were not interchangeable with either Chinese Canteen meal tickets or Foreign Canteen meal tickets, so I always ended up with a pocketful of incompatible plastic coupons.

After dinner in the hot, noisy, and smoke-filled canteen, we took a walk to reacquaint ourselves with relatively fresh air. Eventually we sat down on a bench outside Southwest Dorm, the same one that had been graced by the foreign journalists a short while ago and which remained unusually agitated, even now. A makeshift public-address (PA) system rigged up by the student activists emitted a non-stop crackle and hiss as self-appointed campus leaders took turns making breathless political statements that mirrored Hot Water Shack announcements.

CONTINUE THE STRIKE!

REMEMBER 5-4

FIGHT CORRUPTION

OPPOSE THE APRIL 26TH *PEOPLE'S DAILY* EDITORIAL

The three of us settled into the comfortable cacophony of the courtyard, watching people come and go by, observing a line of thermos-clutching students snake around the water shack, trying to make sense of the latest posters. Political polemics done up in a fine hand of calligraphy were interspersed with dance and drama announcements on rectangles of colored paper, taking on an artful aspect from where we sat.

The homely soot-stained brick walls of the coal-fired shack concealed a utility most indispensable; it provided sterilized drinking water for thousands. Inside the shack, a dozen spigots fed thirsty thermos bottles while an elongated cement sink contained any scalding spills. When things were going full bore, the inside of the shack was like a steam room, thick with fog.

At twilight the atmosphere on campus became borderline magical. The harsh details of unsightly facilities faded into shadow, the little indignities of the day all but forgotten. In the lingering glow of a spring sunset we watched students dodge in and out of billowing clouds of steam.

Nearby, clusters of socially guarded but physically at-ease students lounged about, memorizing vocabulary, singing pop songs, picking their noses, or just hitching up their trouser legs to enjoy a furtive smoke. In addition to the usual joking around, shouts of laughter, and the constant hum of conversation, there was the crackle of announcements about going on strike and heated political talk. The fact that several hundred people were packed and pressed together in a courtyard the size of a tennis court did not make it seem crowded. Places like this only felt crowded when you were in a rush or didn't want to be around other people.

People accustomed to communal living conditions learn to move with a certain grace and agility. The flow of the water gatherers was joined by a stream of bathers, washbowls, shampoo, and towels in hand, going to and from the campus bath. Just around the corner were the pool-sized bathtubs said to serve over ten thousand bathers daily. The bathhouse generously accommodated a seemingly endless stream of sweaty, sticky, and smelly individuals, only to emit, an hour or so later, an equal number of squeaky clean, rosy-cheeked students with wet hair dripping on towels wrapped around the neck.

Wafts of steam and the scent of shampoo permeated the dusty evening air. Freshly scrubbed students paused to chat on their way back to their congested rooms in nightclothes and pajamas. Campus life was not luxurious by most standards, but the sheer mass synchronicity of little rituals centered around procuring one's daily dose of hot rice, hot water, and a hot shower made for poignant moments.

This evening the mood was grounded in just such habitual rhythms, so calming and restful, but it was also laced with a touch of political idealism; life in China at its best.

PART I

NEW MOON

MAY 3

◖

In Search of the Real China

The night is young. Bright and I decide to visit a friend at his home near the Lama Temple. His place is at least a half-hour bike ride from Shida, so we amble over to the main road to search for a taxi. Cui Jian, a budding rock star, has been on campus a few times, including at the Insider Guest House, where he humored me by playing guitar with me and listening to some of my songs. He is disarmingly quiet but shrewd; it is his own cautious personality as much as the conservative Communist culture that keeps him from getting the big bucks and big head associated with successful rock musicians in the West.

He and fellow band member Liu Yuan had both left the security of performing for a state-sponsored troupe to try their luck on their own. For years, the best they could aspire to was the foreign dance and party circuit. Such events were primarily held within the confines of diplomatic enclaves, such as the International Club, a restaurant in Ritan Park, or at embassy parties. It's not that Chinese didn't like the new music—though it was clear that certain party elders strongly disapproved—but there simply wasn't a club scene or media access for such rugged independents.

As a result, Cui Jian and Liu Yuan, not unlike Chen Kaige and other newly emerging filmmakers and artists, played mainly to a foreign crowd and, if they sometimes tried to please foreign tastes, it was in part an act of artistic survival, as venues for locals barely existed and media access was strictly curtailed. Foreign students, diplomats, and businessmen were the fundamental fan base for a number of Chinese artists in the 1980s, which made it easy

for party hacks and envious contemporaries to ridicule them as being enter-
tainers for foreigners.

When I saw Cui Jian play in London a month earlier, he wore a red headband over his eyes and sang with a passion bordering on anger while Liu Yuan
played his heart out as they performed briefly as part of an Asian music
festival.

I attended the concert at the Royal Albert Hall with David Hinton, a
witty British director who I had collaborated with on the behind-the-scenes
documentary *Bertolucci: The Last Emperor* and subsequently traveled with to
Yunnan, where we watched the Chen Kaige film *King of the Children* until being expelled for not having proper internal travel permits. During my visit to
London he helped edit my *Chinabeat* script while we also met various movie
people such as Zhang Yimou, Zhang Tielin, and Eva Radnowska.

Dave and I hosted a party for Cui Jian, Liu Yuan, and their friend and
guide, Boreana Song, after the concert, and the next day we toured the sights
of London, from Brixton and the South Bank to Chinatown.

Still not a taxi in sight. Depending on the time of day, minutes could lapse
without a single car passing by. Landing a taxi could take half an hour. Bright
and I were standing in the road outside East Gate wondering if we should
have gone by bike when at last a metered car pulled over.

We had the driver let us off at Lama Temple, then crossed to the north
side of the road where there stood several tall housing blocks. Cui Jian's
apartment would have been impossible to find had I not been there before,
but once inside, his modest flat was not just another room in an anonymous
high-rise. Entering his residence was rather more like invading the hidden
lair of an American suburban kid who had decked out his room as an asylum
from the world.

Entering a room decked out in posters and exotic bolts of cloth was comforting and familiar, more like a college dorm room in the States than anything
I had seen in China. Under posters of Stevie Wonder and Sting lay two guitars, boxy stereo speakers, cassette players, tape reels, and mixing equipment.

Our host gestured for us to sit down on a bed draped in Indian-patterned
cloth and put on some music. I almost forgot I was in one of those tacky
housing blocks so typical of socialist China. Then again, people said China
was changing.

As we drank tea, Cui Jian mumbled in rapid-fire Beijing dialect with
Bright, while using a more standard Chinese when addressing me. He seemed
a little more taciturn than usual this evening. I asked him if recent political
tensions were having any effect on his freedom to perform.

"Not really," he said, measuring his words. "But I've got to be careful. I am watched very closely."

"Yeah, what a drag. But you're making progress; you've got your own room now. Nice place," I said, not in the mood for a depressing talk about surveillance. "Only last year you were still living upstairs with your parents."

"It's okay," he said. After a pause, as if weighing whether or not to confide, he launched into a quiet tirade about taxes. "You know the government is on my back about taxes. I have to spend May Fourth at the tax bureau."

Ah, the taxman. Cui Jian was already suffering the financial woes of rock and roll's rich and famous, though he had yet to enjoy the fruits of success.

The conversation turned to music. He had recently finished recording some new material and asked if we would like to listen to it. He put on a tape.

"Jin," he said, using my Chinese name in a natural way, "what do you think of this?"

"Kind of cool, I like the melody," I said. "Yeah, I like the repetitive guitar in that, it has a very Asian sound."

We listened to more music and sipped tea while Cui Jian took a phone call from his band manager. He was invited to meet some people at the Jianguo Hotel, including a music executive visiting from Taiwan, and asked us to come along.

The band manager had a car, so we didn't have to endure an interminable wait for a taxi. He pulled up to the back door in a beat-up jalopy. We all squeezed in, and with a shiver of adventure and foreboding we were off. The car reeked of fumes and vibrated as if ready to fall apart, but it was a novelty to be on wheels not under government control.

We entered the Jianguo Hotel through revolving doors, stepping into an intimate lobby that was a popular meeting place for foreign businessmen and reporters. The smallest and most practical of Beijing's overpriced hotels for foreigners, the Jianguo was said to be "slipping" since it had recently reverted back to Chinese management. Nonetheless it still looked like a Holiday Inn and even had lounge music, but instead of an over-the-hill crooner there was a gowned graduate from the Central Conservatory of Music playing challenging classical tunes on the piano. A focal point for expatriate life for over five years, the Jianguo was the first hotel permitted to allow Chinese visitors to enter without signing in.

Due to the unique registration-free visiting policy, the lobby was home to various plainclothes agents, some of them quite obvious, sitting around smoking all day in the corner, with a brief to monitor illicit Chinese-foreign interactions.

Cui Jian's manager told the guard the room number and we were let upstairs without further question. We were greeted at the door by Lao Ni, described as a record producer from Taiwan and agent for Chyi Chin, a Taiwan rocker who was popular on the mainland. Lao Ni welcomed us into an ordinary hotel room that had been transformed into something of a salon by his guests. Several conversations, intense and intelligent, were taking place simultaneously, but there were also some guys just lounging around, comfortably slouched in chairs and sprawled out on the twin beds with an almost comical lack of concern for appearances. Our arrival went almost unnoticed as various discussions progressed under a veil of cigarette smoke. Bright, Cui Jian, and I were invited to sit on one of the beds, sending its previous occupant looking for an alternate place to recline. We just sat there watching, soaking up the alcohol-enhanced talk with quiet amusement.

I liked Lao Ni right away. He spoke the Chinese I learned in the classroom, crystal-clear Mandarin softened by just a touch of Taiwan accent. He could speak some Japanese as well, asking me about the Japan pop music scene when he learned that I spent some time in Tokyo. He had a slightly formal bearing, perhaps appropriate to his status as a respected businessman, but he was free of pretension, not averse to trying new things. One of his schemes was to get Chyi Chin, whose song "Wolf" was immensely popular, to come and tour in China while arranging something of a reciprocal visit for Cui Jian to perform in Taiwan.

That such a thing could even be discussed was a testament to how much China had liberalized since 1983, when Taiwan pop music had been banned and denounced as "spiritual pollution." To think that musicians might travel back and forth now!

And that wasn't all. Right here in the hotel room of a Taiwan businessman, one could hear freewheeling political talk by men from both sides of the straits. The TV, which had been left on as background noise, suddenly became the focus of attention when a news bulletin showed Yuan Mu, a long-faced Beijing government spokesman, talking on camera. Someone turned the sound up. Just the sound of the man's voice was enough to invite a long string of boos and loud hisses.

Yuan Mu was shown talking to a small group of students and journalists in what was being billed as "dialogue," presumably showing that the government was responsive and willing to meet the protesters halfway. Not everyone was convinced.

"Dialogue? Dialogue my ass," said one of the guests with a Beijing accent.

"Those students, just look at 'em! What a joke! Definitely hand-picked by the government," said a very fast-tongued man nicknamed Black Horse. "Just look at those goody two-shoes!"

"And if you ask me, Yuan Mu looks like a fox. Look at that face, what a liar!"

"So condescending . . . "

When the news bulletin ended, Black Horse got up to do some impersonations. First off, he made a show of talking and acting like former party chief Hu Yaobang. Here was none of the reverence, real or manufactured, that student activists showed for the dead leader. Rather, Hu became the butt of playful jokes based on snippets of real incidents, such as how all Chinese should eat with forks and all Japanese should come study in China. That was fair game, but what really got the rest of the room quiet, and more deeply on edge, was a caustic imitation of top leader Deng Xiaoping. Black Horse had a knack for acting and mimicking speech patterns down to the regional accent, but it was his irreverence that so electrified this select audience.

"More, more!" Having thrilled us by lancing political taboos, by speaking the unspeakable out loud in a performance so amusing, he was egged on for an encore.

"And did you hear the one about Hu Yaobang and Li Peng?"

A few minutes later, just when Black Horse had everybody buckled over laughing and he could finally take a breather, he suddenly got half serious, looked around, and said, "I hope none of you work for Public Security or I'm finished."

For a fleeting moment Black Horse had scared all of us into complete silence. Then he flashed a smile and continued, "And this man, why this man is supposed to be the leader of a country of one billion, and look at him, he is so short! Why, he looked like a little kid standing next to Reagan!"

If Black Horse was scared, he masked it well. He had an irrepressible wit and couldn't help himself, and we were grateful for it. His jokes had effectively broken the ice. Soon everyone started talking about the recent unrest and wondered if the rumored May Fourth demo would take place tomorrow.

"Only one way to find out," announced Black Horse, gaining an attentive silence. "Anyone want to take a ride to Beida?"

The Beijing University campus was clear across town, a long ride even by car. At first we thought he was joking, but he wasn't, and soon he was counting hands for a ride on the wild side.

Bright looked at her watch. It was already midnight. Campus curfew long since violated, she said she had better go home to her parents' compound.

We saw her off in front of the hotel where she got a taxi, ignoring the not-so-subtle invitations from some of the more inebriated men present.

It was a little past midnight by the time Cui Jian, Lao Ni, and a few others crammed into the beat-up sedan with Black Horse behind the wheel. We sped along in the near-total darkness, traversing eerily deserted downtown pavement all the way to the outlying district where Beijing University was located. We practically had the streets to ourselves, which was just as well because there was alcohol breath coming from the front of the car in addition to the gas fumes in the back.

"During the Cultural Revolution, if you wanted to know what was happening in the country, you had to read the wall posters," said Black Horse, who was probably old enough to remember those days clearly. "So when we get there, read the big character posters, so we can figure out what's really going on."

"Yeah, Wang Guangmei went to the Qinghua campus at midnight to read posters, to find out the fate of her husband Liu Shaoqi," I said, laboring to edge my way into a fascinating but fast-paced conversation. I was showing off nothing but book knowledge, but I also had met Liu's daughters in New York, which made the famous incident seem a little more personal and real.

"That's right. Well, we'll also be arriving about midnight, so whose fate do we want to know about?" asked Black Horse, taking his eyes off the road to look at us as if more concerned with the direction of the conversation than that of the car.

"I don't know if this is such a good idea," said Cui Jian, who was looking as unenthusiastic and queasy as I was feeling, and we weren't alone.

"Yeah, I have to go back to Taiwan tomorrow. I don't want to be accused as a Taiwan spy and end up in some Beijing prison," added Lao Ni.

"What are you, anyway? Are you some kind of specially trained agent?" Black Horse needled. "How else do you explain your perfect Beijing accent?"

"My parents were originally from Beijing," he explained, a bit defensively. "You know what? My father went to college here, he went to Shida."

"Beijing Normal?" I asked, not quite believing it.

"Yes. Before the revolution."

"Really? Wow. Way back then? Have you been there?"

"No, I'd like to go. You know the campus, right?" he asked, turning to me. "Can you show me around?"

It takes a certain amount of cultural humility for a Chinese to ask an American to be his tour guide in Beijing, so I was tickled by Lao Ni's request. In a way we legitimized each other. Being in my presence accentuated his foreign links, despite a Chinese face, while showing him around accentuated my links to China, despite a Caucasian appearance.

The unlikely arrangement reminded me of the time in 1987 when I was working for NBC News and traveled for two weeks around East China with Chinese-American television personality Connie Chung. Everyone thought she was my interpreter and guide but in fact it was the other way around.

Black Horse hit the brake hard when we reached the university gate. After a cursory inspection, a uniformed guard waved us in, although none of us had a student ID or were student age. Once inside, we were free to explore the beautifully landscaped campus in pitch darkness. After several wrong turns we finally arrived at the dimly lit crossroads known as Sanjiaodi, a community corner not unlike the busy intersection by the women's dorm, public baths, and hot water shack at Shida.

As late as it was, well after midnight, there were a number of students milling about, mostly in small groups, reading the freshly painted wall posters. Black Horse parked in the shadows near the signboards, but no one got out when I did, and I did so as much for fresh air as anything else. It was only when I realized that the others were afraid to step outside that I worried. What was it, police? I looked around and didn't see anything out of the ordinary, though it was busy considering the late hour, and there were a plethora of big and small character posters plastered over the public message boards. I skimmed the easy-to-read big character posters; most of them were calling for a student strike. One poster announced tentative meeting points for a May Fourth demo while another poster explained that the demo route details would not be announced in advance for fear of police action.

Lao Ni and Cui Jian remained in the car. Both had higher public profiles than I did, which explained their reticence to come under surveillance. Lao Ni kept asking me what the signs said, which was ridiculous as he was fluent and I wasn't, and at last his curiosity got the better of him. He stepped out of the car as cautiously as if he had just landed on another planet, almost to the extent of holding his breath, as if checking to see if the radical environment had a breathable atmosphere.

"Xiao Jin—Phil? If anyone comes up, talk to me in Japanese, okay?" Lao Ni entreated in a sober whisper, "Say anything, whatever, even *ohaiyo gozaimasu* or any other words you know. Just whatever happens, I don't want anyone to know I am from Taiwan. They might accuse me of being a spy and I'll end up in jail."

A group of Chinese men, teachers perhaps, walked up to us. Were they watching us? I played along with Ni's request, toying with the limits of my Japanese to the point of absurdity.

"*Ah so nan desuka, genki? Tokyo, Osaka, Nagoya, Sapporo ichiban . . .*"

It was a silly ruse but it worked, if indeed anyone had been paying attention at all. The suspicious strangers, or should I say the strangers we were suspicious of, moved on without scrutinizing us further.

For Lao Ni to pretend he was Japanese seemed an unnecessary ruse, but being from Taiwan he had his reasons to be circumspect. After all, look at rock rebel Cui Jian—he wouldn't even get out of the car!

Were the others overly cautious or was I so ignorant not to see the obvious peril of the situation? What might they possibly know that I didn't? The apparent ubiquity of surveillance meant that the more one was in the know, the more paranoid one was likely to seem to those less in the know.

Lao Ni followed me to the signboards, clingingly close, as we studied posters, eavesdropped on some heated arguments, and staged faux chats in nonsense Japanese. A streetlamp or two cast just enough light to read the ink-brush characters as shadowy strangers slipped in and out of the radius of light with eerie effect. It was about two in the morning and quite a few students were in evidence; were they locked out for the night or had curfew restrictions already broken down on this vanguard campus? The scene was exceedingly peaceful, but who knew who watched from the shadows? Cui Jian and the others adamantly refused to get out of the car, so we decided to pack it up.

On the way back to the Jianguo Hotel, Lao Ni, emboldened by his "daring" midnight reconnaissance of Beida, said he would like to visit Shida with me first thing in the morning. Lao Ni had a valid personal reason to visit the historic campus—it was his father's alma mater, after all—but he also wanted to get a glimpse of an antigovernment rally. Neither of us had failed to note the hand-painted notice at Sanjiaodi announcing that Shida would be a staging ground for students from other colleges on the way to Tiananmen.

Wow. Tiananmen again. As Black Horse raced across Beijing, Cui Jian sat in a terse silence, while Lao Ni and I quietly worked out a plan to go to campus at the crack of dawn. He and I shared the voyeuristic curiosity of outsiders; we wanted to stand witness to the genesis of an illegal demonstration, and the policing of it, should the proposed demonstration actually take place.

I spent the night, what little was left of it, across the street from the Jianguo Hotel at a modest inn called the Railway Hostel, thanks to an introduction from Black Horse. It was the sort of working-class facility that few foreigners were "lucky" enough to see the inside of. When I entered my room, I found that none of the electric lights worked except for a single low-watt bulb in the bathroom. The hot water thermos had no water, hot or cold; the tile floor was badly stained and the shower broken. The minute I settled into the dusty bed, however, I fell fast asleep, so the substandard amenities hardly mattered.

MAY 4

◑

The New May Fourth Spirit

The sun is rising. At Beijing Normal University, red flags flutter and unfurl in the early morning breeze above the sports ground. Thousands of students mill about, excitedly falling into groups and lining up to take to the streets and march to Tiananmen Square.

The great May Fourth demonstration is underway despite stern warnings in the press and strict police orders not to take the protest to the streets. That's the real May Fourth spirit! Defiance in the face of danger! Knock down the old, make way for the new! Challenge authority!

The early morning air is refreshingly cool with only the faintest trace of coal dust now that the long winter is over. Animated, nervous, smiling faces bask in the honey-colored glow of a brilliant morning sun. Even the birds, rare as they are in Beijing, add to the defiant chorus!

Seize the hour! Seize the day! Wake up! China, Wake up!

The atmosphere is electric, but the movement of rebel forces is gentle, co-operative, and fluidly choreographed.

Large red banners with bright yellow characters of the kind used in school sports meets announce group affiliations such as History Department, Educational Psychology, and arts choral group, but it is the national flag of China that takes the place of honor in the student color guard.

Self-appointed student leaders run around the thickening assembly of students with battery-operated megaphones trying to get others to listen, trying to instill order and decorum.

"Please remember discipline!" one voice shouts. "Find your department, look for the banners!"

"Stay with your group!" another one screeches, as static and feedback from the megaphones start to obscure the message.

"Remember to stay with people you know!"

"Song sheets are available from the arts choral group."

Cloth headbands are passed around. Student scribes dash off calligraphy calling for dialogue on sheets of plain cloth and cardboard using ink brushes and felt-tip pens.

Already the air is humming with music. In the middle of the gathering, two accordion players are bellowing and bouncing, rehearsing some morale-boosting numbers for the day's march. There are not enough mimeographed song sheets to go around, so marchers scribble down lyrics in their notebooks, copying them off handout sheets and public blackboards. No cribbing is needed for "The Internationale," as everyone knows the anthem inside out.

Why sing a song embraced by the establishment? The idea is brilliant in a way. If you sing it enough, you own it. The Communist-indoctrinated youth of Beijing are waving the red flag to beat the red flag, employing iconic rhetoric of rebellion to remake China in their own image.

"DO WE HAVE TO WAIT ANOTHER SEVENTY YEARS?"

There it is again. The students are willfully making parallels between their situation and the progenitor of all student demonstrations. The social and creative explosion that followed the May Fourth demonstration at Tiananmen Gate in 1919 led to the founding of the Chinese Communist Party. Once the party took power, it enshrined the 1919 student demonstration as an icon of Chinese Communism.

The mood is light, cheerful; the air full of familiar shouts, earthy Beijing greetings, and boisterous sing-alongs. There's a kind of safety in numbers, at least psychological safety. If many people are doing something, and don't start to panic, the risk that an individual will be singled out for punishment decreases. Nonparticipation involves a risk too, the risk of being left on the wrong side of history. Conditioned by decades of campaigns and crackdowns, Chinese understandably look to those around them for clues on how to behave. It's not so much follow the leader as follow other followers.

Standing in the swirling, excited pack of protesters, I am hit with a pang of self-consciousness. Not because I am over six feet tall, a 190-pound blond man in a sea of black hair and thin physiques; this is a political rally in a country where foreigners live in separate buildings, eat in different restaurants, and shop in different stores using different money from local people. Everywhere I go, thousands of curious and sometimes resentful eyes observe my every move. Any lapse of judgment on my part will be magnified many times over because of the stigma of difference.

I am not the only one hit with this sense of not belonging. Beside me stands Lao Ni, who has seen enough excitement for one day. He has seen enough to tell his friends in Taiwan, and he is getting ready to leave.

Bright and Jenny find me by the side of the road watching parade ranks being organized by departmental affiliation.

"Jin Peili! Are you going to join us or just watch?" Bright asks provocatively.

"I don't know," I answer, trying to imagine myself as others see me. "I mean, I'm a *wai-guo-ren*."

"Are you afraid?" Jenny teases, eyebrows arching in disbelief.

"No, not really."

"Then take a stand with us!" Bright is insistent, bordering on seductive.

Without another word she takes me by the arm and leads me past a throng of people into the middle of the arts choral group. Just then there is a ripple of excited whispers whipping across the staging ground. Word has just come in that the student marchers from other colleges have reached Beitaiping Zhuang intersection just north of campus and that it is time to fall into formation behind departmental flags to break out of the gated, guarded campus. "Jin Peili is marching with us," Bright says, assigning me a cohort to march with.

Somehow being placed in the middle of the music section is reassuring.

"Arise, you enslaved people!" cry out a dozen voices in arts choral group, "Do not say we have nothing. We shall be the masters of the world. This is the final struggle . . ."

"The Internationale" is effective in jump-starting the march. It is sung with such repetition that it is soon one of those tunes that you can't get out of your head.

Doubts mount as we are forced to take a roundabout path to find a way past the padlocked bars of the southeast campus gate. The student vanguard discovers a passable exit through the narrow doorway adjacent to the vestibule manned by campus security. A row of policemen is visible just outside the bars of the gate, but we outnumber them by the hundreds, if not thousands.

Guards or no guards, there is no stopping the rush off campus once the first few students squeeze through. We break ranks, forcefully propelled forward through the passageway to face the unknown. Like grains of sand slipping down the thin neck of an hourglass, dropping past a point of no return.

As we emerge on the street, two campus security agents plead with some flustered students to immediately return to campus. The narrowness of the makeshift exit had forced everyone to go more or less single file, causing each marcher to step out alone, momentarily isolated from the group and vulnerable. The procession quickly reassembles into departmental groups aided by the waving of banners and shouts of student facilitators. Cars and buses on the wide thoroughfare outside the school gate are slowed and then halted as the road is inundated by wave after wave of protesters pouring off campus. Traffic on the wide avenue comes to a complete halt.

A long line of police watch intently from the far side of the road. They are ridiculously outnumbered and make no serious attempt to stop the onrush. Immobilized automobiles get swallowed up, lapped by bodies on all sides, like listing ships in a turbulent sea. From the north comes a spirited procession of students from other schools, and in no time students fill the road as far as the eye can see.

Bright banners for Beijing University, Qinghua University, and Political Science and Law University are hoisted above the heads of the crowd on bamboo poles, flapping in the wind, cracking like whips. As the assembly of students flows tentatively south towards Tiananmen Square, the police back off and let the human mass proceed towards the city center. Are the police in shock and intimidated by the stupendous size of the crowd or silently supportive, won over by the contagious, ebullient spirit of the young protesters? Either way, they do nothing but watch.

Pedestrians start gawking, too. Cyclists sit on their bikes, unable to cruise forward, curious about the disturbance. Most of the inconvenienced commuters stare in dumbfounded silence, though a few shout words of support and clap at the ragtag student army marching down the street. Passengers stranded on stalled buses peer out their rectangular windows, surveying the scene.

The police ignore the law-breaking students, but the students do not ignore the police. Instead some fast-thinking students try to win the day with cheerful improvisation and song.

"The people love the People's Police!"

"The People's Police love the people!"

Three policemen climb onto the roof of a stalled bus to better survey the unstoppable horde. They exhibit neither amusement nor anger. Some uniformed officers remove their hats, as if off duty. Others stand stiffly at attention. Are they mesmerized by the irrepressible optimism of the marchers or just waiting for orders? We stream confidently past several lines of police as the rhythmic drone of accordions cues a series of crisp rhyming chants. Word quickly reaches us that police blockades erected a short distance down the road have been penetrated by the vanguard of flag-waving marchers, so spirits mount and the student parade picks up speed. The demonstration flows southward on Xinwai Road, coursing past nondescript walled compounds containing military hospitals, factories, and apartment blocks.

As we approach Xiaoxitian, near the China film building, a few hardy members of the international press corps are in evidence on the side of the road. Ensconced inside a Chinese crowd in motion, I return the gaze of people who look more or less like me as they attempt to capture images of something that might turn out to be a newsworthy event. Caucasian men hastily clamber up ladders and balance heavy cameras on broad shoulders to take aim and record the progress of an unauthorized May Fourth protest that already has a whiff of history about it. Seeing an opportunity, perhaps even protection, in the regard of unblinking black lenses, the arts choral group enthusiastically plunges into song.

"Everyone unite! 'The Internationale' shall certainly be realized . . . "

The marchers around me ham it up, they strut and swing and cry their hearts out, happy to have been observed, at once defiant but eager for validation.

We surge southwards like a river swollen with rain, seeking Tiananmen. Crossing Second Ring Road, one of Beijing's key arteries, we bring east-west traffic to a standstill, leaving taxis and buses stranded and abandoned. Meanwhile, construction workers halt their heavy lifting to line the streets, some of them waving and shouting rowdily. As if on cue, the arts choral group accordion players change tack, "The red sun shall shine all over the globe," fading out on the line, "'The Internationale' shall definitely be realized," to launch a new tune. When I hear the lyrics I know why. It is proletarian agit-prop outreach time.

"Peasants, workers, soldiers, unite together!"

The gaggle explodes in celebration upon hearing the call for solidarity. The rhetoric is not new, but hearing it in this context is.

A strange excitement lifts me. This is the China I have long imagined but never known, the China synonymous with revolution and rebellion that I've read about in history and literature. The energy is inclusive and all-encompassing. Can a peaceful people's uprising be in the making?

As the procession moves south along the narrow tree-lined shopping street leading to Xidan, the choral group starts chanting a ditty to the melody to "Frère Jacques," slyly co-opting a Young Pioneer anthem.

Dadao guandao! Fandui fubai!
Women yaoqiu minzhu! Women yaoqiu ziyou!
Xiang qian jin! Xiang qian jin!
Down with corruption! Down with nepotism!
We seek democracy! We seek freedom!
March forward! March forward!

The mood of the moment is more fun-loving than militant, but the political implications of the word *dadao*, that is to say, "down with," are ominous. The mood can't be forever lighthearted and uplifting, but need it be mean and outright destructive?

Somewhere along the road to Tiananmen the illegal ragtag May Fourth demonstration turns into an unsanctioned but broadly tolerated peace march. The implicit militancy of the demonstration at the outset, understandable given a system of government in which a police action was not only possible but likely, was softened by the nonaction of the police and the positive response of bystanders along the way. Had there been serious scuffles, arrests, or violence between police and marchers or even just conflict between inconvenienced motorists and marchers, the Tiananmen-bound procession would have forced to choose between conflict and surrender. Instead there was virtually no resistance, which permitted marchers to relax and reach out in a way that reflected how others were responding to them.

By the time we reach Chang'an Boulevard, the numbers are swelling beyond count. Everywhere well-wishers come out of their homes, offices, and shops to wave and show support. Police blockades at critical junctions are relaxed as the good-natured vanguard of students wearing sun visors, carrying the sweaters and jackets no longer needed in the midday sun, cheerfully beg cooperation.

A jolt of energy surges through the rapidly moving procession, now numbering ten thousand or more as we reach the northern extremity of the Great Hall of the People and our forbidden destination comes into full view. The protesters around me are sweaty and sunburned, some losing their voices, others already limping from walking miles without a break, but even those unsteady of foot have a bounce in their step, the proud young rebels homing in on the legendary destination that is stage center in Chinese politics.

The crowd picks up speed. Those of us near the front of the procession feel an exhilaration as the parade pours onto the vast emptiness of Tiananmen Square, finally coming to rest near the Martyr's Memorial. My group settles in the shadow of Sun Yatsen's portrait, a wood-framed monolith temporarily erected for the national holiday. As thousands join us in due time from universities situated even further away, the throng thickens and we are surrounded by student contingents on all sides. Yet even now, the vast breadth of the square dwarfs the growing congregation.

I was supposed to meet Cui Jian and Liu Yuan for lunch today. Now I'm in the middle of a crowd in the middle of Tiananmen Square, participating in a demonstration I had merely planned to take a look at.

The rock singer was a musical rebel and effectively expressed his angst in song, but in conversation I rarely found him to be political. If anything, he was cautious, plodding, and methodical in his rebelliousness. He sang songs exactly the way he liked to, which ruffled lots of official feathers the wrong way, but he had no desire to push things to the point that he would become a persona non grata or be forced into exile. So he paid the dues of living in the People's Republic, including taxes, payment of which was extracted as a corollary of his fame.

Daily life in the People's Republic was excellent preparation for the practical and dramatic demands of staging political theater at Tiananmen. It was the art of skirting the edge without crossing the line. It was rebelling within the orthodox vocabulary of rebellion. On what grounds could the May Fourth–inspired Communist Party object to a May Fourth march of students waving red banners and singing Communist anthems?

Already townspeople are swarming towards the protest, and they too know how to play the ambiguity game. If questioned they could say they are watching out of curiosity, not in solidarity.

Meanwhile, the police are melting away, which lessens the likelihood of conflict and actually enhances the sense of order. The crowd can do without police because it self-polices. Everyone is under pressure to stay with his own group, remaining under the watchful eyes of peers. There are no explicit rules but there is much order—order born of years of communal life in a communal society. One instinctively knows how to take turns using the facilities in a family's cramped apartment, to share a single desk with six roommates in a dorm room, to fall into order and march and sing in state-sponsored youth fests. Functioning in a crowd, cooperating, and putting on a show are nothing new to these young Communists. This demonstration, though illegal, is being guided by well-honed instincts. It reflects not so much rebellion as an intense expression of everyday values.

The banners around me are both provocative and orthodox, lifted from slogans uttered in generations past.

FREEDOM
LONG LIVE THE PEOPLE!
DEMOCRACY AND SCIENCE
UNDER THE SKY, ALL FOR THE PEOPLE

Tiananmen Square! As a protest of uncertain duration begins on the monumental chessboard carved out in the heart of the arid, mountain-ringed plain of Beijing, no one knows for sure where things are going or what will happen next, but the location is deliberate. Tiananmen is the ceremonial stage for a nation of a billion. Nowhere in Beijing does the sky seem wider and grander than over Tiananmen, the sky gate—the place where the sky meets the ground. Scorching hot in the sun, magical in the moonlight, lyrical lookout on the cosmos, celestial yet grounded. Open to the heavens, a conduit of the elements, Tiananmen is the place, if such a place exists, where the mandate of heaven resides; not just a place to celebrate history, but a place to make it, inspired by precedent.

"Jin Peili? Jin Peili! Get up! Get up!" Bright implored, pulling me to my feet.

"What?" I was reluctant to stand up. Just minutes before, there had been an angry chant of "Get down! Get down!" directed against a Western photographer with long curly blond hair. He had brazenly climbed atop Sun Yat-sen's portrait for a better angle, only to be chased away. Sensing a racial flashpoint, I wanted to keep the low profile, literally.

"Get up! We must go, quickly!" While keeping a watchful eye on me, Bright also took responsibility for Jenny and Lily.

In no time at all, everyone was up on their feet, trudging slowly to the south, as organizers frantically whipped the student delegations back into parade formation with crackly announcements over their megaphones. We had just been given our marching orders, though by whom or for what reason remained a mystery. The mass exodus accelerated to the point that I found myself running with the student pack away from Tiananmen Square. It was disconcerting to be running with no known destination in mind. The arts choral group was back in formation, led by the accordion players and the flag bearers. The entire Shida contingent was now hoofing it due south, and we eventually exited the square on its southwest corner just beyond the Bank of China building.

"Where are we going?" I asked. "What's the big rush?"

"Keep running, it is discipline of the group!" One of those amplified voices shepherding the herd barked, "You must follow the leaders."

"Can't we walk?" I asked Bright, not wanting to be a sheep blindly moving with the flock. I didn't like taking orders from people I didn't know, and something about running with the group implied a level of commitment that was absent in my mind. It was one thing to walk into trouble, step by step, quite another to race into it. What was going on?

"It's discipline," Lily offered, in between huffs and puffs, carrying her bag of goodies in hand.

"But why do we have to run?" I said, feet pounding in lockstep on the pavement below. Do we just follow orders? Have I become a soldier in an army in which it is out of line to question authority? The lack of information made me feel ill at ease. To make matters worse, I was attracting unwanted attention.

"*Laowai paobu!*" "*Laowai paobu!*" "*Laowai paobu!*"

See whitey run! Is there something innately funny about a white person running? Why do I hear so many people yelling out the exact same phrase?

Soon the students of the arts choral group are all looking at me, smiling and laughing. Some of them picked up the refrain, and chanted in rhythmic cadence: "*Laowai paobu, laowai paobu!*" The newest slogan was a stupid joke at my expense!

Spectators lining both sides of Qianmen Avenue picked up the refrain, and the words "*Laowai paobu! Laowai paobu!*" echoed in the air. Why did they have to call me that? When I was in a good mood, *laowai* sounded teasing and playful, and when I wasn't, it sounded derogatory and racist. One could analyze it as a lighthearted linguistic device used by common Chinese to put uncommon foreigners in place, but even friends bandied about the term. Bright burst out laughing when she heard the rabble yell out "*Laowai paobu!*"

"If you gave me a penny every time someone says that I'll be rich," I told her.

"If we hear it fifty times, I'll treat you to dinner!" Bright laughed.

We jogged at a steady pace down Qianmen Avenue, and every time I thought the verbal barrage was over, a new gaggle of curious onlookers would point to me and shout out "*Laowai paobu!*" triggering a new cacophony of teasing voices. I stopped counting after fifty, an upcoming dinner with Bright being my only consolation.

Who was the first person in the crowd to say "See whitey run"? Did it spread around uniformly or was it such an obvious thing to say that everyone thought it up on his or her own? I doubted most people had ever used the expression before, yet it was on everyone's lips all at once. It made me wonder if there might not be a similar sociolinguistic process at work that enabled a mass of tens of thousands to organize itself, to create a few uniform slogans without direction from above.

Ever since I first came to China I'd noticed that many Chinese used the exact same words in the same situation. This was great for language learning, for one could pick up such phrases and use them safely over and over again. It was not really linguistic lockstep, because phrases seemed to come and go without any coordination from above. Was it born of the Communist tendency to use slogans, or years of memorizing Mao, or was it something more ancient in Chinese culture?

Chinese is full of interesting aphorisms and literary references that are fixed as four-character expressions. I suppose there are similarly rich lodes of fixed expressions in English that come from the Bible or Shakespeare, but Chinese seems to have more of them.

We stopped running as suddenly as we started. Now group discipline called for going at a snail's pace. Our forced jog ended like it started, abruptly and without any explanation. Who was calling the shots here? It was like a conspiracy and I was not in on the secret.

"Who gave the orders to run? Who gave the orders to stop?" I demanded an explanation from my friends.

"Laowai!" was Bright's nonsense response. I ignored her at first because she had a habit of distancing herself from me in front of others, in part to deflect inevitable questions about the nature of our relationship. She used the word again.

"Yes, I know I'm a foreigner, do you think I forgot?" I said, playing along.

"How can I forget when people constantly remind me? So, why were we running?"

A friend of Bright's, who had edged up to us during the forced run, offered an explanation. "Maybe the police are coming."

He had an authoritative air about him. Tall and athletic-looking, he wore a Western jacket over a T-shirt. He sported longish hair, with a telling trace of a moustache over a friendly mouth, but his eyes were inscrutable, hidden behind dark sunglasses.

"They said we must all stay together," added Lily. "Otherwise it is dangerous."

"No, I think Shida was running to catch up with Beida," Bright said, with a knowing nod. Jenny seemed to enjoy the exchange but offered no theory of her own. I knew relations between the two schools were competitive, but I thought that was stretching it.

"Jin Peili," Bright said, getting around belatedly to introductions, "this is Chen Laoshi. He's a teacher, a graduate of Shida."

"I have heard much about you," he said. "Good fortune to meet you on such a splendid and exciting day."

"Nice to meet you."

"So, what do you think of this magnificent march?"

"I wish I knew what was going on."

"Let me explain. We are going back to campus, but first we will stop at the New China News Agency to protest the April twenty-sixth editorial. Some members of the Chinese press have joined us in our demonstration."

"I wonder if it makes sense for me to be here," I said, fishing around a bit to find out what the people around me thought of a foreigner marching with the students.

"Don't worry, I'm not a student either," he said. "We want to show support and march in solidarity with our good friends. Nothing wrong with that, right?"

The sun, although well on its way down, grilled us as we headed west for New China News Agency. I wiped the sweat from my brow several times and I was not alone; it looked like everyone had broken into a sweat the minute we stopped jogging. Bright daintily daubed her face with a yellow facecloth, which she shared with Jenny. Lily used her shirtsleeve. Chen just kept on dripping, seemingly unfazed by the heat.

The movement down Qianmen road was stop and go. Student organizers had staked out strategic points in advance and had appointees directing traffic at big intersections to avoid jam-ups wherever possible. This task was complicated by red and green lights indifferent to the politics of the march plus streets full of curious spectators. Each time a light changed, the flock compressed and expanded like an accordion, with audible grunts and sighs instead of music, but eventually the procession returned to normal marching speed. The more comfortable pace allowed a resumption of conversation, laughter, and celebratory song by the arts choral group.

"LONG LIVE THE NEW MAY FOURTH MOVEMENT!" proclaimed a banner.

From time to time street vendors, mostly older folk, came up to the marchers offering popsicles and little boxes of fruit drink. Despite the talk about discipline, there were several mad scrambles for the limited refreshment, because demand initially outstripped supply.

If my complexion meant I was sometimes the butt of jokes or the source of free entertainment, it also bestowed with it certain perks. Being the only foreigner around, I didn't have to push and shove to get a popsicle—an old lady went out of her way to hand me one and fellow vendors followed suit. In no time at all, I had a red bean ice in my mouth, two milk ices melting in one hand and a container of warm orange drink in the other.

By now most of the vehicular traffic on this key east-west artery had come to a halt or was forced to detour. We occupied the entire westbound side of the wide avenue and managed to screw up much of the north-south traffic as well. We marched into the late afternoon sun, passing the old Catholic cathedral that tentatively peeked out behind an imposing brick wall. At Xuanwumen Intersection we came across another one of those photo opportunity angles where foreign journalists were staked out with their cameras to record the news of the day. When we reached the front of the angular white tower that housed *Xinhua-she*, the New China News Agency, everyone stopped and sat down.

Since the choral group was near the head of the march we sat in the front row facing the main entrance to the rocket-shaped building. Being perpetually out of the loop, it took me a few minutes to realize that we were staging a sit-in. A handsome, fair-skinned Chinese youth got up in front of our group and started screaming chants and slogans at the top of his lungs. His words were unintelligible since he had all but lost his voice. He continued to wave and chant with the gusto of a professional cheerleader. I wasn't in the mood for a pep rally, but the strikers seemed to appreciate the distraction he provided.

"How long are we going to stay here?" I asked.

"This is a sit-in to protest the lack of press freedom," explained Teacher Chen, sounding teacherly in a slightly wooden fashion. "That is why we gather here at Xinhua News Building."

"Isn't that what's-his-name?" I asked, nodding to the male cheerleader who appeared to be dancing or doing some kind of calisthenics.

"That's Wuerkaixi," Chen explained with a grin. "He's from Shida, too."

I had to wonder if the wise guy from Xinjiang, the guy who had the cheek to stage his own press conference in his own dorm, was a principled activist or just a crowd-pleasing performer. I wasn't sure what I thought of him, but other observers apparently were; the chant got louder and louder.

"Come on out, don't be afraid,
True journalists do not fear the truth.
Come on out, don't be afraid!"

None of the "true" journalists came out, none that I could see, but many watched from the windows. The angular skyscraper stuck out from the neighborhood of low-rise Soviet-style architecture as much as I stood out from the crowd. A few workers inside the building leaned out windows and waved, but it was hard to tell construction workers from journalists because parts of the new propaganda headquarters were being worked on and journalists didn't dress that well either. After twenty minutes or so the Shida delegation moved on so that other schools could each in turn stage their own personalized Xinhua sit-in conveyor-belt style.

The arts choral group marched further westwards until we reached the place where the Second Ring Road runs north. It was rush hour, so traffic jams added to the drama of the march as immobilized commuters had no choice but to watch the rally, which greatly increased the number of spectators, waving to us marchers. Hundreds of people stood on bridges and overpasses cheering our procession on. Workers stripped to their waists waved shirts from scaffolding high above the streets. Tired as we were, we got an unexpected burst of energy from the enthusiastic attention, especially when passing under overpasses. The pace quickened, the music got louder, chants and song once again reverberated in the air. Clusters of townspeople applauded and waved wildly at the ranks of student protestors as the sun melted out of sight on the dusty western horizon. The energy of sympathetic citizens helped us complete the circuit. The sudden surge of attention made us want to go on marching, to reach for new heights.

With the sun gone but the sky still glowing, the red-banner day of successful protest came to a close. Things started to break up after we passed Fuchengmen. Though the college campuses were still several kilometers to the north, student protesters, having had enough of a good thing, broke from the pack in search of rest and refreshment. Some limped home to nurse aching muscles and blistered feet, but even they walked with purpose in their step. One could imagine the pride of war heroes, returning home wounded but triumphant.

Bright, Jenny, and I said good-bye to Lily and the remnants of our delegation as we approached Chegong Zhuang, a nondescript subway station along the Second Ring Road. My two apple-cheeked companions asked me if I wanted to take the subway with them and I did.

There was a subtle sense of loss as we crossed the line from participant to spectator. Facing a blood-red sky, we rested on top of the embankment above the Second Ring Road and looked down on the marchers below. We were greeted with smiles and even congratulations from the wall of spectators around us. I climbed up onto a two-wheeled cart that already bore the weight of three spectators to get a better look at the long file of people I had just been part of. A woman on the other side of the cart, who like me was standing, surveyed the traffic in the sunken highway below. It was novel to see a ring road backed up with traffic composed solely of people, not cars. A bobbing flow of bronzed faces surged northwards in the direction of the university district.

While I took in the panorama below, the two people who had been sitting on the other end of the wheeled cart got down, breaking the delicate balance. My side of the seesaw cart plummeted to the ground, launching the poor woman on the other side of the cart into the air. My tumble was absorbed by the soft flesh of five or six hapless spectators beside the cart, while the woman on the other side had a similarly rough landing a few feet away. After dusting off and checking for bruises, everyone apologized profusely and made light of it, exchanging the stoic grins of comrades.

After saying good-bye to Chen Laoshi, Bright, Jenny, and I walked towards the industrial-looking cement and glass entrance to the Beijing subway line. "Come on my laowai," Bright said, teasing me affectionately, "follow me!" There's that word again. I guessed she watched the same English study program as everyone else in China.

As we entered a world of dim lights and flickering shadows, I found myself feeling a bit depressed. It was hard to leave the big family of marchers and not feel that something was missing, that life had suddenly lost a rich, communal aspect. Whether it was the ache of postparty or postpartum loneliness, a gap presented itself. The group ethos provoked a tangible excitement, a sense of something much greater than the sum of its parts but also transient and situation-specific; the feeling could not easily be sustained apart from the crowd.

We descended two flights of stairs into a cool concrete cave, an orderly but unattractive black-and-white world apart from the chaos and color of the streets above. The ticket booth, stairways, and underground platform were plain and functional in comparison to the more exotic subway systems of New York and other world cities. There was no graffiti, advertising, or art to distract the eye. It was as plain and utilitarian as could be imagined. Once we boarded the flimsy, boxy subway cars, I spotted other defectors and refugees from the Tiananmen tribe of marchers. Though the greenish glare of the overhead fluorescent lights and fatigued faces of commuters made for ghostly countenances, a distinct minority looked less ghostly than the others. If the government wanted to round up all the marchers it wouldn't be hard—they just had to look for young people with uncalloused hands, dusty shoes, and sunburned cheeks.

Our underground journey followed the perimeter of the ancient city wall, retracing in a few minutes' time the circuit that had taken half a day to traverse. Bright had considered inviting me along with Jenny to her home, then thought better of it. I was still a laowai in the eyes of others, if not in hers. We enjoyed a quiet stroll before parting, then I searched for a hotel to make a phone call

"Wei? Hello?" Lotus cheerily answered in Chinese and English. I could hear other voices, too. She was apparently busy entertaining guests, so I didn't tell her about the big march.

"Oh, why don't you come over this evening? You remember Belle, don't you? Belle Yang? She's coming over too."

I had known Lotus almost as long as I had known Bright. Lotus and I first met when I showed up at a hotel event wearing clothes more appropriate to the laidback life on campus. I had bicycled over an hour from Shida to the swanky part of town to attend a 1986 breakfast meeting of the Beijing American Club that featured former president Jimmy Carter as guest speaker.

Living the simple student life at the time, it was a luxurious departure from routine just to be in the Jianguo Hotel. But I was there not for the usual reasons—a chance to relish the air-conditioning, use the facilities, or splurge on a coffee—but to attend an expatriate gathering in one of the event rooms in the basement. I had gotten a special invitation from Professor Mike Oksenberg, who was accompanying the former president on a tour of China. After the talk, Oksenberg made a point of calling on his former students, University of Michigan classmate Kathryn Minnick and myself, to step up front to speak with the former president.

As Lotus likes to recall, "After I saw you shaking hands with Jimmy Carter, I just had to meet you. You were the only person in the room wearing a Mao jacket!"

I took a taxi to the Lido Hotel, which is on the road to the airport on the outskirts of town. Adjacent to the sprawling low-rise hotel was a series of residential towers for foreigners working in Beijing. Lotus and Al's apartment was located in this convenient enclave that had a cluster of foreign currency shops, schools, and offices specifically designed for expatriates. It was Beijing's "foreign ghetto," as Lotus often said.

"Good to see you!" Lotus greeted me with her customary hug.

"Same here," I said, patting her on the back. She always made me feel instantly at home.

"Come in, come in. I have exciting news!" she said. "Justin and I took some video pictures of the illegal demonstration at Tiananmen Square today."

"At Tiananmen?"

"Yes, you should have seen it."

"I was in it."

"You were? That's great!" Lotus said, lighting up. "You must tell me all about it!"

"It was unbelievable, it was unreal," I said, struggling to find words to sum up the day's excitement. "I can't believe how things are changing."

"Some of the changes are good, some of them are not so good."

"So far so good, if you ask me." I said. "Boy, I'm wiped out after all that marching."

"Well, there's always room at the inn." She turned the conversation back to practical matters. "The kids have some guests. Sorry I can't offer you a bed, but you are welcome to sleep on the couch in the living room."

"You know me, anywhere's fine."

Albert, an MIT graduate working for a prestigious American firm in Beijing, bounded into the apartment wearing white shorts and a sweaty T-shirt, spinning a basketball in his hands.

"Hi!" he said, then turned to his wife. "Lotus, we gotta do something about the shower, it's not working again."

"Nia, Justin?" Lotus called out. "Have you two said hello to Uncle Philip yet?"

According to the unwritten etiquette of the Chinese-American immigrant culture that Lotus and Al were both raised in, close friends are treated like family. Their young teenage daughter understood this, but she was, after all, a teenager, so I got a practically inaudible "Hi, Uncle" from her before she ran back into her room. Justin, a few years older and far more outgoing, introduced me to Tony, his overnight guest. The boys engaged me in an earnest conversation about the avant-garde art of skateboarding in Beijing.

Maybe I was just overtired from all the walking in the hot sun, but when Belle and some other Americans came over dressed to party, I was about as sociable as little Nia and just wanted to curl up and go to sleep. Belle's parents were also old-world immigrants from China, but she radiated a distinctly modern California charm, sparkling and vivacious. She was studying Chinese folk painting while directing a study abroad program in Beijing. She and I had had many good conversations and long walks across Beijing in the past. This evening, however, she had three exchange students in tow and I was not in the mood for the small talk and forced joviality of American-style interactions. The intensity of the demonstration had sparked something in me and put me on a different wavelength, making it difficult for me to switch gears to the casual "American" mood.

I already missed the company of my fellow marchers. The archipelago of luxury, the self-styled "ghetto" that Lotus and Al inhabited, was less enticing than it had been on previous visits when life in the streets of Beijing was dull and grim. Earlier that day, I had seen the streets of China come alive, making the foreign enclave seem wooden and waxen in comparison.

The conversation turned to the Lido Hotel disco. It was a popular foreigner hangout, but I didn't like patronizing such places on principle because Chinese locals were strictly prohibited. A passport was needed to get in. Not the sort of place I wanted to go, not after protesting corruption in the streets all day. After getting a whiff of the promise of a more egalitarian, idealistic China, after the tacit acceptance I felt marching shoulder to shoulder with the youthful multitude, I was in an idealistic mood. It was enough to make the Lido Hotel complex seem like a corporate theme park, a luxury habitat for foreigners kept at remove from the people.

"I think I'm gonna call it a night," I said, bowing out.

"Phil, cheer up, let's go dancing!" Belle was obviously in bouncier spirits than I.

"I don't know, I'm just not in the mood," I said. "So what did you think about the demonstration today?"

"The demonstration?" she asked.

"At the college they told us not to get involved," answered her young male companion.

"Chinese students making a lot of noise in the streets, who'd want to get involved in that?" quipped the other.

"I did, I was in the march today."

"You were?" Belle asked incredulously, as if I had shown poor judgment. The tone of her remark was innocent enough, but it seemed like an assault on my entire worldview at that fatigued juncture.

"Oh, but it was great, you should have been there," I said. "You know, the original May Fourth was all about young people and rebellion. Today they took back the day, the music, even Tiananmen Square!"

The lovely Californian looked at me with curious incomprehension. I was tired, but pumped up and charged politically. For the not yet initiated, it was just another day, and for the apolitical, the protests at Tiananmen spelled trouble with a capital *T*.

"What are you getting involved in all of that for?" Belle reprimanded gently.

"Well, I don't feel like dancing tonight, so you guys go ahead. You can dance through the revolution."

Belle's rebuke to my sarcasm was still ringing in my ears after she and her friends had gone out and I was dozing off on the couch in Lotus and Albert's living room. "I don't know about you," she had said, "but I'd rather dance than demonstrate."

MAY 10

◐

Ten Thousand Bicycles

Gliding into the east gate of Beijing University on my bicycle, I took a leisurely, breezy circle around the tranquil landscaped campus known as "Beida" in Chinese. Even though I was not a Beida student, I had a fondness for the pavilion- and pagoda-rimmed No Name Lake, a placid font of nature known for being unknowable.

With the springtime rousing of student activism, the Beida campus had gotten a little less tranquil; rules were being broken left and right, no one seemed to be in charge, and boundaries were constantly being redrawn. For those familiar with the shifting winds of Chinese politics, just about the scariest thing was that you might wake up one day and find yourself on the wrong side of the line. There had been no demonstrations in a week, but the antigovernment rhetoric on campus was heating up.

The scratchy shouts of the students' informal PA system assaulted my ears even before I reached the campus crossroads of Sanjiaodi. The narrow triangular plaza, defined by a row of shops, a dorm, and the campus announcement boards, was so packed with students milling about that I had to dismount my bike to enter.

Sanjiaodi had a functioning democracy wall of sorts, which is why Black Horse and Cui Jian had wanted to visit. But now it had taken on a more active countenance, a sort of student-strike central, overflowing with self-appointed student leader types, amplified announcements, strident posters, and heated small group discussions.

"Strike! No more classes! Hit the streets! Demand dialogue!"

A week had gone by since the glorious rally on the fourth, and there was a view gaining momentum, espoused by Bright and some of her generally conservative friends, that the students should leave well enough alone and go back to classes. Hadn't the students made their point? Hadn't the government shown restraint? Was it time to wind things down or not?

There was a bright red poster at Shida right across from the Insider Guest House that expressed the gnawing doubt succinctly:

THE AMAZING MAY FOURTH MARCH IS OVER.

SHALL WE GO BACK TO OUR DESKS AND CLASSROOMS?

WE ACHIEVED ABSOLUTELY NOTHING FOR OUR EFFORTS.

HOW CAN PEOPLE POSSIBLY SPEAK OF VICTORY?

THE OLD RULES AND REGULATIONS HAVEN'T CHANGED A BIT.

Indeed, life was on the verge of going back to normal at Shida and on other campuses, so much so that I had enjoyed a few normal days doing things like playing basketball at the Sports Institute and playing guitar with friends in the Shida foreign student dorm. I had lunch with Cui Jian; had dinner with the writers Gladys and Xianyi Yang; talked screenplay and sound track with Hou Dejian; had lunch with the artist Yao Xiaoping, one of my first friends in Beijing; and had coffee with friends from Japan, one a student in the Shaoyuan dorm at Beida, the other a businessman at the Jianguo Hotel.

Yet here at Sanjiaodi, in this heated triangle, in this hothouse of hotheads, the demonstrating never really ended and the tender shoots for more demonstrations were kept viable.

The radicals' desperate cries for more mobilization seemed in part predicated on the fear that the movement was running out of steam. If and when it ran out of steam, the arrests of the ringleaders would begin in earnest.

STRIKE TO THE END!

OPPOSE THE *PEOPLE'S DAILY* EDITORIAL

DEMAND DIALOGUE!

BA-KE . . . ZIXINGCHE . . . YOU-XING

There was a new message being voiced this morning, but it took me a moment to make sense of it. *Ba-ke* means cut class, referring to the ongoing debate about whether or not to continue the student strike. *You-xing* means to parade or demonstrate. But what in the world did *zixingche*, namely bicycle, have to do with anything?

A bicycle demonstration? The Beida activists were at the vanguard again, with a new strategy designed to bring attention to the problematic editorial and all it represented. Pressing forward, though not without risk, was one way to gauge the uncertain political mood.

The quandary about what to do next was voiced by the friend of a friend who agreed to meet me for lunch at Sanjiaodi that day. Chen Li, a physics student, was torn between her deep pride in her alma mater and the possible dangers of joining fellow students as they invoked school spirit in taking protest to the streets. She had not marched on April 27 or May 4, but she said she was proud of what the students had done, adding, with characteristic school chauvinism, that she was especially proud of the Beida students who naturally had taken the lead.

Her last comment left me with the uncomfortable sense that some of the Beida students might be sufficiently smitten with the elite status of their school as to make faulty decisions based on an exaggerated sense of self-importance. Some of the young geniuses gathering around me were sincere, others snobbish, as if their sole motivation to keep it going was to avoid ceding leadership to less prestigious institutions.

Here at Sanjiaodi, the name of Beida was on the line. If you committed to march, you'd better do so with exemplary school spirit. Go, team, go! Ironically, this gung-ho sporting attitude was less in evidence among the easy-going, athletically gifted jocks at the Sports Institute just down the road.

The flurry of feet to and from the student headquarters and the flapping of tongues blasting out on the PA system grew increasingly up-tempo and strident.

There were few students who sweated the tough entrance exams for top-ranked schools such as Beida unaware of the elite status that society accorded them, but the reward was paid in prestige, not hard cash. Professors were materially poor and lacked clout off campus, but they did have time to read books, except when forced to attend political meetings and indoctrination sessions.

I told Chen Li about a conversation I had with China scholar John Fairbank, who was profoundly concerned about the active impoverishment of Chinese scholars in the face of market reforms. Being smart but poor was a topic she quickly warmed to. She agreed that it was humiliating enough that watermelon vendors and street hustlers could earn more than mathematicians and history professors, but what really worried her was an iffy job assignment.

This was the legacy of the 1986–1987 student demonstrations in Hefei involving outspoken astrophysicist Fang Lizhi and others; the crackdown that followed culminated in the relatively liberal and tolerant party chief Hu Yaobang being ousted from power. That's why the April 26 editorial struck such a raw nerve: it was a signal that the party planned to punish campus activists, essentially exploiting the state-controlled system of job assignment to punish dissent.

What surprised me was not this fear, understandable enough given prevailing conditions, but how quickly it was overcome by the many who demonstrated already.

Chen Li did not strike me as the demonstrating type, but then again neither did Bright or Jenny or Lily. So there was some larger force at work here. As she vocally weighed the pros and cons of joining today's illicit demo, Chen Li finally turned the question onto me.

"What is the right thing to do?"

I had a hard time answering her. It was one thing for me to tag along, another for her. Perhaps the government itself was changing, however reluctantly, with the changing times. Could there be credence to the rumor that Zhao Ziyang was sympathetic with the student cause?

One could go back to class and hope the hard-liners in the government would forgive and forget, or escalate the protest in the hopes that it would strengthen the hand of reform-inclined members of the politburo.

Demonstrating with conspicuous patriotism and expressing discontent in an oblique way that was at least superficially congruent with core Communist ideals; that is to say, using the red flag to beat the red flag, seemed to be a reasonably well-thought-out strategy with some chance of success.

The long-legged Chen Li shifted restlessly on her bicycle as her mind wrestled with indecision. It seemed that Chen Li had almost made up her mind to join the demonstration when some annoying static over the student broadcast system brought to mind another problem.

Just who were the so-called student leaders? They hadn't been voted into office. They just sort of seized the initiative. Chen Li bristled at the idea of taking the lead from such overly ambitious peers, wondering instead what her teachers would counsel. Part of the problem with the student movement, it seemed to her, was that it was run by students.

Judging from the proliferation of paper flyers, however, the number of academic departments that supported the strike had doubled and was growing, which to her suggested at least tacit teacher support. She was more attentive to cues given by the teachers in the background than the students in the foreground.

The more aggressive students were defining the terms of engagement, and were beginning to sway thousands of apathetic and undecided peers with their persistent emotional pleas and florid urgency. In a country accustomed to periodic convulsions of government-initiated political campaigns, the idea of whipping up enthusiasm with banners and slogans and political outreach was a time-honored method. But unlike party-initiated campaigns such as the anti-rightist and anti–spiritual pollution movements, this was not a top-down political wind, at least as far as I could tell, but a popular groundswell from the bottom up. That is not to say it was free of top-down intrigue, a trickle of which was already visible in all the hopeful whispers about Zhao Ziyang, but it had little of the party-line coherence that one might expect of a directed action.

Getting student support for continuing the strike was not hard, even among this swarm of competitive young scholars, not only because it meant a holiday from studies, but because they, too, were vulnerable to the bandwagon effect. The more who joined in, the harder it was not to join, and the later one joined in, the more of a dullard one might be seen by those who joined in earlier. Chen Li was unduly vexed by the thought that she might join too early or too late. The bitter lesson of most Communist-induced campaigns applied here: better to anticipate the trend and join the flow, or at least parrot support, than to resist it and be isolated socially as a laggard or even reactionary element.

If History and Chemistry are going on strike, why not Physics?

Bright had explained it to me this way: "Qinghua University students, mostly in the sciences, have opted to go back to classes because they have a lower political consciousness. Beida is more radical and they want to strike. Shida, usually pretty conservative, is divided down the middle, half for and half against."

"Yeah, and at the Sports Institute," I said in follow up, "They haven't even heard about the strike!"

Chen Li said she was hearing that this day's demonstration was going to be a big one, maybe the biggest ever. You wouldn't want to miss out on the biggest demonstration in the history of China, now would you?

The prior illegal demos attracted huge turnouts with resounding popular support, making them hard acts to follow. So the students hyping the latest Beida demo had to come up with something new—something bigger, better, and more active. It would take something really special to regain the lost momentum, if not exceed, the marches of May 4 and April 27.

We watched headbanded students giving impromptu speeches, voices overlapping with the steady flow of announcements crackling over the activists' makeshift "radio station." Chen Li pointed out a trail of wires running from a set of speakers to a window in the adjacent dorm, saying that a set of rooms inside served as student strike headquarters.

A carnival of shouts and sounds came at us in all directions.

"*Bing-gwer! Bing-gwer!*" shouted matronly saleswomen in thick Beijing accents, "Popsicles for sale!"

"*Jianbing, Jianbing!*" shouted another, selling the popular crepes, made with flour, eggs, scallions, and chopped-up doughnut bits topped with a hot sauce. There were also carts selling ice cream and orange drinks, so the four basic food groups, in fast food that is, were covered.

Flimsy makeshift stalls and food hawkers clogged the busy pedestrian crossroads of Sanjiaodi. The entrepreneurs were not necessarily supportive of the students or their slogans, but business was good and their presence helped fortify the assembly. Steaming food carts provided a whiff of home cooking and normalcy in the rarified political air. Cash-poor patriotic students and petty capitalists forged a symbiotic union to keep the triangular courtyard brimming with life. I wondered what the uneducated but relatively prosperous vendors, among the success stories of Deng's economic program, thought of the students' grousing about vendors getting rich, let alone their antigovernment rhetoric.

I found out one man's view by ordering a *jianbing*. The hawker charged me considerably more than the person before me, which I at first attributed to the time-honored practice of ripping off dumb foreigners. When I pressed for an explanation, however, he claimed he was giving discounts only to activists. I eyed him skeptically while I ate the tasty Beijing pancake. Sure enough, the price varied depending on the customer's appearance. If the buyer was wearing a headband, armband, or shirt inked up with the signatures of friends, they got it cheap.

A stirring melody drifted in the air, cut with the pulsating rhythm of a tacky disco beat. Just behind the solemn, word-drenched bulletin boards, something more visceral competed for attention. Two tinny portable cassette players blasted out bouncy tunes, bringing attention to the sale of dozens of hand-labeled bootleg tapes, pirated and otherwise, which were laid out artfully on blankets. There were cassette tapes featuring Japanese ballads and other bootleg tapes. At the moment, Chyi Chin's "Wolf" was dueling against a bouncy electronic dance tune. But the product in pride of place, and the most justifiably bootlegged product because it had been banned as "spiritual pollution," was by Theresa Teng, Taiwan's leading singer of sentimental love songs. There was also a collection of Cui Jian tunes and a cassette of Hou Dejian's latest work.

Though an oddity as a Taiwan musician living in China, Hou attracted a broader range of domestic listeners than Cui Jian did, in part because he had been at it longer but also because he enjoyed media support from Beijing officials and party propagandists for having created a modern anthem for Chinese on both sides of the Taiwan straits with his hit song, "Descendants of the Dragon."

Hou Dejian's music and quasi-outsider status also earned him more conspicuous income than Cui Jian, because he qualified for a tax break as a native of Taiwan. Hou lived with his wife, Cheng Ling, a local singer and aspiring actress, in a well-appointed apartment in the Overseas Chinese compound near the Friendship Hotel.

During the lull between the demonstrations of May 4 and May 10, I spent time with Hou at his home to talk about collaborating on *Chinabeat*. Although it would be no easy matter to get him and Cui Jian working on the same project—their styles were different and each liked being head honcho—things had calmed down sufficiently on the protest front to think that such explorations were at least possible. Hou was an effervescent host, full of energy, talking late into the night, causing me to miss curfew once again. He put me up at his home for an evening, letting me sleep in his small but functional garage studio, which was right next to where he kept his prized red Mercedes-Benz.

"Buy some May fourth souvenir T-shirts!" someone behind me yelled out.

"Special offer now!" another young voice beckoned.

I turned around to see not another street merchant plying his wares, but students hawking demonstration-related paraphernalia. The most eye-catching item on sale was the mint-green "Democracy and Science" T-shirt, commemorating an antiquated slogan of the 1919 May Fourth movement that had taken on new life due to the role of scientists, such as physicist turned democracy activist Fang Lizhi, in calling for open inquiry in the shared spirit of both science and democracy.

"Can you bring the price down a bit?" I asked, expecting a spirited bargaining session. It's usually a sign of ignorance to pay the first price offered.

"Fixed price," the earnest salesman replied. "These shirts are printed by hand, by Beida students."

Well, that explains it. Beida students deigned to print them, however, so they must be special. Out of the habit, I haggled a bit more, but the student price was as fixed as that of a government-run store and I hit a wall. I liked the color and the slogan, so I bought a bunch of them to hand out to friends.

The Sanjiaodi loudspeakers started crackling with a call to action. Chen Li said they were calling on other schools to join them, or perhaps more accurately, to follow their excellent, courageous, and necessary lead. At noon there would be a rally meeting near the front gate of the university. It was a new form of protest with Chinese characteristics: the bicycle demonstration!

Chen Li and I sat on our bikes under a tree near the front gate of Beida to observe the hatching of this new and unusual type of protest. The "marchers" wheeled in from all directions, mostly walking their bicycles due to the utter congestion. Like earlier protests, which used patriotic anthems as a cover for covert political action, the bicycle demo could hide in plain sight in a city of a million tinkling bicycles. The tree-lined road leading to the main gate on campus attracted black bicycles like crows, watching and waiting for a sign to take sudden flight.

It was one o'clock but there was still no movement in a forward direction. Then a few minutes after the hour, a sudden crescendo of tinkling bicycle bells alerted us that the pent-up energy of the waiting cyclists was about to be unleashed. To the background of jangling bells, screeching brakes, flopping pedals, and the soft thud of rubber tires bumping into the spokes of other bicycle wheels, the demonstration creakily commenced.

Beida professors, some of whom lived in apartments near the south gate, were on the scene talking to students, and in some cases actively cheered, much to Chen Li's delight. But most of the older campus residents kept their distance. Whether it was the wisdom of age or bitter memories of the Cultural Revolution not yet faded, many of them merely watched wistfully from the windows and balconies of the ramshackle teachers' dormitories.

All at once, the mass of a million spokes and wheels, greasy chains and kickstands, heaved into motion again. Enmeshed in a traffic jam at the starting gate, the metallic parade of creaking, entangled bicycles slowly lurched forward, balanced and propelled by feet, more often on the ground than on the pedals. Because it took just a few wobbly bicycles to block a narrow path, the south gate of campus became a bottleneck slowing egress even though the guards did nothing but watch.

Once we rolled off campus and hit the lightly trafficked streets of Haidian District, the mass of bicycles speeded up in concert, a forward movement that felt truly liberating. All demonstrators, from flag bearers to group leaders, were on wheels, so when we finally hit open road, it was possible to race en masse at a flag-whipping speed.

The plan as we understood it was to go around Beijing following the perimeter of the circuitous ring road, but first we had to join forces with allies from other campuses.

"It's a forty-kilometer circle," I heard someone say. "When we get downtown, just follow the old city wall of Beijing."

The circling of an ancient city had a conceptual appeal that transcended the political message of ringing bells for change. We would be doing a historic ring around Beijing following the path of the old city wall that once graced Beijing. Destroyed by the Communists in the name of an illusory openness, the wall was better remembered today as an architectural victim of misguided rule by fiat.

Chen Li was well aware of the historical ironies of the journey, but she was no hotheaded activist. Unlike some late joiners, who pedaled with double the enthusiasm, she continued to show hesitation and review her options at each main juncture along the way. Twice we pulled out from the convoy at her insistence when it looked like there might be trouble from the police. I appreciated her caution; I was a bit worried myself. But what impressed me more was that she did not fall into lockstep behind the bossy student leaders up front, who were by now commanding the metaphorical ten thousand troops. The only thing more surprising than the speed with which a handful of rash students took control was the willingness of so many intelligent individuals to become followers.

True, the march would not have been taking wing if everyone took the cautious wait-and-see attitude the two of us did, and some of the student leaders at Beida, Wang Dan in particular, were considered to be thoughtful and reasonable, but the rapidity with which Chinese students fell into line and accepted groupthink troubled me nonetheless.

But as we cruised breezily down the practically car-free streets picking up other waiting wheeled student contingents, a kind of ragtag mass elation built with each addition to our ranks. Soon we had not only a solid procession of bicycles before us but an uncountable number behind us. So many trailed us we couldn't see the end of the line.

Outside Political Science and Law University there was some confusion over an issue that was to dog the student movement from the beginning to the end: campus rivalries. We waited on the overpass of the Third Ring Road while the student leadership squabbled among themselves to establish a pecking order. Who goes first? Who goes second? Who leads, who follows? Who is in charge? In China every rebel wants to be another Mao.

Chen Li said the other schools were mad because Beida was late and they didn't see why they had to wait. The Beida activists wanted the others to accept the natural pecking order of things, with Beida at the top, of course. Shida was designated second, and I gave some thought to dropping back to join that contingent where I was more likely to run into people I knew, but staying in line seemed the most sensible thing to do, given the crush of traffic and calls for discipline.

Deeply felt school rivalries, sometimes amusing, sometimes petty, persisted till the end of the movement. Bright, a graduate student, had studied at both

Shida and Beida. Wuerkaixi was becoming the mascot for Shida. Wang Dan represented Beida's cool intellectual tradition. Chai Ling was a grad student at Shida, but originally was at Beida. Where did she fit in?

At one particularly tiresome bottleneck along the way, Chen Li and I broke ranks with the Beida contingent to climb on top of a crumbling remnant of the Yuan Dynasty wall to get a better view. From the top we could see that the procession of black bicycles was at least a mile long and ten to fifteen bikes thick. That's not a totally unusual sight in Beijing. After all, rush hour involves cyclists in the hundreds of thousands. But today the traffic was gathered in one concentrated, coordinated burst, lined up and aligned with Tiananmen, like tremulous iron filings reaching towards the mother lode.

Pedestrians and supporters on foot lent their support to the unidirectional traffic flow by standing shoulder to shoulder forming a human wall that effectively sealed off competing traffic at big intersections. Many bystanders were as fearless as those demonstrating, energized and militant in their expression. I could detect no opposition to the sight of student "rioters" on wheels. Instead, there was much cheering and waving, as on May Fourth.

The people peering from windows and lining both sides of the streets could see with their own eyes that the demonstrators were not monsters. They could hear with their own ears plainspoken slogans calling for change. They had been young once, during the Cultural Revolution, and might feel, not without a certain trepidation, that the essence of being young in China was to be bold and to rebel. Did those already middle-aged men and women on the sidewalks look upon the rally with nostalgia or tragic portent?

We scrambled down the crumbling section of the old city ramparts and hopped back on our bikes to join the cycling multitudes as the Shida contingent weighed in, grinding past the traffic jam at Academy South Road, but eventually picking up speed as we streamed toward Second Ring Road. It was smooth sailing most of the way until we reached an overpass near West Chang'an Boulevard. Traffic came to a total halt at Muxudi, a strategic intersection en route to the square.

Even though the road was wide at this point, there was a monumental bicycle jam; stalled cyclists sporting red flags and bandannas were visible for almost a mile back. Chen Li and I got off our bicycles and patiently inched along on foot, poking and being poked by the wide handlebars of other sturdy black bikes, until we got to the overpass. Word had it that the student leaders up front had been confronted by the traffic police, who temporarily halted their movement, while the rear guard, unaware of the problem, kept moving until the whole procession had collapsed upon itself.

We put down the kickstands and rested while the procession regrouped. For the first time I noticed the participation of demonstrators who were old enough to be teachers. The traffic tie-up thrust us into proximity of a writers' delegation, a spirited contingent, mostly men in their thirties, who had a distinct subculture of their own. They had even longer hair than the students, for whom longish hair was the norm, and some of them sported beards. They wore the simple cotton clothing of their generation, which few teenagers could be seen wearing then, and had a wizened, bohemian look. During the hour-long delay, we chatted with the writers and watched them entertain their younger brothers and sisters with artful calligraphy, painted on the backs of shirts. Someone was distributing red headbands and someone even gave me a school pin to make me feel more included. One of the older participants had his shirt inked with lyrics from China's national anthem.

ARISE, YE WHO REFUSE TO BE SLAVES!

A group of writers and poets in support of the students dashed out the twin ideographs for *ziyou* and *minzhu* on the shirts of their younger brethren. The painted shirts proclaimed in black ink what a thousand voices had been saying:

FREEDOM AND DEMOCRACY!

Democracy, what is it anyway? *Minzhu*, meaning the rule of the people, is both new and old in China. Old, because it was the slogan of the students in 1919 and it even inspired late Qing Dynasty reformers at the turn of the century. New, because rule by the people still eluded China, even after decades of fighting in the name of the people.

Ziyou, usually translated as freedom, sounded good, but it was a step short of chaos and anarchy to the control-conscious. It had civil war and Cold War connotations as in "Free China," meaning Taiwan. *Ziyou* also meant "liberal" in some contexts, further freighting it with mixed connotations, such bourgeois liberalization. Seeking to be free or merely liberal in liberated China was not easy.

Word drifted back that the demonstration could resume, but not along the route mapped out in advance. The traffic impasse was resolved when the vanguard row of bicycles signaled a change in direction to the west. To head west, as everyone knew, was to go in the opposite direction of Tiananmen, a dispiriting thought. But the promise of being on the move, regardless of direction, had a strong appeal. Sitting on a bicycle going nowhere in the hot, hazy sunlight was an exercise in frustration. We picked up speed, and with it the appearance of a breeze, and with that the illusion of progress. It was good to be moving again, even if it was the wrong way.

The road to Tiananmen had been blocked by police. We could see them standing there as we made our big right turn. Word was that the police had been firm but not unfriendly, and there was no fighting or confrontation. The traffic police were just doing their job, cordoning off the section of Chang'an Boulevard that went past the leadership headquarters at Zhongnanhai on the way to Tiananmen. If the men in uniform had been sticklers about not allowing a left turn towards the square, they showed little concern for what the demonstrators might do elsewhere. That was someone else's responsibility.

Beijing's gridlike layout of large east/west avenues crisscrossed by north/south roads made it nearly impossible to lose one's bearings. It became immediately obvious to me when we turned south after a feint to the west that we were still headed for Tiananmen after all, only in a roundabout way.

The snakelike chain of cycles doubled back to head for our unspoken destination. Successfully overcoming the police roadblock doubled the good spirits; the collective mood was ecstatic and electric. The indirect route to the square offered no obstacle to our forward motion. I couldn't believe the traffic police were so dim-witted as to fall for the ruse. It seems more likely they were following orders to the letter without enthusiasm. Once they had stopped us from turning east onto Chang'an Boulevard, they didn't seem to care where we went. It was as if they put up a perfunctory show of opposition to the march, not in real opposition, but so as not to get in trouble for not doing their job. Bureaucracy at its best!

When we got to broad Qianmen Avenue we veered east, making a nosedive to Tiananmen, as inexorably as if pulled by gravity. It was here, as the audience thickened, that Chen Li heard a variation of *laowai paobu* that she was kind enough to share with me. What were people saying at the sight of me today? *Laowai qi zixingche!*—whitey rides the bike!

As we picked up speed, spirits soared. The flying wedge leading the pack thinned out to about five bicycles abreast, stretching and doubling the procession in length. It was a race to beat the police to the square, or so we thought as we hit our clunky bike pedals with an accelerating clip. This got the adrenaline going. There was no stopping our unauthorized procession now. Whatever residual indecisiveness one might feel was largely overcome by the bold and inspiring spirit of fellow cyclists. Butterflies in the stomach took flight as we made the invigorating plunge towards the square.

As the bicycle procession reached the outskirts of the Tiananmen area, I couldn't imagine pulling out, even if there were police waiting. I didn't want to miss the thrill of streaming across the symbolic plaza in a swift convoy of thousands, holding aloft fluttering flags while wheeling it for free speech.

The mad dash across Tiananmen Square was the high point of the day. A defiant burst of energy propelled us clear across the forbidden ground in a giant, diagonal slash. There were pockets of urban well-wishers and curious rural tourists, who out of friendly support or fear of speeding bicycles stepped back from the bicycle course to form a line of observers on both sides. We sped along like chessboard knights across the graphlike matrix of the square, starting in the lower left-hand corner going two steps north, one step east, then one step north and two steps east, finally exiting on the upper right-hand side.

The vivid pathway cut by us cyclists swooshing across the square was volatile and transient; it lasted only as long as the last bicycle in the procession. Banners strapped to bicycles and some huge red flags were held high in the air, balanced deftly by skilled cyclists. The way the flags whipped in the wind created an air of excitement. The red headbands, representing blood, rebellion, and speed, were perfect for the course. How else could we identify our cyclists in a city of several million bicycles?

From the vantage point of a gliding bicycle, it was a magnificent scene. Before us and behind us, red flags and banners lashed the air and unfurled in the jet stream of rushing cycles. This gave the illusion that flags and banners, some strapped to bicycles, others held aloft by skilled cyclists, were flying above the crowd under their own power, like the magical brooms of the sorcerer's apprentice.

As the vanguard zigzagged and sought openings through the crowd ahead of us, I suddenly had to wonder, where did all the spectators come from, anyway? At least some of the onlookers were supporters, because they lined up, holding up traffic, creating a protective corridor for the bicycles to slip through. By the time we reached the northeast quadrant of the square, the banks of spectators were four or five deep on each side, shouting in unison and clapping in support.

The mood was relaxed and confident, not only because the police backed off, but because there was a sense of safety due to the tacit support of townspeople and the growing camaraderie of fellow cyclists. Thanks to the elation of the experience, all my doubts, and I think those of Chen Li, about whether or not one should get involved in such an event vanished. I was exactly where I wanted to be.

The streaming rivulet of bicycles got dammed up at Nanchizi Intersection just beyond the square while group facilitators conferred on which way to go. Tires against tires, the procession scrunched up into a mass of protesters resting with feet on the ground for balance. The signal to continue was passed back one voice at a time and a million shiny spokes were soon creaking back in motion, revolving confidently down Chang'an Boulevard towards the diplomatic section of town.

And look, over there! Foreign journalists!

In front of the Beijing Hotel we could see foreign film crews scrambling to set up their cameras to capture this unusual and uniquely Chinese demonstration on film. Unlike the well-documented marches of April 27 and May 4, it seemed like the foreign press had been caught unprepared by this one. But that was a relief in a way, for cameras have an unnatural effect on people on both sides of the lens. As the brusque men with big cameras scrambled up their ladders, taking aim at us, there was a tinge of humiliation in being hunted by the roving lenses, being reduced to a kind of native wildlife.

We weren't sure if being on TV was good news or bad news. Had the press been tipped off by the government about an imminent crackdown, or tipped off by the students about the rally? To see newsmen arrive on the scene was a bit like sighting vultures; their appearance was usually a sign of trouble. As we ignored the cameras and sped on our way, I heard students complain that a bunch of journalists showed up the other day at the last minute when it looked like the police might stage a crackdown and left just as quickly when the crisis passed.

What was their take on the story? So far, Western reports seemed mildly amused at the unexpected protests, usually framed as a sidebar to the Gorbachev story. Depending on how reasonable the students were perceived and portrayed, it could go either way. In Iran in 1979, student protesters were the bad guys, but generally speaking there was a press bias towards students because they were relatively powerless in the larger scheme of things. Although I hadn't seen any foreign broadcasts, I had no reason to think the Western reports had been unfriendly to the Chinese students.

But being on the inside looking out and hearing some of the unkind comments that were stimulated by the sight of "laowai" with cameras got me thinking. Who were these alien invaders who thought nothing of sticking mikes, cameras, and notepads in the faces of people who had good reason to value anonymity and good reason not to have their pictures taken? Since most of the journalists did not speak Chinese, they depended on government-provided interpreters, another risk for the rebels.

The bicycle convoy passed Jianwai, the handsome apartment blocks where the Western press lived in assigned housing with assigned telephone numbers and worked in assigned offices with assigned drivers and interpreters. It was an open secret that the Chinese government assigned spies to work in the offices of foreign journalists, and, as if to justify such craven controls, it was whispered that foreign journalists were really spies.

Bright told me that most foreigners did not fully comprehend the degree to which their activities were being monitored. She and her friends had grown up under surveillance and were inured to the lack of privacy as a part of daily life. They felt that foreign reporters were not careful enough in their dealings with Chinese informants and interviewees.

I had seen this firsthand freelancing for American TV crews. In a one-on-one situation, Chinese students were often quite content to pour their hearts out to foreigners on the reasonable assumption that the foreigner in question was not likely to be working for the Chinese police. Yet the same interview subjects would freeze up the moment the big camera was brought in and the lights went on, because recorded statements were incriminating. There was also a detectable shift in mood during an interview when a government interpreter arrived on the scene, and with good reason. In a land of ubiquitous spying, better safe than sorry.

At the same time, there were those who let themselves be interviewed without fully comprehending the gravity of speaking on camera. The presence of the camera is both disconcerting and seductive in its effect, much in the way that an armed soldier can be both fearsome and admirable. The magnetic polarity of television both attracts and repels fear.

After cruising past the "no Chinese allowed" enclave for foreigners centered around the foreigner-friendly Friendship Store, the bicycle convoy heaved forward. To our immediate left on the north side of the road was the solidly built Qijiayuan residential compound, where two friends of mine lived: Jimmy Florcruz, a Filipino who worked for *Time* magazine, and John Woodruff, a correspondent for the *Baltimore Sun*. I knew from them that being accredited as a journalist in Beijing was an occupational hazard; it forced China watchers to become the watched. On a slightly more positive note, it created an esprit de corps among reporters, exotics stuck in the same foreign-only fishbowl.

Covering a country of a billion-plus people is a daunting task even under the best of conditions. But when journalists are forced to live in monitored luxury housing, life in the gilded cage exerts a subtle pressure of its own. Add to that the pressure to meet deadlines and accommodate the wish list of the home office, and reportage gets even further skewed. When I worked for NBC as an interpreter in Beijing and Shanghai in 1987, I found it particularly disheartening to see how their coverage of China went from one cliché to another, from panda to ping-pong to dissidents and dictatorship, and then back to pandas again. The expert producers put on a good show for the home audience, to be sure, but I felt the truth got lost somewhere over the Pacific.

Chances were I knew this part of town much better than my fellow cyclists. It was a kind of modern-day foreign legation, a comfort zone for foreigners, and while it was heavily surveilled, it was not without its attractions. The road we had just passed was littered with the grand architectural monuments of expatriate Beijing: the International Club, the Jianguo Hotel, the CITIC Building, the Friendship Store, and apartments for diplomats and journalists.

The lengthy convoy of bicycles kept slithering eastward until we reached a mammoth hole in the ground, a new construction slated to be something called Guo Mao, or China Trade Center. From there we made a ninety-degree turn to the north, gliding onto Third Ring Road where we met only light vehicular traffic. We cruised briskly without interruption along the broad pavement of the ring road, amazingly devoid of cars, heading north, and then turned east for the home stretch on our way to the most tactically precise protest point of the day. Tired legs were urged to press on and thirsty throats had to wait until we reached the front gate of the word factory that printed the incendiary accusation of "fomenting turmoil."

At the main gate of the *People's Daily* compound, the convoy of ten thousand bicycles came to a complete and utter halt. There was some halfhearted chanting, led by a familiar, exceptionally strident female voice. "Sounds like Chai Ling, she was at Beida," my companion said.

"*People's Daily*!
Full of nonsense!
Telling lies to the people!
Where is your conscience?"

Arrival was anticlimactic because we were tired and thirsty and there was no place to go and nothing to do. Immobile, and soon immobilized by the crush of bicycles around us, we stoically endured the lapse of leadership and a master plan as bikes bunched up near the front gate. Banners were waved and slogans shouted, but due to creeping fatigue, it seemed like what little energy was left might better be conserved for the long ride home.

The joy and elation of the rolling protest had peaked for me at Tiananmen Square because the geomancy of the place was so appealing, its very openness an invitation to big thoughts, its embrace of the sky an inspiration for ideals with universal significance. Dismounting in front of the *People's Daily* office on a crowded suburban street to protest—far from Tiananmen, far from campus—made perfect sense politically, but it lacked the aesthetic grandeur of the Square or the appealing centrality of the route followed on the fourth of May.

While I fully supported calls for a free press, it didn't suit my style to yell out angry slogans in unison with those barking out announcements.

Likewise, Chen Li's lips barely moved. But there were no shortage of noisy shouts, strident sloganeering, and menacing fists being thrust into the air

Physical exhaustion was probably a factor, but more than anything else it was the lack of forward movement that caused the march to implode. The target had been reached, a message had been conveyed with great repetition, and there was nothing more to do, not as a group anyway. Unlike a march on foot, where eye contact abounds and small talk is plentiful, one doesn't really get to know one's neighbors in a bicycle marathon.

The return to campus in northwest Beijing was an unorganized free-for-all, everyone on his own, and the carefully observed discipline of the first half of the bicycle procession got lax as students took shortcuts home or made stops along the way for food and drink.

Chen Li and I took a much-sought-after break at a local snack bar, knocking off a few bottles of warm orange soda and sharpening our teeth on rock-hard chunks of stale cake. The saleslady stared without smiling, which I took to be a variation of the typical rude stare afforded to foreigners by someone unfamiliar with the species. Then I realized what caught her eye was not so much the blond hair and blue-green eyes as the red headband, school identification pin, and baggy pants. The long hard look she gave me got me wondering again whether or not I was pushing my luck by getting involved in Chinese student demonstrations.

But it was also in the snack bar where we finally got to meet some of our fellow "long marchers." Spirits were generally high because yet another successful act of defiance had been pulled off without a hitch. We got to talking about the beauty of the humble black hunk of metal and chain called a bicycle. The bicycle was a necessary and appreciated vehicle of the masses. It offered physical freedom from bus schedules, long lines, and the tempers of other people.

Cars were for important people and rich people; that was the unspoken message. Officials and political commissars in the "people's" government cruised in Mercedes limousines with tinted windows, an import said to be favored by Deng Xiaoping himself.

The procession of ten thousand bicycles might have moved too fast to draw thick crowds, but it was a crowd-pleaser, especially around the square. The cash-poor, bicycle-bound students had been successful in generating instant rapport because the materially humble world they inhabited was not far removed from that of the working class. The vast majority of city dwellers did not ride in cars; having access to an automobile was a perk or a privilege of power. The banners of the day were ostensibly about press freedom, but anger at corruption and unfair privilege were an unspoken undercurrent of the movement.

The moving demonstration had also brought into the open, for the first time in a long time, the proliferation of revolutionary accoutrements, as the wary gaze of the waitress reminded me. Headbands—inexpensive, easy to make, easy to see—helped to psychologically unite a disparate gathering of idiosyncratic individuals. Waving red flags increased the aura of rebellion and placed current actions within the orthodox revolutionary tradition. Sharing little strips of cloth with school names gave the sense of membership in units allied with the movement. Hand-painted posters and banners were expressive of both original views and the emerging student party line.

Boisterous voices, wildly unkempt hair, youthful sunburned faces, and sweat-sopped clothes made the protesters easy to recognize anywhere in town, even after headbands and armbands were removed. Since students in China have to wash their own clothes by hand, thin synthetic fabrics that dry overnight on a hanger have long been favored over more fashionable wear, though there was no shortage of imitation designer shirts, golf hats, and visor caps.

Shoulder bags and army book bags carried snacks, books, and eyeglass cases while keeping hands free to steer bikes and negotiate traffic. Windbreakers and baggy jackets protected against rain and the desertlike range of temperature, from scorching day to chilly night.

In order to prevent outside interference and infiltration, and to readily identify who was who, personalized armbands, headbands, school pins, and school T-shirts became the name cards and informal ID passes for the students. Another effective means of maintaining order in the ranks was the grouping by school and department, as I learned the hard way on May 4 when I stepped away from the Shida contingent to take a walk and was denied re-entry until vouched for by Bright and friends. By sticking to well-defined groups, unaffiliated outsiders could be quickly identified and questioned, perhaps even denied admittance to what appeared to be an unorganized freewheeling crowd of thousands.

Unlike the shouting match with the Western photographer on the fourth, I witnessed no hostility towards the press during the parade on wheels. If anything, there was almost a palpable sense of disappointment that the Western press had not turned out in bigger numbers. With the Chinese press immobilized by Deng's malevolent characterization of the students as rioters, it fell on the foreigners to report the facts. If the cameras weren't there, there was the danger that a major publicity-seeking event would go unnoticed and uncertified in the eyes of the outside world.

I for one hoped it was dawning on students hungry for publicity that the Western press was not just an elite foreign presence—spies in disguise as government hacks would have it—but a professional force of information collectors who could help get the truth out. But suspicions lingered and I found a number of Chinese students were under pressure from their peers not to talk to the media, at least not without prior approval.

We stretched our aching legs and gradually rejoined what was left of the ragtag bicycle brigade, peddling slowly back to Beida. Despite the late hour of our long-delayed return, we were met by applause and rousing cheers from a waiting committee of campus supporters, including quite a few professors and other adults. For a few moments at least, the sense of accomplishment and the warm recognition made all the aches and pains go away. Chen Li was simply beaming with pride during our victory lap. Given her cautious nature, it said a lot about the movement that someone like her was willing to join in. In the space of a few days she had gone from someone who didn't want to cut class to a lukewarm supporter to a proud participant.

For dinner, we settled on a small state-run restaurant a few hundred yards down the road from the front gate. Once we got inside, we ordered sodas and beer, trying to quench a thirst that wouldn't go away. We were joined by other tired cyclists inside and struck up easy conversation as we rested our sore rumps on padded chairs. Soon the place filled up. Although it was a state-run joint, the food was good and the service fast and friendly. Here in the shadow of Beida, bound, for the moment, by shared bonds of subversive celebration, I felt at one with the others.

PART II

WAXING MOON

MAY 13

◑

Hunger Strike

Honey-colored sunlight pours into my room. The sun is up, time to make a move. Today's a special day, so I hurry over to the foreign dorm for a shower. Running hot water in the morning is a rare joy, even if it comes out of an unadorned pipe; balls of hot liquid pound my neck and shoulders, washing away drowsiness and unsettled dreams of the night.

I opt for a full breakfast on this, my first day of work, to gear up for an assignment that I face not without a tremor of reluctance. I'd spent most of the day before walking around the tranquil lake district of Houhai with Jenny and Bright, talking about the pros and cons of working for the Western media.

Two bottles of fresh yogurt for starters, then toast and fried eggs, which taste like they should even if they were served as stir-fry. The whole meal, including a cup of hot milk, sets me back less than a buck in meal tickets.

In that sense, my new job pays well. I can expect one hundred US dollars a day for helping the British Broadcasting Corporation (BBC) produce news coverage for the duration of the Sino-Soviet Summit, five days at the max. The job offer came indirectly through a friend who I had previously worked with at NBC, a Canadian cameraman who had seen me marching with the students on the fourth. I remember seeing Fritz, a powerfully built man with red hair and a winning grin, take aim with a big camera from the side of the road. He later told me about the BBC, and the BBC about me, and they hired me on his recommendation.

I appreciated the tip, but was not without misgivings, for the imperatives of work would, on the one hand, take away my freedom to march with friends and follow the flow of things as I was wont to do, but also might, paradoxically, put me back on the street amidst my friends in the guise of a journalist, which made me, in effect, a paid spy and informer for a foreign news agency. That the information I was being hired to collect was collected in good faith with the intent of sharing it with a large public, albeit mostly foreign TV viewers in a foreign land, helped diffuse my nagging doubts, and there was a touch of ironic consolation in the notion that it was a two-way street. Among the people I would report on, some were no doubt already reporting on me. The ethical barriers of working as a paid hack for a network were not insurmountable, not in political terms, but I feared it might put me on the other side of the wall from my Chinese friends.

The lengthy taxi ride across town burned up a pocketful of cash, paid in crisp foreign exchange certificates (FEC) scrip, because the destination I instructed the driver to take me to bespoke luxury, thus reducing my leverage to haggle. I bounded into the airy chrome-columned atrium of the Great Wall Hotel, an international island of air-conditioned calm and thick-walleted cachet.

I knew the layout well. While working as a tour guide for Lindblad luxury tours, I had taken pampered American tourists here when it first opened and was the only hotel of its kind. It was also where the press stayed during President Reagan's visit to Beijing and where, by sheer chance, I bumped into American journalist Ted Koppel in an elevator only to be greeted with the TV announcer's trademark grin and a quick lesson in journalism. "You're lucky you are not stuck in this hotel like the rest of us," he said, wryly taking note of my weathered Mao jacket. "I'm sure it's much more interesting outside."

The glass elevator transported me above and beyond the roof of the atrium to a quiet, carpeted residential floor where the temporary BBC TV office was located. The first person I noticed when I stepped in the room was a kindly looking man with short, unkempt blond hair and a rugged tan. I could tell right away he was the reporter in the room. He smiled, stood up, and offered his hand, breaking the bemused stares of various producers and technicians, some of whom glared at me as if I had just intruded on a private club.

"Hello, I'm Brian Barron, you must be Phil!" he said, putting a cheerful emphasis on my name. His instant friendliness, his safari shirt, his observant eyes, and his award-winning smile were not just part of his personality; they were part and parcel of his job as an ace foreign correspondent for the BBC. Next, I shook hands with the senior producer, a pale man with a weak, sweaty handshake. Still more stares. Then the reporter kindly indicated that I was to be welcomed on board and the others, one by one, stopped what they were doing to offer their hands in greeting. The conviviality lasted another minute or so until the producer called the room to order. That was the moment when I realized the warm and dashing Brian was not the one in charge.

"Phil—it's all right if we call you Phil, isn't it?" the producer asked, betraying a boarding-school reluctance to use first names. "You will be out with the crew and help them get around. I'm told you speak Chinese and you were a student here for a while? Right, well that takes care of that. Also, you can translate some things for us here in the office."

"Sure, I'd be glad to, but I thought you needed help reporting, you know the summit and all the stuff going on."

"We have enough people on Gorby. You can help us if we go to the campuses. Tell us, Phil. What's going on with the students now? Anything interesting?"

I found myself talking about the bicycle demonstration and then about seeing Chinese student friends during the two-day lull in protest activity that followed when it occurred to me that I might want to choose my words more carefully. It didn't feel right, talking about friends to a room of strangers, especially since the unspoken pact was that anything we discussed would be fair game as a news subject. If the BBC sought interviews, the easiest people to contact were people I knew already, but I couldn't get used to the idea of my friends being interview subjects. It seemed unfair to them and might even get them in trouble. I paused, weighing what to tell, what not to.

"No, it's pretty quiet. The main debate is whether, well, at Beida there are posters calling for more action, continuing the strike, but the campus I'm staying at is a bit more conservative."

"Could you tell us more about—" started the reporter.

"Say, Brian," interrupted a lanky, pale-skinned producer, pulling rank. "Brian, what do you have planned for today? I think I might come along for the ride."

"I thought we'd ask Phil here to take us to the, what is it called, the Shedan Democracy Wall, and maybe I'll do a piece to camera there."

Xidan Democracy Wall? That was torn down ten years ago, just a bunch of billboards now. Oh well, it's the first day of work, better keep my mouth shut. The BBC must have their reasons. But if one really wants to see a functioning democracy wall these days, a campus such as Beida or Shida is the place to go.

When the camera crew assembled, I suggested to Brian that we politely exclude the government-appointed interpreter, a type of barbarian handler that experience had taught me to give wide berth to. He immediately understood and readily agreed. He was a pro who had, after all, covered the fall of Saigon and other big news events.

Downstairs I was introduced to the "BBC driver," a timid man who wore the white gloves of a chauffeur, but who made it clear from the moment he nervously tried to start the engine that he was a novice behind the wheel. In a free-market situation, we would have opted for another car, but we had no choice. He was assigned to the BBC by a state-controlled dispatcher and we couldn't drive ourselves. We could wing it on translation, though, and the government-assigned interpreter was given busywork in the office to keep him out of the car.

The driver, who introduced himself as "Min from Beijing," was relieved to hear that I could speak Chinese, but he thought it irregular that we were traveling without a Chinese escort and made several queries to that effect.

"Just take us to the democracy wall," Brian told the driver, and I duly translated and gave directions.

Min didn't know a thing about the wall, but the *d* word gave him pause. About a half hour later we reached to the corner of Chang'an Boulevard and the ancient shopping street known as Xidan.

"Well, Brian," I said. "Here we are, only it doesn't exist anymore." I pointed to the right. "That's what's left of what used to be the democracy wall."

The driver had slowed down at the intersection but had not come to complete halt when Brian impulsively swung open the passenger door and jumped out of the still-moving vehicle onto the busy road. Acting like he had just been parachuted into a war zone, the reporter brusquely motioned for the crew to follow him. The driver stopped the car from rolling, but turned red and nearly had a fit. Cars behind us were starting to honk.

"Tell him to get back in! Tell him to get back in!" Min waved his hands frantically. "This is a no-stopping zone, I will get a fine. Please! Tell him I will . . . "

I called after Brian to no avail, for he was almost out of shouting range, skillfully dodging the erratic flow of bicycles and cars now trying to worm their way past the halted van.

"I cannot tolerate this. I am going back!" the driver said.

Min inched the van forward, getting a heap of verbal abuse from other drivers. His natural excitability and timidity only made matters worse and soon he had the van on the diagonal, blocking two lanes of traffic.

Cursing until he worked up a sweat, Min got out of the car and disappeared without explanation.

"Phil?" asked Brian, peering into the tinted windows of the van, driver's seat abandoned. "Where's the driver?"

"Don't know," I said. "He was angry. But look, at least he left us the van!"

"What the hell is he angry for? It's his fucking job!"

I walked around the thickly peopled intersection on the lookout for a slightly plump Chinese man with a fierce crew cut. I found him on the sidewalk, wiping his forehead with a thin towel, all steamed up. I pleaded with him to return to the van. "Come on, *shifu*, come on master, let's go," I said, using the honorific to calm him.

"They force me to break traffic rules. I will not go!"

"Don't let them get you angry, that's just the way they are."

"They break the rules!"

"Yes, sometimes reporters can be hard to understand," I said. "But look, they are all obediently waiting in the van now."

"If I drive, they must listen to me!" Min pleaded. "I am the driver!"

Drivers had a certain social cachet in car-scarce China, but the mere fact of being the designated operator of an expensive imported van failed to impress the Londoners, and he suspected as much. I explained that drivers were routinely referred to as "master."

The van turned right and then crawled slowly but steadily north on a congested two-lane street. Along the way, Brian explained that he wasn't really interested in the democracy wall; what he was really after was some evidence of political posters.

Anxious that my first outing with the BBC not be a total failure, I decided to tell him about the hot water shack at Shida.

"The water shack?" questioned the slightly aloof cameraman. It was the first thing he said all day and it seemed freighted with skepticism.

"It's like, how can I explain? It's the place you go to find out what's happening."

"Do you think Min the Master would be good enough to take us there?" asked Brian.

"Um, the university is to the north of here. I mean, if worst comes to worst we could actually go on foot if we had to." I was already beginning to worry about Min's reaction to the idea that we drive onto a crowded campus full of striking students.

"Walking?" Brian asked sarcastically. "Not with all the gear, Phil. What do you think we have a van for?"

I gave Min directions to Xinwai Road without mentioning the university.

The van rumbled past weathered walls, gray brick houses, and inner courtyards decorated with colorful laundry. We slid through narrow *hutong*, passed small gardens and children playing and—*screech*! The van skidded to a stop and all its passengers were whipped forward as the driver made an uncharacteristically sudden, unscheduled stop.

Min was now cursing violently in Chinese. He cursed us. He cursed the bicycles in front of us and behind us. But he saved his choicest comments for the man on the rickety old bicycle cart who tried to squeeze past our car.

"Your mother's a . . . you fool, watch out for my car!"

The crew, momentarily appeased by what they thought was Min's attempt to make a beeline to the university, was not the slightest bit amused when the white-gloved driver got out of his van and made a time-consuming search for scratches.

"Phil, what is going on?" Brian asked, glancing at me, then the producer in the backseat.

"Beats me," I said.

"Come on, let's go," I urged Min. "No scratches, right?"

Min got back in, giving a long pleading look at Brian, whom he clearly took for the boss. To him Brian was much more of a boss than I or the real boss sitting in the backseat.

"Tell him to pull ahead now," said Brian. "I'll watch on this side for our mate, the master."

"Turn right here," I told the driver, who was still unaware that we were heading for Shida, "then a left there and go straight." I wanted to save the argument about not being able to visit a university without permission for the last minute so we could get within striking distance and, if necessary, walk onto campus.

We came shooting out of the alley into the bright sunlight at Xisi and put-putted north towards Xinjiekou Intersection, picking up speed. Suddenly everyone was in good spirits again, after being delivered from the dark, narrow lane onto the colorful thoroughfare with calligraphic signboards advertising clothes, musical instruments, cigarettes, and lamb kebabs.

"Phil, if you should see anything interesting along the way, please tell the driver to stop." Brian asked gingerly, ceding some decision-making clout.

Under the billboards that grace the southwest corner of Huokou Intersection, I spotted a thick gathering of townspeople. It was not the usual throng of shoppers picking out cabbages and carrots, but a cluster of pedestrians gathered around a man speaking from the top of a cart.

"Stop here! *Shifu*, please. Stop right here!"

Min the master stopped on a dime, practically jerking us out of our seats again.

"Phil, why don't you get out and see what's going on first?" Brian said good-naturedly. "I'll sit here and keep our man Min company."

I came back with a glowing report. "Well, we found our posters, plenty of 'em. Politically charged ones too." The scene before us was good news for the students and good news for the crew. We needed a story, they needed publicity. The crew deftly unloaded the gear over Min's protests about parking regulations to record, perchance for broadcast, an agitprop performance in progress. While the crew did their white balance checks and attended to technical details, a few heads turned, a few bodies moved out of the way, either camera-shy or deferential in a well-meaning way that inadvertently robbed the shot of its local color, but the lion's share of attention went to the emotional oratory of the student speaker. Brian probed bystanders on his own, but couldn't find anyone who spoke English. "What is going on here, Phil?"

"Seems to be a group of Beida students doing political outreach, you know, to the common citizens. That's unprecedented, in my experience here," I answered. "Why, look, they've even got a small printing press!"

We had stumbled into the heart of things despite the best efforts of our driver. This urban guerilla outpost was the advance party for a new, perhaps final, thrust at Tiananmen.

Much to Min's dismay, the BBC crew went about doing what they did best, capturing vivid images under trying conditions. They were unperturbed by Min's moaning and the din of oncoming vehicles. After all, what's a bit of unruly traffic or a parking ticket compared to filming under live fire or rushing into a disaster zone?

The students' mobile propaganda unit was an interesting development because it represented yet another daring ploy in the psychological standoff with the government. The students first protested on campus, then took their message, fleetingly, to the streets. Now they were building links with the ordinary citizens of Beijing. If workers or entrepreneurs were encouraged to actively support or even participate in the movement, then the students' poker game with the government took on a new aspect.

The party jealously guarded the power to manipulate the masses by keeping apart, or playing off one against the other, broad social strata such as intellectuals, merchants, workers, farmers, and the military. For even a fraction of one group to forge an alliance with a fraction of another group threatened party control.

I collected a handful of the blue leaflets that were being inked and printed on a primitive silk-screen press. The broad billboard that marked the Huokou Intersection as seen from Second Ring Road was already plastered with hand-painted posters describing student complaints about corruption, the lack of press freedom, and the unwillingness of the government to recognize the demand for dialogue.

In the skittish and somewhat ill-defined swarm of one hundred or so spectators, I could find only five students, all from Beida. They were enthusiastic facilitators, helping us worm our way through the thicket of curious onlookers to get the best angle on the scene. One student used a megaphone like a movie director, realigning the malleable group of lookers-on composed mainly of workers, merchants, and idlers of indeterminate vocational status to help us get good close-up shots of the printing press.

After ten minutes of quick study, observations hastily scribbled into a script, Brian did a standup introduction filmed at an expert angle that simultaneously captured the strident speaker, the political posters, and the commercial billboards behind. My job for the moment was to keep curious onlookers out of the shot. The ready cooperation of the local citizens was commendable, thus it was all the more annoying when a foreign photographer with long frizzy blond hair walked into our setup. I was almost sure he was the same athletic lensman who had climbed to the top of the giant Sun Yatsen portrait on the square.

While the BBC crew grumbled about the breakdown in order, the unrepentant, the photographer himself, either unaware or unfazed at having interfered with our work, approached me softly, smiling. He was an American who worked for *Newsweek*. He said he saw our crew as he was passing by and had just heard me speaking Chinese. What I could tell him about what was going on?

I told him he was in our shot, and he just grinned. I took that as an apology and explained that the Beida students were taking their protest off campus, trying to explain it to the people. Satisfied, he walked away and started snapping pictures. I had seen this dynamic in action before. It was one of those piggyback events where one film crew would be stimulated into action by the sight of a rival, thus transforming what might possibly be a media-worthy event into a too-important-to-be-missed media event. If there are cameras, there must be fire. If there isn't fire, wait a while, there will be. The heat of media attention, like a magnifying glass focusing the sun's rays, tends to get incendiary after a while.

If our stuff made it onto the air, BBC viewers in England would be treated to their first view of a Chinese mobile propaganda unit narrated by Brian Barron, with an unidentified blond photographer walking through the shot.

Min, of course, had by now gone missing, so while we waited for the van to reappear, I stood in a small circle with the crew. Brian belatedly introduced me to my fellow passengers on the BBC magical mystery tour. The producer was introduced as "someone you already know," so I didn't catch the name, but thought it was Mark. Then there was Eric, a tall, supple, and lithe cameraman who had also covered Vietnam and, like Brian, had been based in Hong Kong for many years. His soundman, Fred, so pensive-looking at times in his dark-rimmed glasses, was a warmly ironic artist from California, also based in Hong Kong. Soft-spoken Fred—I didn't realize he was American at first—could have passed for a distant relative of mine, given his fair complexion and wavy dirty-blond hair. Fred's girlfriend, also American, introduced herself with a cordial smile, explaining that she was more or less along for the ride, but also doing some odd jobs for the BBC as a courier.

If I could mistake fellow American Fred for being English because of his placement in the midst of a BBC crew, I could understand why the Chinese I was talking to made the same assumption about me. While my Irish forebears might chuckle to see me playing the Brit, such a confusion could work to my advantage if Public Security got on my case. The mistaken assumption that I might be an Englishman would buy time for Philip Cunningham, citizen of the USA, who had been, over the past six years of pushing boundaries and breaking little rules, twice arrested for activities incompatible with being a foreigner and thus endowed with a thick security file. By 1984 alone I had a file so thick with detail, according to a well-placed person who was questioned about his connection to me, that it was said to contain paraphrased conversations with strangers I met on an "unauthorized" train journey—which is to say I failed to get official permission from the East China Normal foreign student office to leave Shanghai for Xian.

Still no sign of the van. While the rest of the crew stood in the shade of a lone tree to escape the beating down of the noontime sun, Brian continued to explore the scene with admirable energy, seeming very much in his element in the dry, ovenlike heat.

Then Min showed up. He was in a cooperative mood—he hopped out of the van to slide open the door and help us load the gear—his bearing almost apologetic even, as he labored under the mistaken idea that the day's outing was over and he had only to drive us back to the hotel. Brian relinquished the front seat to me so I could give Min the bad news. Go straight north until you get to the east gate of Beijing Normal University. He immediately started cursing under his breath and dreaming up absurd excuses.

I had only narrowly convinced the crew to take a look at a "real" democracy wall. Now Min was engaged in a civil disobedience strategy that threatened to derail our fragile itinerary. He may have been alarmed upon hearing the dangerous *d* word mentioned so frequently, assuming he understood that much English. How else to explain the nervous driver's sudden resolve to make an uncalled-for right turn, hit the pedal, and start racing in the direction of the hotel?

The visceral pleasure of being back on the open road again, wind whipping in the window, allowed the driver to put a few kilometers between the van and the mobile propaganda unit. It took considerable cajoling to get Min to make a U-turn and deliver us to the university.

We arrived at Shida shortly after twelve and then I realized there was a simpler explanation for the driver's stubborn behavior. It was lunchtime. The second east gate was not under strict watch. We got through without as much as a glance in our direction. Having passed that hurdle, we tooled cautiously towards the inspirational quote by Mao engraved on a blood-red billboard, a famous line exhorting students to face the future brightly. I showed the crew the spot on campus where I had witnessed the once-obligatory Mao statue being torn down in the middle of the night two years before.

"That's all very interesting, Phil," Brian said, "but we didn't come here for a campus tour."

"The student dorms are up ahead, you'll see," I said, telling the driver to cross the plaza in between the library and the administration building and follow the single-lane road directly west. The spacious, leafy campus looked unnaturally deserted. After having convinced a time-lagged crew and truculent driver to delay lunch in the name of the "Democracy Wall of 1989," it must have been a bit of a letdown to subject them to a tour across such a sleepy, leafy campus with nothing to gaze at but empty pathways and nonexistent statues.

"Where are the students?" the ever-alert Brian asked. "Are they on holiday now?"

"Well, lunch just ended," I said, looking at my watch, "so I guess it's nap time." It was probably a mistake to suggest that our intended subjects were enjoying food and rest while the crew had to endure growling stomachs and heat-induced stupor, but I told the driver to press on.

It was a pleasure to switch into Chinese, for it allowed me to extricate myself, if only momentarily, from an awkward conversation in English. I had Min drive past the graduate dorms and then Zhongnan women's dorm along familiar byways until we reached the hot water shack. On the rear wall of the shack there were some bright blue-and-yellow posters incendiary enough in content to draw student attention even during nap hour.

AN OPEN LETTER TO GORBACHEV

The crew got out, as much to stretch as anything else, as I read out loud for them as best I could the contents of the scroll-like document, executed in beautiful calligraphy. Notation next to the text explained that it was a handwritten copy of a student letter sent to the Soviet Embassy. The diplomatic missive bombastically requested that the Russian leader come to Shida to meet with student representatives. A poster on the right said there would be a hunger strike if the government did not acquiesce to the student demands for both dialogue and safety from reprisals. A hunger strike!

Next, I turned to study a shocking example of political graffiti, this one scrawled on the gray wall of the most familiar building on campus. A vertical couplet was painted in huge purple characters on the end wall of the Insider Guest House.

XIAOPING NIHAO!

"What's that one say, Phil?"

"It means 'Hello,' or you might say, 'Greetings, Xiaoping!' It refers to Deng Xiaoping, of course."

But why was the most powerful man in China being referred to in the familial way reserved for fellow comrades? The students, as brave and reckless as they might be, were not poking fun at Deng Xiaoping, were they?

And what about the matching couplet?

HE DONGCHANG, DO YOU FEEL NO GUILT?

This glib reference to the Minister of Education signaled disapproval for the harsh treatment of an earlier wave of student demonstrators, punishment meted out by the ministry through the controversial job assignment system.

I led the BBC team into the alleyway in between the women's dorm and the Insider Guest House. We found a suitable angle on the water shack, pausing to admire how it had been covered from top to bottom with student notices. Behind the shack, the recreation space enclosed and defined by the contours of a large U-shaped dormitory, the very spot where I had sat with Bright, Jenny, and Ling a week earlier, had transformed into something much less playful than usual. The shaded courtyard was being paced purposefully by sober-looking student organizers wearing headbands of different colors. The normally popular ping-pong tables were not in use. Gone was the relaxed, idyllic sitting-around-doing-nothing atmosphere of normal campus life. As the crew searched for colorful posters and good visuals, I watched a flood of activists stream into the courtyard from parts unknown. Another demonstration was dawning, but the mood was unlike anything I had seen before.

Before our eyes, the narrow recreation space wedged between nondescript buildings and stumpy gray trees transformed itself into an urban "liberated base," a banner-bedecked command and control center for the students' propaganda war with the government. Here, rabble-rouser Wuerkaixi and his friends held court.

Here, never before published information was pasted onto public walls for the world to see. Here was the leaked news that you would not read about in the official party mouthpieces such as *People's Daily*. One sign proclaimed that Mayor Chen Xitong was hugely corrupt; another that Zhao Ziyang's daughter held a posh position at the Great Wall Hotel.

The long bulletin board and the north wall of the women's dorm were papered with tattered posters, each layer boasting a new stridency. There were a host of missives exposing the ills of the government in point-blank terms. Information-hungry students with enthusiastic eyes and a schadenfreude fueled by pent-up frustration pressed forward for access, frantically copying down tabloid tidbits that had been brush-written on thin, easily tattered paper.

It brought to mind the plight of the bookless denizens of Ray Bradbury's *Fahrenheit 451*, memorizing books to save them for posterity. I half expected to see progovernment vigilantes come rushing in to torch or tear down the antigovernment posters at any moment, but no such thing happened. It was exhilarating and yet somehow also mildly disconcerting to see such unfettered political expression on the staid Shida campus.

A visceral resentment bubbled. Rage against corruption, rather than paeans to democracy or freedom, animated many of the posts. Some anonymous posters outlined the startlingly complex business connections of top leaders, singling out those presumed guilty by name. Members of the so-called *taizi dang*, that is to say, the princeling faction of the party, were singled out for reportedly making a killing due to the heredity privileges obtained by high Communist birth, a marriage of political connection, or commercial opportunity. Who leaked the information? There were some speculative overseas tracts written on the topic, but the level of detail suggested inside access. Was one group of leaders trying to discredit their allegedly corrupt rivals by leaking financial data?

Not only were information norms being violated, the very walls and gates and buildings—all heretofore strictly guarded university property—were also up for grabs. Dorm rooms were commandeered for strategic meetings, public walls were scrawled with graffiti, and public loudspeakers were rigged to trees and posts to broadcast student announcements.

And yet, for some inexplicable reason, there was no detectible policing of campus, nor had there been any obvious attempt by the regular retinue of campus security agents to stop this potent focusing of political opposition at its source. What happened to all the busybodies? Normally there were students, some under party instruction, others mere self-appointed tattletales, who spied on fellow students for school authorities and security organs, like the vigilantes who maliciously reported seeing Bright and Jenny in the company of me, the foreigner, at the Insider Guest House during the 1987 crackdown on "spiritual pollution" of which I was presumably an exemplary practitioner.

Where had all the vigilantes gone? Was this a Cultural Revolution–style dynamic in which the campus party secretaries and school presidents got the message from higher levels to look the other way or even abet the uprising? Or was it rather a complete absence of coherent policy, a mixture of mixed signals and no signals, that was in play? Were the students knowingly or unknowingly being prodded by an unseen hand that empowered them to face the risks they were facing?

Two years before, I performed a song about Mao set to a rock beat for a student talent show on this campus, backed by Nokura and a visitor from Hawaii. That it was a spoof was obvious to just about everyone but the president of Shida and the assorted VIP teachers, administrators, and judges of the televised contest. When I introduced the band as *Gong-nong-bing*, meaning worker-peasant-soldier, there was a drawn-out moment of silence. For three foreigners to assume such a name in itself poked fun at the pillars of the old socialist society. Then a few foreign students laughed, joined by knowing smirks and a flood of whispers among the Chinese students. The teachers and administrators in the front row sat motionless.

We started out by singing "Dongfanghong," "The East Is Red," a tuneful song of praise about Mao. This song was out of date but iconic, and we knew we were playing with fire. Legend had it that this catchy tune was the first thing broadcast from China's first satellite in space, appropriately named *Dongfanghong*. In the mid-eighties, Mao's reputation was facing a precipitous decline, but he was still an icon, more of a demigod than a demi-demon in the eyes of many common folk. Even those who suffered under Mao had trouble extricating him from their lives, for they had been brought up to understand that he was an indelible part and parcel of the new China.

It was bound to get a rise out of the audience, and it did. We got through the first verse, done more or less straight-faced, without much reaction except some sporadic hoots and clapping. For the second verse, however, we launched into a rock-style version and caused a ruckus. Imperceptibly, but rather intentionally, we crossed into a forbidden zone.

The students in the room, Chinese and foreign, cheered, but most of the school officials were silent. We were hopelessly amateur in our performance, but that was beside the point. The talent judges were in a quandary as to how to evaluate the song. Even a bad rating was too good for us. The solution? Our song disappeared from the contest, excluded from the competition. It was literally outside the realm of consideration. That saved us the humility of getting a low score, but it took some Orwellian editing to get us out of the Beijing Television's broadcast version of the event.

With the current escalation of protest, the campus commissars faced a no-win situation. Was it a time for action or inaction? No matter what they did, someone in a high place was likely to be unhappy. Word had it that Zhao Ziyang was saying the student demonstrations were patriotic, that restrictions on the press could be loosened up a bit, but it wasn't clear if his allegedly conciliatory stance merely softened Deng's earlier criticism of the students or brazenly negated it. Such open fissures among China's top leaders, while a welcome change from the steely united front they normally presented to the nation, might augur a political earthquake to come.

What was a campus party secretary to do? Follow the hard line of Li Peng, the premier, or the soft line of Zhao Ziyang, the secretary-general of the Communist Party of China?

In democratic societies such as the U.S., the handling of student unrest was tricky enough, as politicians deliberated, under the weight of the Constitution, whether to ignore, co-opt, or tackle unrest by force. How much less room to maneuver was there here, in authoritarian China, at a time when the unelected leadership spoke in two voices? The impasse at the top made possible a modicum of tactical freedom on the ground, but it also threatened to raise the stakes to the level of an undeclared civil war.

The fact that Shida appeared to be under student control struck me as being a dangerous illusion. Bright said campus life had changed for the better, and on May 4 I could see the soaring of that new spirit. But what if the whiff of freedom turned into a mockery of the same, a transient window of openness that served to make people implicate themselves? It had happened before in the 1950s, when Mao urged "a hundred schools of thought to contend," only to punish those who expressed themselves too freely.

More pertinent to the situation at hand was Deng Xiaoping's encouragement of free speech and talk of democracy in 1978. Former Red Guard Wei Jingsheng rose to the occasion, saying Deng had dictatorial tendencies and China needed democracy. A few months later, Wei and several outspoken colleagues were left high and dry when Deng reined in the movement, putting the young idealists behind bars as an example to others.

To date, the campus strike was having its desired effect of keeping people out of class, but cutting class does not a revolution make. Sleeping late and not doing homework is a temptation few students can easily refuse. The non-action implicit in not going to class had to be accompanied by some kind of action to have any meaning at all.

The courtyard was abuzz with loud announcements blurting out of the hijacked, jerry-rigged amplification system. What might in theory be freewheeling talk akin to the ramblings of a college radio station was instead sounding uncompromising and strident, like a new party line. The drive to convince the moderate student body not to attend class, having largely succeeded, cleared the way for more radical action. The buzz was all about a big hunger strike.

As the BBC crew continued to track down colorful visuals, I approached a forlorn-looking young man who was sitting alone amidst the swirl of activity kicking up in the middle of the dusty courtyard. He was wearing a white headband with two black characters inked on: JUE-SHI.

"Why do you write 'refuse food' on your headband?" I asked, adopting the tone of a reporter without really thinking about it.

"The government just ignores us. We want dialogue. Maybe if we starve ourselves they will pay attention," he said.

There was something off-putting about his explanation. It was unfathomable to me that a young person would starve to death as an attention-grabbing stunt. Here the stated cause was laughably hollow—risking the ultimate sacrifice for a chance to talk with Li Peng. I pressed the would-be martyr on the matter, curious about his personal reason for joining.

"I don't know," he said dully, no doubt taken aback by the volley of questions from the inquisitive foreigner. "It's not personal."

"What if the government ignores you?" I moved closer to him and lowered my voice, aware that our conversation was attracting curious ears.

"We demand dialogue and a reversal of the unjust April twenty-sixth editorial!" he declared with unexpected volume, to the approval of his contemporaries, who were now tightly squeezing in around us.

"What if there is no dialogue?"

"Then we die," he said, winning somber nods of approval. His performance gave me the goose bumps.

I moved on, but subsequent conversations with other individuals quickly turned into group affairs. It was sad and frustrating to meet such earnest young men and women, all apparently willing to put their lives on the line, only to hear them give pat answers, sometimes even grandiose answers, magnified by peer pressure. Did those nodding in approval realize they were urging psychologically confused, approval-hungry classmates to court death? To what end?

Things were polarizing rapidly, making me feel hopelessly lost in the middle. Overturning the unjust verdict of an incendiary newspaper editorial was an aim both discreet and desirable, but what could possibly be the end goal of "dialogue"? Who was to say that dialogue had been achieved, or not? If hunger strikers started to drop, where would it all end?

The May 4 rally and the May 10 protest were framed largely in the name of free speech. Both events were peaceful and good-spirited and I supported them wholeheartedly. I had plunged into a turbulent sea of confusion in both instances, trusting the instincts and judgment of friends. The result was up-lifting; I was pleased to lend moral support to a movement driven by good cheer and an idealistic outlook. But now things were taking a potentially de-structive turn, for a hunger strike implied a kind of self-inflicted violence.

A hunger strike also introduced a ticking time bomb into the equation; things must be resolved in less time than it takes to die of starvation. It sub-jected both supporters and "the enemy" to emotional blackmail, not unlike a person who threatens suicide to manipulate or punish others for their lack of attention. Short of capitulation, terms of which were left dangerously un-defined, on the government side, the unspoken end result would be death. This was no celebratory parade calling for free speech and cultural revival; it was a veritable death march.

Sitting on the steps of the small monument in the middle of the courtyard I watched as more and more grim-looking young men emerged from the res-idence hall wearing white headbands emblazoned with JUE-SHI painted in black. The strikers gathered around the monument in the middle of the rec-tangular quad, bringing to mind the way the protesters in recent days had gravitated to the Monument of the People's Heroes, which commemorated martyrdom in Mao's calligraphy, in the very heart of Tiananmen Square.

Headbanded delegations of students from other colleges began to arrive, giving Shida the doom and gloom of a kamikaze camp. Whither the joyous, life-affirming spirit of May 4?

We had stumbled upon this radical stab for attention quite fortuitously, through a combination of Brian's quest for a nonexistent wall, Min's erratic driving, and my curiosity to see what was happening on my home campus. I mingled with the strikers and their supporters, aware I was being watched more closely than before, but curious to see where the idea of a hunger strike came from. I couldn't think of any examples in Chinese history, though In-dia had elevated the hunger strike to an almost spiritual art. I had just seen some quotes by the progressive Indian writer Rabindranath Tagore in one of the student posters, but no mention of Mahatma Gandhi. Were the student admirers of Tagore aware of his famous criticism of Gandhi, saying that even nonviolent tactics were a hurtful weapon of sorts?

None of those queried could point to a precedent for this type of protest in China. The strikers I talked to tended to give knee-jerk answers to my questions, to the tune of dialogue or death, unwilling to consider the implications of the strike in honest terms or even begin to question decisions made by their "leaders." It bothered me to see such courage coupled with an unquestioning attitude. To me, these young patriots had lost perspective and were fired up by peer pressure to take part in a dangerous "quest."

As with the kamikaze pilots of Japan and the daring guerilla martyrs of the Chinese Revolution, extreme devotion coupled with intense social pressure made it possible to cast a false glow on pointlessly suicidal activities. But I was baffled that otherwise privileged students in a nation that had known much too much hunger should starve themselves for any abstraction, let alone such a poorly conceived one.

Brian found me, asking if I had lined up some students to interview.

"Well, it's hard to say. I just talked with a few students over there. They are on a hunger strike," I explained. "They demand dialogue with the government. There's one of them, see, with the headband?"

"How good is his English?" he asked.

"I don't know. I wasn't speaking English."

"What's the point of talking to someone in Chinese?" he said, which I thought was a pretty incredible statement to make in China. But he had a job to do, and an overseas audience in mind, whereas I was indulging my own curiosity.

"Well, I say we have enough. We're finished doing the posters. That's what we came for, isn't it?"

"But I think this is a good chance to talk to some of the hunger strikers."

"Phil? We can talk to them later."

We were on the verge of going back to the hotel for lunch when I learned that the hunger strikers were signing "wills" and making pledges to maintain group unity, to be unswerving in their determination to the death. The courtyard was now swirling with students wearing the ominous white headbands. Then I saw a familiar face among the hard-core strikers.

Lily! What was she doing with the radical contingent?

My gut reaction was that Lily, a simple, honest soul from a small farming village, an appreciative young woman who didn't hide her thrill at attending a university in the national capital, was caving in to peer pressure. Bright and Jenny had the self-esteem and instincts of self-preservation to avoid the trap of something like a hunger strike, but Lily? I approached her stealthily, aware that she was surrounded by strike organizers. When she spotted me, she couldn't suppress a cordial smile, but watchful stares from her peers signaled that she ought to assume a less communicative, more appropriately solemn demeanor. She wasn't free to be Lily, the delightful woman of an impoverished province, who I liked and knew. She was now an anonymous comrade, a patriotic hunger striker.

We talked briefly, but the conversation was limited to platitudes. She had never been particularly articulate about politics to begin with, and my presence, a foreign male hanging out with a TV crew of unknown provenance, made her extremely self-conscious. I made reference to people and places we both enjoyed, hoping to jump-start a conversation, but she had lost her normal playfulness and sense of humor. When I pressed her as to why she was going on a hunger strike, she gave me the same pat answers as everybody else.

"We want open dialogue with the government."

"Oh, come on, what do you really want?"

"Hmm, I'm not sure, but . . ."

One of Lily's headbanded comrades intervened silently, poking his head into our conversation with the precision of a directional mike. I gave him an exasperated look, hoping to continue a bit longer.

"What were you saying?" I pressed for an answer.

"We want a reversal of the April twenty-sixth verdict!"

I had to wonder if she was fearful or if she already felt the effects of fasting since breakfast. Most Chinese students I knew couldn't even skip a meal without feeling ill effects. Already, her lips were parched and dry. I really felt bad for her and tried to "reach" her, but couldn't get through.

There was some kind of indoctrination going on, but that's not to say there was a mastermind or that the process was coercive in any way. Rather, for students such as she, who had endured years of rote learning and considered it a privilege to be in the city, there was a readiness to take cues from the environment and allow a kind of autoindoctrination to kick in. In the end, all I could do was wish her luck as she went back to her group and I went back to mine.

A short while later there were excited shouts.

"Beida is here!"

"Political Science and Law is here!"

"Shida! Get ready for the march," a cheerleader shouted. "Assemble into your groups!"

The hunger strikers and supporters from other schools came pouring onto campus. Once again a mass of students converged on the sports ground. Once again the dusty basketball court was transformed into a sea of enthusiastic young people waving red flags to the singsong rhythm of rote slogans, redundant chants, and crackling voices on megaphones. Beida, Qinghua, Political Science and Law, and People's University contingents gathered and joined forces to map out a joint strategy.

The final march to the square was about to begin. A march unlike the previous ones, because this time the young people were vowing to sit in at Tiananmen till death or till they achieved "dialogue," whichever came first. The stakes were as high as they could be: total victory or total defeat. The government's hand was being forced, the strikers threatening, in effect, "accept our demands or take the blame for our deaths."

Seeing young people play poker with their lives made me very uncomfortable. If Lily was a typical striker, however, a cynical dynamic was at work. An elite corps of group leaders was jostling for control, upping the stakes, urging others to make the ultimate sacrifice. Could the stated aspirations of dialogue, openness, democracy, and freedom be achieved by violence against the self? Did not violence beget more violence; did it not deaden the spirit and turn the oppressed into oppressors?

Although I failed to produce the English sound bites desired by the taciturn producer and his ace reporter, and they in turn refused to authorize interviews conducted in Chinese, the growing size of the gathering, with the ever-present implicit possibility of violence, convinced the alert camera crew that we should stick around a bit longer.

Conflict that can be represented visually is the stuff TV news is made from. The day's BBC news report from China would not include interviews with student hunger strikers, because the Chinese students couldn't speak, or were less than fluent in, the native language of a boggy island in the northeast Atlantic. Then again, the BBC had a world of news to cover in addition to China. The voices of a few random demonstrators at Shida might seem insignificant in the context of such imperial reach. Furthermore, the hunger strikers, like my friend Lily, did not have much to say at the moment; or, more precisely, lacked the will and motivation to share nuanced thoughts with a bunch of foreigners carrying fancy recording equipment.

While I argued the merits of English sound bites with the reporter and producer, at least there was the satisfaction of seeing a skilled camera crew recording the big picture, something that the media had failed to do on May 10 and the days leading up to this moment. But the decision not to record conversations in Chinese was a lost opportunity.

Any hopes of comprehensive coverage were further dashed by the decision of the producer to go back to his hotel. He said he couldn't possibly find it by himself, and he wanted me to come along. He said something about lunch, and a day's pay for a day's work, though I protested, saying I was more than content to continue working beyond scheduled hours if events demanded it. Then I realized he was talking about himself.

Finding ourselves for the moment, if only serendipitously, in the middle of this big, unfolding story, I took it for granted that normal working hours just didn't apply. Yet I shouldn't have been surprised that a powerful producer wanted what he wanted when he wanted it, even if his desire for lunch in a nice hotel came at the expense of the story. I had seen crazier things happen with the NBC *Today Show* in Shanghai. But this was the BBC, a world leader in news, and I had been expecting a higher standard.

In fact, we would have left then and there if the producer had his way, but he didn't. Our nervous Nellie driver had pulled another disappearing act. If Min's earlier diversions had the effect of keeping us away from anything that smacked of politics, his fear of implicating himself in political trouble now caused him to put himself at such a remove from the students and the crew that he left us stranded and inadvertently well-positioned in the middle of a great breaking story.

The producer was not pleased. When he learned that Min had bolted, his milky complexion reddened. Arms flailing, he explained that he simply had to get back to the office, not just for lunch, but also for a tape deadline. Though he had spurned my earlier offer to find him a taxi at the Shida foreign student dorm, he was now desperate enough to give it a try. After leaving instructions with the crew to find the van, among other things, he and I walked across campus to the east gate together, which gave us a chance to clear up our misunderstanding. I had not been cognizant of the pressures he was under, feeding tapes to London on a tight schedule. He heard me out as to why I thought it was worth keeping the camera crew on campus longer, overtime or otherwise. Pleased to find himself seated in a clean taxi with an agreeable driver under strict instructions to take him directly to his hotel, he gave me the authorization I wanted; I was free to keep the crew and keep on filming.

Flagging down a taxi was one thing, trying to find our van was another. The campus was large, but there were few roads and only four gates. I surveyed an expanse of weedy lots on the neglected east side of campus, an area still under development and relatively distant from where the strikers gathered. Partially hidden behind a row of trees and bushes about one hundred yards away, I spied what looked like our van. I hadn't noticed it on the first sweep, for it was artfully inconspicuous, tucked away between the wing of an old classroom building and a profusion of thick foliage.

Our man Min was napping in the van. When I tapped on the glass, he rolled down the window and sheepishly explained he had moved the car to protect it from getting scratched by the student turmoil. I raised my eyebrows in incredulity, and he pleaded for understanding. He seemed truly spooked by the protesters, perhaps taking a cue from Deng Xiaoping's editorial, which had cast these young demonstrators as rioters fomenting turmoil.

I told him he could go on napping if he promised to wait for us. Then I hoofed it to the basketball courts, the unofficial campus staging ground for big demonstrations, where I found the film crew recording snippets of the genesis of what promised to be another big march on Tiananmen.

At times we stuck out like sore thumbs, but there were other times we were rendered all but invisible, given the way we were jostled, bumped, and swallowed up by the slightly unruly and self-absorbed crowd. Recalling the logistics of the May 4 rally, I helped the crew stake out likely positions to film the progress of the rally. Once the marchers passed through the small east gate and made it to the open streets, it was almost impossible to follow the twists and turns of the student current, so we ended up running alongside the demonstrators, much as I had done at the outset of the May 4 rally. Once again I saw friends marching, and once again I was called to join in. Last time, I took snapshots for myself and had the option of marching with my friends. This time, my marching orders came from the BBC; joining the students was out of the question.

Work is work, but I felt distracted, pulled by the historical imperative that tugged at the marchers, repelled by my own skepticism. I didn't agree with the hunger strike, and was unnerved by the deadly, single-minded seriousness of the marchers in white headbands, so much so that it came as a comfort to hear them break into song. Although I had crossed a line, taking the stance of a professional observer, I had the satisfaction that my new job was not totally irrelevant to what was going on in the streets of Beijing.

We could follow the hunger strikers only so far on foot as they marched intently south on Xinwai Street, headed for Huokou and Xinjiekou. Weighed down by gear and desirous of staying within a reasonable radius of the van, we watch the strikers take the exact same route I had traversed with the arts choral group ten days before. The day's marchers were fewer in number and more narrowly focused than the May 4 march, which seemed, with hindsight, to have been nothing short of boisterous and happy-go-lucky in comparison. The pleasant variety of melodies sung on May 4 was replaced by the endless repetition of the lyric "the final struggle." "The Internationale" was now, by default, the unofficial anthem of the movement.

The wild variety of slogans had been weeded down, too, suggesting new concerns and new strategies. There was scant mention of corruption or press freedom. The issue, in a nutshell, was "dialogue."

When I marched, I was content to be seen and not heard; I didn't feel in a position to be asking pointed questions. Now, as stringer for the media, I couldn't content myself with mere observation. It was my job to probe.

To ascertain if there was in fact an unseen power behind the demonstrations, I started to ask intrusive questions.

"Is there a black hand supporting the students?"

"There is no black hand!" was the usual answer. "This is a spontaneous movement!"

"If it's spontaneous, then who determines what the slogans are?"

"The slogans represent the people's righteous grievances," said one.

"Everyone is free to write his or her own slogan," said another.

"What about corruption? I don't see much about that today. At whom was that charge aimed?"

"The government is corrupt."

"But who? Zhao? Li Peng?"

"No, you don't understand, it is not about corruption. Our two main goals are dialogue and the reversal of the *People's Daily* April twenty-sixth editorial."

I trotted over to a somber group of students carrying the banner of Shida History Department.

"Why are you marching?" I asked.

"To protest the *People's Daily* April twenty-sixth editorial," said one.

"We want dialogue!" shouted the next.

"Is there a black hand behind the movement?" I asked.

"This is a spontaneous movement!" was the indignant answer.

"It is a spontaneous, patriotic movement!" said yet another. And so on.

What I had seen so far could very well have been spontaneous, but why did the students uniformly, and self-consciously, describe it as such? The hunger strikers possessed tight discipline, a discipline that went beyond marching formation and extended to political order and the drumbeat of the mass mind. A party line was being put into effect. Ready-made answers to inevitable questions were already in circulation. Whether or not the word democracy appeared on their banners, and there was little evidence of that today, their whole approach was redolent of hard-core party-liners, with a defensive, nationalistic component.

Was it my racial identity that caused those I asked questions of to give me pat answers, to click into an instinctive "how-can-we-possibly-explain" mode? Was it a chauvinistic reluctance to express subtle and sublime Sinitic thoughts to an ignorant foreigner? Was it realistic to expect them to tell me, this outside-country person with fair hair and a funny accent, their most profound hopes and deepest fears?

I was an inexperienced reporter. Perhaps my use of the politicized buzzword *black hand* put people on the defensive, causing them to make a blanket denial of behind-the-scenes manipulation without really thinking about it. Or maybe student ringleaders had set the tone, inculcating fellow students through pamphlets, posters, and speaker-amplified announcements, providing followers a host of nearly identical ready-made answers, the memes for which were already in circulation.

Still, I considered the term *spontaneous movement* to be something of an oxymoron in Chinese political terminology. The ragtag collection of quirky, eccentric individuals that marched towards the square certainly had a spontaneous look and feel, but the crisp uniformity of slogans and pat answers was disconcerting.

Due to my own "indoctrination" at the seminar table with charismatic American China specialists such as University of Michigan professor Michel Oksenberg, who shared his expert insights into the dynamics of the Cultural Revolution by role-playing—he was Mao, I was Liu Shaoqi—I suppose I too had unwittingly imbibed a catalogue of ready-made answers, reflective of a Western social science approach to Chinese studies. For I found it impossible to believe that such marches could take place without someone somewhere giving a green light from above. I had felt this way on May 4, May 10, and again today. You don't just go marching in the streets in China. It is Public Security's job to make sure that doesn't happen. It wasn't that I wanted them to do what they typically did, namely nipping protest in the bud, but I just couldn't understand why they didn't.

I was curious about the students' new direction of attack. It seemed to be veering away from Zhao and focusing more and more on Li. Who was Zhao if not just another politburo fat cat? Wasn't he the one who presided over the phony May Fourth Communist Youth League commemoration in the Great Hall on the third of May, when the real inheritors of the May Fourth tradition were plotting to take to the streets?

If this demonstration were truly spontaneous, one would expect a cacophony of different voices every time the students marched. That was my experience at demonstrations in New York and Washington. But then again, American obsession with individuality robbed many such gatherings of a unity of purpose, and many a big American rally self-imploded into the divisive clamoring for attention of fractured splinter groups.

I bore down on the tired BBC crew with all the political import I could muster to persuade them to follow the demonstration all the way to the square. As veteran news professionals, they were game, but to shadow this sober pilgrimage, as I was drawn to do, I had to first fetch the driver and win his cooperation.

Min's face dropped when I asked him to follow the demonstration.

"That's impossible!" he protested. "I can't do that!"

"Just try, follow from behind. Just go as far as you can."

"*Ni fuzeren!*" he said, meaning I had to bear the consequences if anything happened.

"If it's impossible or dangerous, obviously you don't have to do it," I said, "but it is your job to drive us, so please do your best."

"*Ni fuzeren!*"

"What makes you say it is I who is responsible?"

"We shouldn't go there, that's what I'm saying."

Saying "*ni fuzeren,*" in essence putting all potential blame on me, was in effect a ploy to get me to agree with him. He reluctantly agreed when I said I would bear the consequences. He switched on the ignition, having finally heard what he wanted to hear from me. Given appropriate incentive, he did not hesitate to shout, "Get out of my way!" to the "dangerous" student rioters, and he quickly cut a trail of dust to the campus gate.

Crew all aboard, encouraged by the miraculous restoration of the driver's driving skills, I tried to steer him south, in the direction of the demo. But when I asked him to turn right, to follow the students, he turned left.

The out-of-town driver did not know the roads around the university and I did, so I used his contrary personality to beat him at his own game.

"Now, how do we get back to the hotel?"

"Well, I think if you make a right, and then another right," I offered, "You'll end up back in the crowd." The deliberately disobedient Min made three consecutive left turns that got us exactly where I wanted to go, stuck in traffic blocked by the passing procession.

Student marchers swelled and traffic at Xinjiekou came to a halt. The crew saw a good shot and couldn't resist it. Once Min got locked into the flow of the march on Tiananmen, it was almost impossible to turn around. He tooled reluctantly forward, cursing the students under each and every breath. The camera crew managed to get out twice, filming at Xinjiekou and Xisi intersections. Shoppers and ordinary folk going about their daily business, living their life in public on the street as was the custom in this part of town, stopped what they were doing to gape in amazement, spellbound by the fearless procession of students singing "The Internationale" with the gallant desperation of troops going into battle.

Civilian spectators on both sides of Xisi Street responded first in silence, then cautious applause, and finally in cheers. By raising the stakes and tightening the focus of protest with a newfound intensity, the radical core of the student movement had seized the moment, if not the day.

In effect, the hunger strikers were pulling a coup, wresting control of the movement from more moderate student voices. If this bold initiative succeeded, the leadership of the fledgling movement would be firmly in the hands of the dare-to-die radicals. If they succeeded, their success might one day be compared to the brazenly defiant moves that propelled the likes of Mao Zedong to assume the lead of a divided Chinese Communist Party (CCP) at the outset of the Long March half a century ago.

The tentative show of onlooker support marked a small victory. If the students could not win the sympathy and support of people outside their ranks, the cause was lost. If they lost the initiative, they lost the mantle, and if the demonstrations stopped altogether, the initiators would be the first to be arrested and punished. But if the attention-grabbers succeeded in winning broad sympathy and support, then more moderate voices would have no choice but to follow suit or pull out.

Peer pressure is hard for young people to resist, perhaps more so in China given intensely communal conditions. Even strong-minded Bright had deliberately ignored me at times to avoid fueling the flames of campus gossip.

The BBC's wonderfully inept driver managed to get lost again, this time in the back alleys west of Xisi, giving the tired crew a needed rest and another involuntary tour of a charming maze of *hutong* (byways or back alleys) lined with sturdy brick walls and half-hidden courtyard homes. A dozen defiant turns later, due to sheer chance and no thanks to the driver or my inadequate directions, we bumped into the demonstration again, this time as it cut a swath through the congested Xidan shopping district. By now the march had gained numerous civilian followers, giving it the kind of momentum it needed to make it all the way to Tiananmen. Pedestrians and cyclists stuck in traffic did not complain, and rioters, to Min's evident relief, did not once scratch the van.

Once we got to Chang'an Boulevard, the importance of the event spoke for itself and the crew was happy to work overtime to get some good shots of the ragtag headbanded army streaming towards the square, an event imbued with historic resonance even as it happened. By the time we reached the expanse of Beijing's greatest public plaza, even Min had stopped complaining. We pulled over and watched in quiet awe as Tiananmen was breached by the vanguard of the student procession, followed by a dispersed trail of civilians following the core like a comet's tail.

A provocative sit-in at Tiananmen was underway. The empty square was being claimed by a controversial vanguard of China's restive youth.

As daylight faded, the BBC called it a wrap. Min, by now almost an honorary member of the crew, took us with great dispatch back to the hotel, where he was rewarded with a wad of cash. A day's work, a day's pay.

But the day was far from over. It was not just that the impending sit-in was too interesting to miss. The sky was clear, the air was dry. It was perfect weather for being out of doors. What better place to go than Tiananmen, the one place where everyone from prime minister to peasant felt welcome. I wanted to go back there. I had to go back.

I called Bright and arranged to meet her on the square a short time later. I was standing halfway between Mao's portrait and the Martyrs' Monument on the central axis of Tiananmen surveying the square when she found me. She guessed correctly I would be near the center of action and had no trouble spotting me, a lone Caucasian wandering amidst the Shida student contingent near the hunger strikers' temporary camp. Word of mouth had already alerted Beijing city folk: the students had marched again and this time they were holding a sit-in, vowing not leave until the demand for dialogue was met. We talked about the events of the day, pondering what it all meant, meandering around the ever-widening perimeter of the mass sit-in. Student security ropes and markers were constantly being adjusted and widened every few minutes to make room for new arrivals.

Who was the first person to sit down and officially start the occupation of Tiananmen? It was impossible to determine, but the growth of the crowd was exponential, from one to two to four to sixteen to two hundred and fifty-six, and it was still expanding. I imagined how the crowd might look from the air, myriad tiny dots moving about, joining, doubling, dividing, and expanding. There was something organic and beautiful about the way myriad individuals were coming together as a single body, something more profound and far-reaching than the discrete political irritants around which the crowd coalesced in the first place.

According to some invisible formula, individuals in proximity and in communication with one another created a larger-than-life organism of breathtaking size and complexity. At the heart of it all were the strikers, organized in cells—by school, of course—and there were the supporters of the strikers, who provided a protective epithelial layer around the nucleus of the throbbing crowd. There were thinkers writing political tracts and students blaring out commands by megaphone, the brain and mouth of the movement. Student bodyguards and self-appointed student marshals were the limbs of the beast, providing some muscle and self-defense capacity. Around them, an even wider perimeter of halfhearted supporters and curious onlookers, the outer skin. Above and beyond that buzzed the flies and mosquitoes, namely curious onlookers and film crews who examined the growing organism with devious delight.

By the time the flaming orange orb in the western sky was about to disappear for the night, Bright and I were standing on the steps of the Martyrs' Monument looking north over the heads of thousands towards stately Tiananmen Gate. We were joined in silent solidarity by hundreds of others who watched as the square absorbed the flood of rush-hour traffic. Not all the tens of thousands of people traversing the clogged north face of the square on foot, bus, or bicycle were supporters. There were undoubtedly many Mins out there as well; put-out commuters who could care less about the students and just wanted to get home. But regardless of their inner convictions they blended into the tableau and could be counted, superficially at least, as part of the crowd.

Bright and I milled around the square under clear skies illuminated by a half moon on the rise, marveling at the giant sit-in that was warming the cold flagstones of Tiananmen. The day had been exuberant and erratic, full of little missteps and pleasant surprises. Despite my initial doubts about the sanity of a hunger strike, the protesters had precipitated something beautiful, something bigger than the petty politics of the day. As midnight loomed, there was a subtle shift in mood. There were whispers among students on the square, saying that confrontation, should it come, would come at this hour. A tense all-night vigil got underway.

MAY 14

◑

Laying Claim to the Square

Daylight brought a mood of its own; if nothing else, the start of a new work-day promised to augment the number of bus and bike commuters streaming past the square. As I was learning from my peregrinations, the line between witnessing something, being seen as part of it, and being part of it was a fine one. Many bystanders tread this fine line. Commuters would watch and gawk and scratch their heads in disbelief, maybe move in closer, watch some more, wave, flash a V sign, or perhaps shout words of encouragement. As they fanned off to work across the city, they would spread the word, serving to stimulate an even bigger rush-hour rush in the evening.

The new epicenter of discontent was in plain sight for everyone to see, a bold stroke, and it was working, though it was not without a downside. It was one thing to strike and cut classes while living in the dorms, quite another to sustain oneself round the clock at Tiananmen Square, which lay an hour's bike ride from where most students slept, showered, changed clothes, and fed themselves.

The square was exposed; it offered no warren of dorm rooms or dark alleys or wooded grounds where one could talk in privacy or even hide, as was pos-sible within the sprawling, leafy campuses that ringed the northern edge of town.

The early, tentative stabs at the prized real estate of the square, each spaced about a week apart, took the form of marches and brief rallies in front of the Great Hall. Defiant and dangerous though such demonstrating was, the rebels had only gone as far as to skirt the square or congregate briefly, not occupy it.

Conversely, now that the strikers were hunkered down on the square and weakening by hour, there was no easy way to move them, even if that were agreed to be desirable.

Gorbachev's itinerary included a welcome ceremony at the square. Would he see the strikers? Anticipating the world cameras that would be rolling, some students made direct appeals in English. All of a sudden, a Russian name was on everybody's lips, even though Russian names are torture to pronounce in Chinese. For the first time, a laowai, albeit an important one, was a topic for demonstrators to ponder.

WE NEED SUCH LEADER AS GORBACHEV.

Whatever lens one chose to look at things through, one had to track a moving target, a changeling. It was about corruption, it was about school conditions, it was about press freedom, it was about the May Fourth spirit. It was ten thousand bicycles protesting the *People's Daily*; it was a hunger strike calling for dialogue.

And now the hunger strike was going full bore.

The hunger strike did it, of course, and was now the heart and soul of the movement. As unseen "heroes" faced self-inflicted starvation, a giant countdown clock clicked into action; it was a matter of days before the famished youth would begin to collapse and die. This created a sense of urgency and struck a sympathetic chord in a cowed populace willing and wanting to believe that times were a-changing.

WE STAND TOGETHER WITH THE HUNGER STRIKERS! proclaimed a typical banner.

Arousing instant empathy with a resounding éclat, the hunger strike fired up a defiant mood. The strikers were seen as heroic almost from the outset, heroic because they courted death. That's what made this new phase of demonstrating different. A solemn assembly of unprecedented proportions was gathered round the Monument of the People's Heroes to show support for the self-sacrificing heroes, mass curiosity piqued by the specter of martyrdom.

An oral tradition was flourishing on the vast plaza, rumor no small part of it, and then there were the moveable texts, calligraphic posters, printed proclamations, scribbled communiqués, graffiti, and hand-painted banners.

As we went along, I tried to jot down slogans and take snapshots of banners.

THE STUDENT MOVEMENT IS DEMOCRACY'S BEST HOPE.

A bilingual sign, in Chinese and Korean, offered a simple formulation that summed up the goal of the protests stripped clean of shifting targets and idiosyncratic detail: FOR A BETTER TOMORROW.

A yellow banner put up by Beida's physics department hinted that it was time for a new generation to assert itself: OH FATHER, BENT BACK WITH AGE, IF ONLY I HAD THE SPINE TO TAKE OVER YOUR STRUGGLE.

In a related sentiment, another poster called on the "bright flame of youth" to STAND PROUD AND ERECT.

The central monument was the most coveted location; it provided two elevated pedestals with platforms facing the four cardinal directions, each backed by photogenic revolutionary tableaus carved in bas-relief. The strikers were sprawled on the pavement like homeless ne'er-do-wells along the north face of the monument, their rectangular-shaped turf initially defined by the row of flagpoles where the giant box portrait of Sun Yatsen had stood on May 4. This sanctuary was later refined with a web of ropes and guarded entrances.

Long slender bamboo poles were used to hoist hand-painted slogans and departmental banners into the sky, staking out turf on a first come, first claims it basis. Orange cables slung from pole to pole connected the student PA system to a remote power source. Students in charge of discipline and those desirous of chiding and inspiring the captive audience in chant were quick to acquire battery-operated megaphones, drawn from campus supplies and newly purchased, to boost vocal range.

White-jacketed medics, clearly older than the students, offered first aid and monitored the condition of the hunger strikers under a homespun Red Cross banner. Thick army surplus jackets were distributed to strikers, some of whom bedded down to insulate themselves or nap under the covers.

Outside the core, which was occupied by strikers and their handlers, ran a concentric ring of students, mostly organized by academic affiliation, pulled into the fray by bonds of friendship and school spirit. Night and day, straw hats and caps with visors were popular, as were sweaters and Windbreaker jackets. All-purpose clothing, comfortable in heat or cold, loose enough to nap in, durable enough for sitting on the ground, was the norm, including sport shirts, baggy trousers, sweatpants, and sneakers. A high percentage of demonstrators, particularly in the student-dominated zones, wore glasses; others donned the bug-eyed sunglasses popular at the time.

Students were still sticking together as units, moving mostly with friends from the same department and more generally with classmates from the same campus. But the hunger strike, though it started at Beida and had a huge Shida contingent, was so grand a concept that it somehow transcended sharp college rivalries and started to capture the general imagination as a unifying force.

Bright and I were well enough recognized by the Shida contingent to be given ready entrance into the protected zone where the hunger strikers rested, giving us a chance to quietly commiserate with Lily and other strikers from campus. Later in the day we climbed up on the pedestal of the monument to gaze out upon the sea of people we had been swimming in. An uncountable mass of bodies bobbled and undulated before us, stretching from the foot of the monument to Chang'an Boulevard, covering the entire northern half of the square. It was a diverse multitude on close examination, but almost uniformly infused with good cheer and thoroughly peaceful. Standing on a monument to history, gazing at such a vast and defiant gathering, now at least a hundred thousand strong, it was not hard to have the impression that history was being made.

Spending the entire night on the Square left me sleepy and disoriented; maybe I was just getting dopey, but I loved being in the middle of it. Tiananmen was a place of rare alchemy, a place that could turn disputatious and distrusting people into a unitary mass; people with little in common could feel like comrades in arms.

Taking foreign TV crews deep inside a nationalistic demonstration proved physically demanding and psychologically trying. It was not enough to be alert to danger, flexible, and well-informed; there was the practical side, like where one could find a restroom or buy drinks, locate a power source or find a taxi.

As evening fell, the BBC crew had to employ bright portable lights to feed its light-hungry cameras. Bespectacled demonstrators, when they weren't overtly attracted or repelled, gazed blankly our way with comic effect as our lights reflected brightly off the big lenses of dozens of black-framed glasses. I was reminded of Steven Spielberg's instructions during the shooting of *Empire of the Sun* crowd scenes. "Phil, make sure they take off their glasses. The reflections will ruin the shot."

Reflections were the least of the problems for the BBC. It wasn't the fault of "extras"—we were ruining our own shots. Our lights attracted trouble like moths.

But we pressed on. I had now done a dizzying number of "tours" of Tiananmen, all in the past thirty hours, including an outing with diplomatic correspondent Brian Hanrahan and his crew, as good an indication as any that the BBC had begun to hedge its bets about which story to give top billing to. This was not a vote of confidence in tour quality; rather, the presence of students on the square was proving to be so disruptive of Gorbachev's itinerary that the diplomatic story and the riffraff story started to merge into one.

Change was in the air. What kind of change remained open to question and interpretation, but the desire for change was palpable. There were too many indignities and injustices under Communist rule for it to be otherwise.

MAY 15

◑

Looking for Gorbachev

I found Lily shortly before dawn. I chanced upon her while I was escorting the first BBC crew of the day—or was it the last one of the previous day—after spending the night on the square. My friend the hunger striker was sitting glumly among her white headbanded comrades just as the sky started to lighten in the east. She stood up and greeted me enthusiastically, but adamantly refused to talk to the big BBC camera. She was wearing a red jacket, carrying the hefty army jacket that had kept her warm through the night, and had a dust-busting scarf around her neck.

She said she hadn't slept much but was otherwise well, hungry but coping. I tried to encourage her without goading her on. I didn't want to add to the social pressure that was making a hero out of this ordinary young woman. I told her to take care, and that I would come back to see her again. I wished her luck.

As the sun broke through the horizon and climbed over the roof of the Museum of the Chinese Revolution, a parade of fresh civilian contingents arrived on the square, announcing solidarity with the cause. The nonstudent marchers took a cue from the student vanguard by marching in groups, announcing their work affiliation with the same variety of red occupational banners and hand-painted posters, waving flags and donning headbands. Like the students, the working people brought a sense of order and decorum to what might appear at a distance to be an undifferentiated mass by looking out for one another and sticking together as units, which generally seemed to correspond to *danwei*, or work units.

It was precisely this extraordinary, understated discipline that made free-wheeling, seemingly unfettered civil disobedience possible. An individual in the crowd was both at liberty and under intense peer pressure. The boisterous collective defiance simultaneously inspired, defined, and limited one's freedom of movement.

I reluctantly pried myself away from the magnetic pull of the monument and the charismatic tug of the crowd to taxi across town for a BBC meeting. The producers were apparently pleased with the tireless assistance I had been giving to news crews on the square and, tired though I was, it pleased me to learn that they wanted me to personally escort a newly arrived senior correspondent for an evening shoot. I'd never heard of John Simpson, though I could get a measure of his fame in Britain from the hushed way others spoke about him. I was suitably impressed once he and I were introduced and got talking; he was a good listener, eager to learn and distinctly more interested in the emerging story of street politics rather than the scheduled pomp and circumstance of the summit. By taking him to my beat, Tiananmen Square, I hoped to convey to him, and thus indirectly the British television public, the historic importance of the students' scrappy but spirited sideshow.

Observing John Simpson in conversation with his colleagues was telling; he wasn't as approachable as Brian, but aloof in a way that was strangely effective. He had a way of keeping at arm's length the logistics-obsessed producers. He had a congenial gravitas that lent itself well to the job. He was mindful of his appearance, precise in his choice of words. He dressed dapper and fresh, rather like a politician, or at least a man of some importance. On this particular day he wore a beige suit and striped tie.

We traveled by hired car from the Great Wall Hotel to the outskirts of Tiananmen Square, then had the driver stop at the point where automotive traffic thinned out and the footsteps of protesters began to dominate. Cameraman, foreign correspondent, and soundman exited the car with all their gear and stood there; now it was for me to lead the way. I plunged right into the humming throng, turning around now and then to make sure the crew stayed close as we waded our way inside, going single file, opportunistically looking for cracks in the crowd. The crew moved with practiced ease as a single unit, staying as close together as we reasonably could, while negotiating throngs of youthful demonstrators and thickets of excited citizens. I dragged the crew deeper and deeper into the morass, my morass, hoping to get the BBC the kind of access I had been able to get on my own, hoping to excite them with the theatrics of the makeshift student center, but it quickly became apparent that student pins and student ID mattered more than journalistic credentials when it came to getting inside.

The going got slower and slower as we pressed towards the center of the square. Eventually we were stopped by student security, who let me but not the BBC cross the perimeter rope line. The cameraman paused to survey the panorama and gave a thumbs-up to set up a shot. We were about a hundred yards or so to the east of the hunger strikers and with night falling and security tightening, it was unlikely we would get any closer.

Squeezing our way in this far had sufficed to give the visiting correspondent a visceral "feel" for the protest. There were inevitable toes stepped on, accidental collisions, and reflexive shoves; one lifted one's foot tentatively, uncertain if there would be a foot's worth of open pavement to put it down on again.

As we set up shop, I could see in the eyes of those who followed our awkward movements a mix of bemusement and resentment. What's with those big white guys? What are the laowai up to? Where's their Chinese minder? Who's watching them?

We were weighted down with preconceptions of our own, not to mention clunky professional gear. We lacked the official escorts that might better define us, place us in a locally sanctioned context.

Although the BBC's desire to shoot a standup to camera with Mao's portrait in the distance and a big crowd in the foreground did not strike me as being the height of journalistic endeavor—for starters, I wanted to know more about the mind-set of the rabble who were regarding us with uncertain emotion—at least the BBC had been willing to spare a TV star and one of its top crews for the square.

At any rate, I was having a hard time fielding questions from spectators who demanded to know what we were up to. How does one explain a "standup" in the midst of an illegal demonstration to Communist citizens who have never watched any television news but the narrated pabulum on CCTV? How could we, lugging around heavy-duty gear that we at times pointed at the throng like an unwieldy weapon, reassure those around us that we were, if not precisely on their side, not on the other side, either.

"Please move out of the way, we are England Television," I found myself shouting over the din of a thousand muffled voices, coming off a bit more imperious than intended. Not without a bit of discomfort did I don the group identity; it was no longer me being me, it was we. We, as in the BBC.

No doubt there were those who viewed us through the prism of their own paranoia as intelligence agents under journalistic cover or rich foreigners looking down on poor Chinese. No amount of explanation was likely to convince the truly suspicious, but there were many others who deserved some sort of explanation for our periodically odd and oddly aggressive behavior.

Already I missed the easy access and rapport with demonstrators I enjoyed as a sole foreigner surrounded by Chinese. Though utterly defenseless when I moved solo through the crowd, I always felt much freer and less threatened, in part because I trod lightly and provoked little fear. A lone wolf, a somewhat Sinocized one at that, was less threatening than a pack of foreign ones.

Setting up a shot in a methodical manner—tripods incrementally adjusted, white balance achieved, illumination enhanced—allowed for the recording of clean, well-lit images worthy of prime-time TV, but much of it came at the price of spontaneity. That which we sought to observe was constantly reacting to us and regrouping due to our presence. Cameramen know all about this of course, and a long lens can, with some foreshortening, capture unadulterated spontaneity, but more than once we simply scrapped the shot when members of the crowd seized up or returned our curiosity in an obvious way.

Which brought us back full circle to the solipsism of the TV standup; one of the few tasks we could film convincingly was a phony setup in which one member of our crew talked to the red light of the camera, hoping to simulate an intimate conversation with unseen viewers in faraway lands in the not-too-distant future.

It was hard to get away from the feeling that television news was at least as much about "television" as it was about "news." The starving students and their rowdy supporters on Tiananmen Square were, for our current purposes, but a colorful backdrop; the BBC wanted to shine light on one of its own. But even that proved an elusive task.

To get the desired angle necessary to see both the correspondent and the crowd, and, if humanly possible, Mao's distant portrait floating somewhere in the foggy night air, we had to find some way to put the solidly built, silver-haired John Simpson head and shoulders above everyone else. But a plaza as wide and unadorned as Tiananmen Square offers few natural promontories other than the monument, which was already staked out by students and at this juncture off-limits to the crew.

After Eric, the cameraman, made it clear he needed something, anything, to elevate the correspondent, I procured, at length, two flatbed bicycle carts to serve as platforms, one for the correspondent, one for the cameraman.

The trishaw drivers were most cooperative at first; no haggling was involved. In fact I chose not to discuss cash compensation in advance, because it seemed to go against the prevailing spirit of shared idealism and mutual aid that I had been experiencing on the square ever since the giant sit-in had started, especially once they got the not entirely representative impression from *me* that *we*, too, supported the students. Plus, I had hinted at a tip.

Working as a China tour guide I had learned to tip generously to lubricate little transactions. As much as I hated greasing the wheels, it really worked, but I also knew from experience that one should avoid doing so in too blunt or obvious a way.

The cameraman signaled he was ready to roll, which was John Simpson's cue to mount the flatbed cart and commence his standup. He squeezed past curious spectators in a reasonably dignified manner, but he had to step out of the dignity of his persona in order to clamber up on the cart, one knee at a time, and rise, tentatively and awkwardly, to a standing position on the top of the slightly wobbly cart.

Eric was perched atop the other bicycle cart, which he and his soundman Fred had expertly aligned with John Simpson's temporary pedestal to obtain optimal background visuals, effective depth of field, and a precise focal length for the standup shot. Yet even they, despite their workaday clothing and self-effacing work style, created through their silent labors enough commotion to draw a circle of onlookers.

Technical delays provided time enough for a growing throng to precipitate around what must have been an anomalous, if not intriguing, sight. The instant Fred switched on the powerful portable lights, the noose of spectators who encircled us drew inward, tightening ominously. Not only was there no room to escape, but there was hardly enough room to adjust position for a better shot. A throng of adult onlookers, wearing white shirts open at the collar, jackets loose and unbuttoned, sweat-streaked faces made shiny by the light, leaned in, pushed, and stood up on tiptoe, craning to get a better view. One man, who wisely kept his distance from the knot of people desirous to be up front, casually hoisted a kid up on his shoulders.

As eager onlookers inched forward to see what was going on, they pressed against one cart or the other. Even the slightest wobble or shift in position caused the shot to fall out of alignment, ruining the setup and creating a new delay.

Fred, curly blond hair sprouting every which way from the black frames of his glasses and big black headphones, attended to technical difficulties in his usual calm and unruffled way, expertly handling both sound and illumination, while trying to detect the source of the trouble. He adjusted the lights, hoisting the sound boom in place while Eric and I tried to realign the carts. The "talent" remained aloft, only slightly ruffled from two near-miss tumbles, his shiny, neatly groomed hair now mussed up from the effects of a light breeze.

Simpson did what any conscientious television anchor or on-air reporter would do, which was to focus on making himself as presentable as possible while silently practicing his lines for the unforgiving eye of his intended audience in television land, but in doing so, he made himself look, to his unintended local audience at least, like a madman on a soapbox.

In a random gathering of bored and fatigued men aching for spectacle, gawking at a distinctively dressed foreign man fussing with his hair and going through the tics of his prebroadcast routines under a spotlight and above the assembled masses was a kind of entertainment. Spectators who had presumably come to Tiananmen to see the cosseted students on strike had, for now at least, to content themselves with a bizarre pantomime put on by an exotic stranger.

The correspondent got about halfway through his stentorian address to an unseen audience when peals of laughter ruined the sound and a shake of the cart ruined the shot. Eric called "cut" and requested another take. Again the cart was bumped or shaken; again it was hard to keep the spectators quiet. What was an imperceptible movement to the rest of us Eric saw magnified through the shaking viewfinder and concluded to be intentional sabotage. He made a grimace, turned off the camera, and pleaded with me to address the onlookers, to demand that everyone be still.

Wary of issuing orders with no authority at an illegal gathering where, to put it lightly, the forces of law and order were neither in view nor on our side, I superpolitely requested of those around me their cooperation. Satisfied, Eric gave the correspondent the signal to start over again.

On the third take, a young Chinese man, perhaps inspired by sight of foreign journalists taping what appeared to be an important speech, lifted his own tape recorder, a cheap cassette player, high over his head. His outstretched arm mimicked Fred's boom mike, shoving the tape recorder right in front of the important white man to better capture his important, if indecipherable, words.

"Cut!"

The subsequent take was also ruined, this time by a comically aggressive onlooker who was straining to smile for the camera. The take after that was nixed by the soundman, as two of the standers-by next to him started a loud, animated conversation the minute the lights went on.

Seeing the exasperated faces of the BBC crew, I formally addressed the crush of bodies around us, hoping to win some cooperation. In response I was told that we foreigners were offending the dignity of the Chinese people due to our arrogance.

"*Tongzhimen* . . . Comrades," I said out of textbook habit, then softened it to reflect changing times.

"*Peng-you-men.* Friends. Please help us here tonight," I offered, desperately trying to strike the right tone. "We are making a news report for BBC English television. Would it be possible for everyone to be quiet and still for just a minute?"

"We can talk if we want to!" a voice shot out from the back.

"Of course you can," I sallied back, "but please, talk quietly."

"This is China!" he said indignantly. "You're foreigners."

Because this xenophobic line of thought with its unhappy echoes of foiled past encounters truly irritated me, I turned my back on the man, which riled him up all the more.

"I demand that you translate everything the 'old whitey' is saying," a man in a cheap Mao jacket said, giving us the look-over with a jaundiced eye. "Otherwise we, that is, we Chinese, we will not cooperate!"

"Hey, listen, friend," I said sarcastically, my patience straining, "I will translate for you, but after we are finished filming, okay?"

"We demand you tell us now!" he shouted, rallying for support.

"Where are you from?" asked another young man.

"It will only take a few minutes and then we will have lots of time to talk," I promised. "Okay?"

"Foreigners!" a new voice rang out.

"Look at old whitey up on the cart!" shouted another, followed by a caustic laugh.

I tried to ignore the provocations and instead work quietly with the more cooperatively inclined spectators, greeting individuals with short introductions about who we were and what we were doing, asking for their understanding. Such individual entreaties won a high degree of compliance, but there was always some joker in the back who wanted to show off, or someone who had just squeezed up front, demanding to know what was going on.

With at least a hundred people now pressing in on us in a deeply congested corner of a plaza containing, all told, over a hundred thousand demonstrators, we were vulnerable, at the complete mercy of the illegal assembly.

Meanwhile, the big, important man on the cart continued to attract special attention, even with the lights out. Oblivious to what was being said but undoubtedly aware there was some snafu, the foreign correspondent gamely continued to practice his lines. Again, this is perfectly normal practice for actors and newsreaders, and incidentally not unknown in China, as students would often stroll around campus talking to themselves as an aid to memorization. But on this evening, it only added to the mystery of who we were and what we were up to.

My entreaties may well have backfired. Here was this tall blond man, wearing cheap local clothes, mixing with the masses, speaking unbidden to strangers, having the nerve to ask "friends and comrades" for their cooperation in strangely accented Chinese. If all that was not awkward and amusing enough, the important man with silver hair whose waist was level with the eyes of spectators had one hand thrust deep in his trouser pocket, fidgeting with the small tape recorder he used to record memos and prompts.

"Today a crowd of millions gathers in peaceful protest at Tianan—" Simpson started. "Hello! Hey—who's shaking the cart?" After almost getting knocked over by a particularly violent thrust, he regained his balance, but not his composure.

The deliberate thrust against our man felt like an attack on all of us. "Who did that?" I asked sternly, studying the faces closest to the cart. My interrogative glance was met with indignant protestations of innocence, sullen stares, and a few weak smiles.

"What is your relationship with the foreigners?" I overheard someone quizzing the bicycle cart drivers. The vigilante-style interrogation that followed left both drivers looking shaken and worried. One driver approached me sheepishly, saying he'd like to get his cart back. I indicated I understood. The other driver sportingly agreed to wait, and even went so far as to ask the troublemakers for their cooperation. He did so in a culturally sensitive way, asking his fellow citizens to quiet down so that the "laowai" would get done already and he could go home to eat, but it didn't placate everyone.

"Oh, you're a fine one, telling us to shut up because you are in the pay of the foreigners," challenged a young man with an unruly mop of hair.

"That's it," chimed another, "how much are the laowai paying you?"

"How much, traitor? That's what we want to know!" another unfriendly voice cried out.

The almost magical, all-encompassing harmony I had experienced moving amidst the student-dominated crowd in the past two days had evaporated, causing me to wonder how much of the harmony had been in my mind.

Part of the difference was in the timing; early in the day it was mostly students, now that evening rush hour had ended, there were lots of workers from all walks of life. Anybody and everybody could come to Tiananmen for an evening stroll or look-see. But most of the ordinary folk, cowed enough as they were by toiling for low wages under imperious commissars, were modest if not mild-mannered. They kept to themselves and maintained a low profile out of habit. If anything, the workers were more cautious and gun-shy than the rambunctious students. But in every crowd there's a wise guy or two, isn't there?

And then there was us. Nearly everyone in monoracial, nationalistic China had a visceral reaction to foreigners, a slight but perceptible visual shock followed by a curious gaze that sometimes betrayed a hint of envy. Being an honored foreign guest made it easy to make friends, but not everyone believed in friendship. Xenophobia was the other side of that coin.

"So, how much is the foreign boss paying?" shouted a threatening voice.

"Yes! How much? How much?" echoed several others.

Oblivious to the content of the arguments storming around them but hypersensitive to vibrations as perceived through the lens and microphone, the crew gamely tried to accelerate the shoot, attempting to race through the short standup while I worked the crowd. At last, Eric, who struck me as being a most sensible and patient man, started cursing under his breath.

"Phil," he whispered, "There's someone doing it on purpose. They wait until the lights are on and then they deliberately shake the cart. Can you find out who it is?"

I carefully watched both carts, but honestly couldn't pin down the culprit. As it was, I was hearing preemptive pleas of innocence.

"It wasn't me. Nope, wasn't me. Wasn't me either."

It was on the ninth or tenth take that I heard a shockingly stupid rumor going around. The distinguished-looking Caucasian man up on the cart was said to be a famous politician. A really famous one.

"That's Gor-ba-chev!" a voice cried out, as if in confirmation, "Look, they're interviewing the leader of the Soviet Union!" A momentary hush was followed by a wave of excited murmurs and a forward thrust of onlookers. Then there was a sudden, total breakdown in order as the Soviet leader's name was chanted in Chinese.

"Ge-er-ba-qiao-fu! Ge-er-ba-qiao-fu! Ge-er-ba-qiao-fu!"

Something hit the cart hard, knocking John Simpson off balance. He broke his fall with an outstretched arm, tumbling safely into the arms of the crew. Pale and shaken, he tried to regain his sangfroid by batting the dust off his jacket. "Can someone tell me what is going on?"

I didn't want to say that the rumor of the Soviet leader appearing on the square to mix with Chinese protesters was a positively explosive development, plus Simpson wouldn't understand how two white men who looked so different could be confused, so I let it go.

The rhythmic incantation about Gorbachev, though apparently incomprehensible to the crew, was alarming enough that they knew it was time to beat a quick exit. I emptied my pocket, handing each of the drivers a wad of small bills, crisp FEC notes mixed with wrinkled renminbi (RMB).

"Are you trying to buy us Chinese with your foreign money?" an eagle-eyed spokesman for the masses asked maliciously. "Foreigners! Imperialists. Ha!"

The drivers, now completely intimidated, refused all money, hastily mounted their bikes, and slid away into the darkness, begging cooperation as they pedaled against the inward push of the throng. It was terrifying to realize that just a handful of malicious hangers-on could put so many decent people in jeopardy. At a time of uncertain political outcome such as this, it didn't take much to manipulate the mood of listless bystanders, and I despaired to see how a small misunderstanding could trump the overall mood of solidarity.

"You see that? The arrogant foreigners used the cart," one of the more devious troublemakers said in accusatory tone, after scaring the drivers away, "and didn't even pay!"

"They are taking advantage of the Chinese people!" yelled his coconspirator.

"Who the hell are you?" I shot back in rude Chinese. By now I had had it. I didn't want to fight, but gambled that a strong response might get the wise guys off our backs and stop the conflict from escalating. We were surrounded, so if the crush got any more hostile, it might be hard to extract ourselves without a bloody fight.

"Don't you dare talk to me like that," the man steamed angrily. "This is China!"

"China? China has nothing to do with it," I shouted back. "The problem is you. What kind of thing are you?"

I had really lost my cool, and it was wrong to use such a coarse expression, even though I heard Chinese use it among themselves. The situation had deteriorated in a way that needed no translation. The BBC crew wasted no time in packing up and packing off while I tried to hold my ground in an intemperate verbal exchange.

Just as my crew was on the verge of extracting themselves from the scene, a middle-aged man with a thin beard came up to me, effectively blocking my exit. He spoke fluent, educated English with a soft American accent.

"You should not have talked to that man like that!" he chided me.

"He shouldn't have made so much trouble for us!" I answered in Chinese. "Who does he think he is?" And who do you think you are, I might have asked.

"Your Chinese is very good, but you must be careful," the soft-spoken man said, continuing to speak in impeccable English. "This is a very special night for the Chinese people."

"What do you mean? That guy was bothering us."

"It is very important that people like him be here," he said. "They may seem rude to you, but they support the students. It is especially dangerous for common Chinese to be here."

Who deemed it important for the "common people" to be here tonight? The man passed for what in China is called a "knowledgeable element" or intellectual. He was clearly educated, confident, and had something of a superior air.

Who was he? He reminded me of Zhu Jiaming, a Zhao protégé I had met at the University of Michigan, and was not unlike other brilliant young intellectuals in government think tanks such as the Academy of Social Sciences, many of whom had studied on American campuses. Was he one of those reformist intellectuals working behind the scenes for Zhao Ziyang?

"And if I may, just what unit are you with?" I asked in Chinese, to the apparent delight of a few in the now momentarily subdued mob who had been straining to understand the exchange in English. The soft-spoken man had a definable presence, an unassailable font of self-assurance, almost a cockiness that reminded me of film director Chen Kaige. His erudition and elitist élan could not be completely disguised by his untended facial hair or his baggy trousers and plain shirt.

"Never you mind that," he said dismissively, steering the conversation back into English, "But I know your country. I did research at the University of Chicago."

"Why are you talking to me in English?"

"I don't want them to understand."

"So where do you work?"

"The Academy of Sciences," he said. "And you? Tell me about yourself."

"Well, we're from BBC," I said, turning only to discover that my colleagues were out of sight. It was my responsibility to get them back to the Great Wall Hotel, after which we could safely commiserate about the dangers of the mob over cold beer in the lobby bar.

A familiar feeling swept over me, pulling me two ways at once. I wanted to talk more to this enigmatic man who had been observing us and the people's reaction to us with insight and attention. But I had agreed to take the crew to the square and worried, probably unnecessarily, given their finely honed vocational resourcefulness, about them finding their way back to the hotel without a word of Chinese between them, so I pulled myself away.

"It's interesting talking to you," I told the self-possessed intellectual. "And I'd love to chat more, but I gotta catch up with the crew. See ya."

On the way back, I explained to the crew that John Simpson had been mistaken for Gorbachev, and we all got a good laugh out of an otherwise harrowing experience. If our ace reporter had been frustrated by the failure to do a proper standup, or if his ego had in any way been bruised by the public humiliation of being forced off the cart, at least he could console himself with the thought that he had been mistaken for a great man.

MAY 16

◑

Working-Class Heroes

On the fine day of May 16, Bright, Jenny, and I lost one another in the thick of a swarm bubbling with eye-catching distractions. All morning we had been subject to the tug and pull of a crowd with energy to burn, much of it dissipated in mindless Brownian motion, but some of it creative and constructive. The stake out of prestigious ground near the hunger strikers now began to refine itself as activists started to develop their subdivisions of pavement, using piles of coats and blankets as beds, newspapers as seats, and stacking bottled drinks and paper-wrapped edibles in makeshift dining halls, marking places to nap and places to nibble. It was like a giant campground, young people gathering in tight circles to sing, strum guitars, tell jokes, and otherwise entertain themselves.

Getting lost in such a sea of people was almost a given, and it was not as if we didn't see it coming. Pulled in different directions by the lure of different acquaintances and curious chance encounters, attracted in unequal measure to solemn political pronouncements and impromptu guitar jams, going off on our own to buy some bottled drink or search for a restroom, it was all but guaranteed that the three of us would lose sight of one another.

Providently we had prepared a back-up plan to meet at a small intersection near a row of shops on the eastern face of the square not far from the Mao Memorial Hall. We called our prearranged meeting spot the "Wonton Place," as there was a small noodle and dumpling shack on the corner there.

I got there first, mounting the low promontory on which the shack was built to get a more comprehensive view of the square. Knowing Bright and

Jenny were in there somewhere, though impossible to single out from such a distance, I joined a long line of hungry protestors to order some food.

The sweat-drenched kitchen cooks and limping waitstaff of this modest eatery were sorely overworked, having seen business jump exponentially in the last few days without advance warning. They rose to the challenge, though as state employees there was no financial incentive to do so, ladling out wonton soup and noodles to multiple hundreds of hungry diners, a tiny but not insignificant contribution to keeping the Tiananmen congregation replenished and refreshed. When it came to food and commercial outlets, the square was a sterile zone, not unlike the symbolic mall of Washington DC. It was the kind of place most people made a short visit to, took photos, and then went somewhere else for lunch. Now, with people here around the clock and the midday swell easily reaching half a million or more, the pressure to find food and drink was almost Malthusian.

Yet, though the lines were long, I didn't see any line-cutting, nor any of the indignant grumbling and argument that usually goes with it. Service was slow, maybe even slower than usual, but there were few complaints because complaining somehow violated the spirit of selflessness emanating from the hunger strikers on the square. Indeed, anyone on line could consider themselves lucky to be in line at all, for the heroes of the moment were conspicuously hungry. And even for those not on strike, food within walking distance to the square was hard to come by.

Under more normal conditions, one might easily walk past a greasy chopstick joint such as this without giving it a second glance. The only prominent eatery in the area was the venerable Quan Ju De Beijing Duck restaurant a bit further down a road that seemed devoted to greasy eateries.

Pricey menu aside, there was something obscene about hunger strike supporters dining on rich fatty duck at a time like this, so the homely noodle stall fit the bill. Inexpensive nourishment promised satiation without the guilt.

It was basically a soup stand, but what could better replenish liquid lost to perspiration and appease cramps of hunger than hot soup and dumplings? What better place to rest and recharge while remaining within view of the square?

As the line snaked slowly closer to the sweltering kitchen, I ordered for Bright and Jenny, but despaired of actually finding a place to sit. Every last wobbly plastic chair and weather-warped table was accounted for, not just by diners already sitting down, enjoying their repast, but by contenders for those precious chairs. Dozens balanced bowls of hot soup and bottles of beer while closely eyeing those who supped, awaiting a sudden opening.

It was long after lunch hour but the kitchen staff continued to stand stoically on the grease-splattered cement, tending huge boiling vats of broth, kneading dough, and ladling out portions to impatient eaters, restoring the flagging spirits of tired protesters and nurturing the dehydrated bodies of the sun-exposed men and women weary of foot. Cooks, cashiers, and cleaners who toiled in low-rent, ramshackle shops such as this had no illusions about their social status. They were among the losers in Deng's new hybrid system of socialism mixed with capitalism.

Such work wasn't entrepreneurial, with all possible risks and benefits that entailed, but it was not much of a socialist sinecure either. They worked long hours for low pay in a job both physically demanding and accident-prone. Deng Xiaoping famously said to get rich is glorious, but that was for other people, special people. The workers in the "iron rice bowl" trades could at best look forward to sipping tea and reading newspapers in between shifts, a life of low productivity punctuated by long stretches of boredom.

But the Wonton Place met the needs of cash-starved, dialect-shouting rural pilgrims visiting the capital, diners who might only dream about eating in Quan Ju De, where duck was served up according to social class, with VIP rooms for wining and dining foreign dignitaries such as Kim Il Sung along with less efficiently air-conditioned rooms for local hotshots and, as a gesture to the hoi polloi, a fast-food-style canteen on the ground level where the tables and floor were never free of cigarette butts, discarded bones, and duck bits.

Here, in contrast, the menu was simple and there was but one class of service. Deliveries were made by bicycle and the coal-fired kitchen hummed along with a hardy functionality, so low-tech it could operate at full blast even during a black out.

A worker in a food-stained white uniform took a break from the infernal heat of the kitchen, stepping outside to wipe her brow, then briefly surveyed the insatiable army that she was helping to feed. Transfixed by the size of the crowd assembling on the square, her eyes brightened with pride and amazement, as if it had just dawned on her that she too had a part to play in the unfolding drama.

The words "it is important for people like that to be here" came to mind. The neglected wageworker, who made a bare-bones living by slopping out soupy servings to day tourists on the edge of a plaza that memorialized revolutions past, was she not also an inheritor of the revolutionary tradition? The sudden upsurge in "serve the people" politics was transformational. These men and women in their soiled aprons were working class heroes, playing an appreciated role, feeding pass-by revolutionaries and slaking the thirst of the throng.

I had seen a similar transformation of kitchen crew and menial workers on campus, even the sassy rural attendants in the Insider Guest House, who, far from being critical of the students, were proud to be proximate to history in the making. The nervy defiance of the students, however opaque and abstract their goals might be in political terms, was seductive to bored ordinary folk, for it offered both spectacle and a hint of better things to come. Egalitarianism and self-sacrifice were back in circulation with a vengeance after a decade that saw socialist values eroded by a get-rich-quick mentality.

Bright finds me and hurries over just in time to help me carry our bowls of hot soup while Jenny looks for a seat. We thank the kitchen staff for the food they ladle out, and we are not alone in doing so; others too express admiration for the way the kitchen crew efficiently filled so many stomachs.

By a stroke of luck, two seats opened up just as we had resigned ourselves to eating on our feet. There was no table, but two sturdy stools were available along the railing on the edge of the earthen promontory. We swiftly took possession of the coveted seats, taking turns to rest our legs and greedily slurping hot soup in full view of the square.

The outdoor eating area of the Wonton Place was like a rough-hewn balcony, offering a rare, unobstructed view of the drum-flat plaza in front of us. Beyond the railing and a mass of entangled bicycles, a pent-up political procession unscrolled before our eyes.

Given the elevation of our humble perch, we could not only see the south-to-north pattern of flow of the demonstrators treading closest to us, but could detect an equal and opposite movement clear across the square where the other side of the human cyclone moved north to south.

We gobbled up the dumplings and savored the hot broth to the last drop. I was proud to have been a tiny cog in that giant rotating human clockwork out there, but at the same time it was a relief to be a more or less autonomous individual again, a few paces apart from the hypnotic beat of other footsteps.

I needed space and distance to order my thoughts, a quiet time-out to jot down some notes. For some reason I found it hard to think in the midst of the crowd. It was as if some ancient communal subconscious ruled when I was walled in on all sides by thick human traffic; it was hard to reflect with any clarity from the inside out. But then again, I would not have much to reflect on afterwards from the sidelines had I not first lost myself on the inside. To me the two emerging sweet spots in a rotating vortex of protesters pushing a million were to be either in the center of the crowd or on its outer edge. There was a crunching intensity in one view, an aloof clarity in the other. The two poles were buffered by an indeterminate zone of halfhearted student agitators and partially politicized townspeople.

Maybe the BBC's tussle with militant onlookers last night had been in just such an in-between location, but it might just have been a bout of bad luck, bad vibes provoked by fears of a nocturnal crackdown. This morning I had seen little of the volatility I normally associated with tight knots of people on the street, where loud arguments, even shoving matches and fist fights routinely took place in full public view. It was not so much ironclad discipline that enabled the crowd out there to enjoy such an unusual degree of freedom from untoward incident or petty fights, it was rather a kind of mass elation combined with a collapse of individual boundaries; the mass somehow pulled itself together and sedated itself.

Several times I tried taking pictures of the kinetic marching with my fixed-lens Olympus, but only a wide-angle could do the broad panorama real justice, and even then, the result would be too static to convey the constant motion. I settled for a series of snaps in succession, thinking I might be able to fit them together like pieces of a puzzle later.

The spectacle of so many people in motion was so mesmerizing, the effect of delicious noodles and a warm beer on empty stomachs so soporific, that we lingered in our ringside seats overlooking the square even after lunch hour ended. Eyes locked in a hundred-yard stare, body immobile with fatigue and slightly off-balance from a touch of inebriation, I felt myself being tugged and transported back into the thick of it without lifting a finger. I was overwhelmed with a sense of awe and an ecstatic sense of well-being to see so many people moving together with so much spirit and so little friction. The square had become a font of revolutionary renewal tempered, mercifully, by an all-encompassing harmony.

The marchers at Tiananmen moved to the drumbeat of the Chinese language hypnotically, almost in unison. Did the rhythmic repetition of slogans have a mantralike calming effect? Or was it the simple unalloyed delight of the warm spring breeze that blew under the embrace of a blue sky? Or was it perhaps the cool, silvery light of a moon on the rise, daring to follow in the trail of the scorching sun. There was a communal joy in being part of something so much bigger than oneself, but there was also a rare assertion of self, the realization of a long-suppressed need to take the helm of one's life.

I crouched forward and leaned on the railing, the warm restorative broth and warm beer having some effect, not to mention the delayed onset of drowsiness from a sleepless night on the square. But what was really immobilizing me was the confusion of running two different ways, leading two different lives.

I had mixed feelings about experiencing this rare moment in China's history in the employ of English journalists; diverse and engaging as they were in their own right, as useful as the modest income and a chance to learn about their craft was, somehow the timing was all wrong. I didn't want to eat with them or drink with them or otherwise indulge in the work hard, play hard hotel expatriate life with them, at least not at a time like this.

I yearned to be in China and among Chinese people on my own terms, especially now that a subtle transformation was underway, visible in the new-found confidence and bounce in the step of friends. Although many of the things going on right before my eyes eluded easy intellectual comprehension, I was moved by the spirit of the day. It was thrilling to be in a nation waking up to a new dawn; it was empowering to witness the empowerment of the downtrodden. Something important was going on, touching all levels of society, and I wanted to be close to the beating heart of it.

For every hour I worked with the BBC in such a setting, I felt a need to match it with time spent with Chinese friends and acquaintances, and if none were available, even out-and-out Chinese strangers would do. Burning it on both ends of the cultural spectrum, the fatigue alone was enough to make me reconsider my freelance deal, which the BBC had offered to extend. To be an effective journalist in a competitive market might well require a kind of invasive aggressiveness. One had to pin down reluctant interviews and fight for scoops, one had to seduce and abandon informants to get the "get." For stunning visuals, one had to sometimes step on feet, or shoot surreptitiously, or boldly trespass. All was deemed fair in the name of a good shot.

It was also dawning on me that Bright wasn't exactly pleased with my working for the BBC, though I initially thought she might be. She wasn't like Yao Xiaoping, a family friend who hammered me to get a "real" job, any old job, when I visited her at her uncle's place at Beida a few days after the May 4 rally.

Bright, in contrast, clearly conveyed her doubts about my new job without saying a word about it. She had a habit of disappearing as soon as the BBC arrived and wouldn't meet me until they had left. In this regard, the BBC was blameless, for more than once she had been specifically invited to join us.

Of course, given the nature of the news that the BBC was, partly at my insistence, looking to take measure of and shoot, collaring a Beijing student active in the demonstrations was an ace in the hole. It's not like they were extending invitations to her, or to me, for that matter, to help them with VIP interviews or summit photo ops.

No, it was obvious they wanted some guidance regarding the sideshow on the streets. By signing up for one hundred dollars a day I was contracted to help, and wanted to help, but Bright was free of such obligations and once she finally made her views clear, I fully supported her decision not to perform for them.

It was one thing to take risks with one's peers in hopes of making permanent improvements in one's native country. It was quite another to risk it all for professional war reporters and ambulance chasers, here today, gone tomorrow, ever in search of shock and spectacle to sell to the home audience.

As for me, I was attracted to journalism in principle, but not in the way it was practiced. Not in China.

The difficulty of being a bridge between two cultures had been driven home when I worked as a China tour guide and cruise director. The vacillations were extreme. There were hours of the day when I resented the foreigners and identified with the Chinese and vice versa, and the polarity could switch almost instantly.

Like the time an emergency struck while I was dining with American tourists on what was once Mao's private riverboat. Due to rough waters, an American woman fell and cracked her head open. Her limp body was lifted onto a dining table, and even after first aid, the bleeding continued until the white tablecloth was soaked red. I had to argue vociferously with a timid captain and a truculent on-board commissar to change course and turn the boat around for a medical evacuation in the nearest big river port of Wuhan, a demand which they ultimately complied with, only to find myself then being pounced upon by irate American tourists demanding to know if they would still get to "see the monkey temple" and demanding a refund if they couldn't because of the hours lost to the medical emergency.

The injured woman survived, thanks in part to a capable and competent Chinese crew that rose to the occasion. After her condition stabilized she was eventually flown to Beijing and out of the country, but we never did make it to the monkey temple.

A more subtle occupational hazard was the constant shifting back and forth of languages, and the implied identities that went with them. Frequently I found myself more in the mood for one language than the other, in the same way one might crave Chinese food for one meal, something Western at the next.

As to how someone so overwhelmingly Caucasian in appearance might find common cause with the Chinese, there's clearly a contrary streak in my nature, a willingness to take a stand in favor of the perceived underdog, a curiosity to try new things and try to imagine the world as others see it. It's a road taken not without pitfalls and pratfalls; it is the sort of thing that once had me rooting for a Chinese team playing an American team in New York, to the extreme puzzlement of both Chinese and Americans sitting with me.

Although Irish by family background and more generally American culturally, I have always been fascinated by Asia, China in particular, and have tended to assume the guise of eager cultural exchange student, enthusiastic, perhaps naively so, for any experience that might deepen my appreciation of the language and culture.

Just three-and-a-half days with the BBC had been enough to bring such conflicting thoughts back to the surface. I knew it was part of the game to work as late or early as asked and also knew it was an honor of sorts to be invited to kick back a few beers with the crew afterwards, but last night I had said yes to beers after work only to miss dorm curfew and end up stranded.

It was BBC producer Mark Thompson, one of the more difficult people to take around—not just because he perpetually operated on London time, but because he expected China to follow suit—who inadvertently put me straight.

After a round of beers and a round of "thanks, Phil," "See you bright and early tomorrow morning, Phil," I plodded out in the midnight gloom of the hotel parking lot while everyone else went up to their rooms. Given an ungodly early start for the next morning, I had asked if I could sleep on the carpeted office floor, but that was nixed, so I scoured the parking lot for a BBC car to see if a driver could take me across town. The drivers were off-duty, planning to sleep in their vehicles, a courtesy they extended to me.

Thompson, who had come down to greet a late-night arrival, spotted me as I lay curled up in the back seat of a BBC rented car trying to get some shut-eye.

"Look at Phil, poor old sod!"

His coworker asked why I didn't have a hotel room and the producer said something to the effect that I didn't really work for them. Then they went back into the hotel.

No BBC hotel room for me, no per diem either, not even carfare home. I'd spent one night sleeping on the square, and was poised to spend another in a car, on call round the clock, ready to rise to the demands of a demanding job.

But as I lay scrunched up in the back of that car, physically exhausted, mind wide awake, I had to wonder why I was allowing a crappy short-term, low-pay job with no security and innumerable risks to come between me and my sleep, let alone me and China?

I didn't like having to leave the square when the crew wanted to go back to the hotel and I didn't like Bright avoiding me when I was with the others. She hinted that my hanging out with the BBC had already affected my attitude, making me impatient with Chinese people. It was causing me, more and more, to view her people as "they" did—primarily as news subjects. It was true in a way. Just the act of taking aim and filming "subjects" and interviewing "them" cast a slightly unreal, objectified quality upon the Chinese, not unlike viewing nature through a lens. I tried to explain to her the time constraints of the job, an unusually erratic but demanding schedule that had more to do with Greenwich Mean Time than events on the ground.

In a different environment, one in which I had invested less of my life, dreams, and aspiration, I could imagine how being with the BBC during an uprising would seem like the best of both worlds, making money in an exotic setting, bonding with fellow foreigners as the natives went amok, then retiring to the womblike comfort of the dark hotel bar.

But this wasn't just any news story. And China wasn't just any country, at least not to me.

If I had been working for an American news crew, as I had on previous occasions in Shanghai and elsewhere, I might have felt more like one of the guys, if only because being American is such an indelible part of me. A British news crew, on the other hand, while culturally familiar, was just different enough that I could, in effect, elect not to fully identify with them. Being not quite British and yet clearly un-Chinese made it possible for me to occupy a third space, somewhat equidistant between "English television" and the "native informants."

Tossing back and forth in the cramped back seat of a cab that night made for a fitful sleep, but it had a salutary effect. I decided to get a room of my own, not in the Great Wall or the Palace but in the considerably more affordable and centrally located Beijing Hotel. It was a strain on my budget, but it would be good for body and mind. The alternative was to quit the BBC altogether and go back to campus.

The white-capped workers at the Wonton Place were now sitting outside too, taking a much-needed break. I drained my beer. I think we all felt uplifted by the outburst of communal enthusiasm, and the seemingly unbreakable spirit of people power led us to relax for the first time in days. History was marching before us, but not so fast that one couldn't enjoy a beer chaser to wash down the delicious Chinese dumplings.

"Anyway, I'm glad I got the room," I said, explaining my decision to book into the Beijing. "You and Jenny can visit any time."

"But that's a hotel for foreigners," Bright protested, "and expensive, too."

She was right. There was much less social division here, out in the open, under the sky. Tiananmen was starting to feel like an old friend.

We plunged back into the mix. No matter which way we turned, we found people interacting smoothly, in a neutral and matter-of-fact way. After telling Bright and Jenny about the case of mistaken identity of the BBC's own Gorbachev, I marveled at how, in contrast, I had been able to spend the early morning escorting another BBC crew around the square without incident. Same place, different mood. We filmed freely, did spot interviews, squeezed in close to the students and completed standups, all without incident.

As we drifted with the people currents, the real Gorbachev was meeting behind closed doors with Zhao Ziyang and Li Peng, and there was to be a state banquet with Deng. Meanwhile the students refused to budge and the crowd just kept getting bigger.

The mood today was hearty and purposeful in comparison to the ambiguous mood of previous days. There was a shared sense of mission—to hold the high ground while the Soviet leader was in town—and a contagious optimism working to unify the protest movement.

From the plethora of big character posters and hand-painted banners one could discern themes old and new, calls for dialogue and openness and democracy and science and job opportunity and transparency and free speech and, oh, but how could one possibly tie all that together?

The anticorruption slogans, so central to early forays off campus, were all but gone. If one slogan started to emerge from the cacophony of voices trudging clockwise around the giant plaza on this red-banner day, it was not an active call for democracy or press freedom nor was it an angry denunciation of corruption and dictatorial rule. Nor did it have anything to do with Gorbachev. Instead it was something simple, if not overly simplistic, something positive with a neutral ring.

"SHENGYUAN XUESHENG!"

"Shengyuan xuesheng?" That's it? I conferred with Bright on the possible nuances of the four-character phrase, failing to find any satisfactory depth to it. The latest articulation of the movement's highest aspiration was simply "Support the students!"

For better or worse "shengyuan xuesheng!" was the mantra of the moment. It was easy to grasp, it sounded vaguely humanitarian, and it was hard to disagree with as long as some students were putting their lives on the line.

What? Which students? All students? Beijing students? The student vanguard? It was a simple formulation, but not without conflicts of interpretation, given so many different ideas and personalities out there vying for influence.

In practical terms, "the students" most worthy of support were those on hunger strike, and perhaps by self-serving extension, the activist core in the zizhihui or autonomous federation who policed and stage-managed the strike. More generally to support the students might mean to support all the students, mostly from Beijing colleges, who put themselves in conflict with the authorities by demonstrating.

There were other slogans that were easy to agree with, too; after all, who wasn't against corruption? But the "down with" this and "down with" that slogans, some of which I heard vociferously shouted in the May 4 demonstration, were too negative to be inspiring. The almost Darwinian evolution and winnowing of slogans to suit the mood of the day meant that yesterday's shouts were ancient history, yesterday's banners detritus in today's parade.

The term *democracy* was gaining a certain purchase on the popular imagination as well, though it was not without its slippery side. Given the predictable confusion about what the students were really up to, given the abstraction and ambiguity inherent in the political term *minzhu* within the confines of a Communist society that fancied itself to be democratic in a roundabout sort of way, democracy meant very different things to different people. It had such a bafflingly wide range of meaning, it was so easily co-opted and distorted, that one could better appreciate the efficacy of a banal but concrete cry.

Thus "support the students" became one of those rare phrases, polished and spit out by the crowd, that a million voices could safely agree to say in unison.

SUPPORT THE STUDENTS!

The frictionless interactions I was enjoying with Bright, Jenny, Lily, and other friends from Shida also bolstered my confidence, my sense of being part of a giant, magnificent sort of drama that had a role for everyone and anyone willing to step up on stage.

The spirit of the day permitted ample interaction of the sort I liked best. Not above, not below, just side by side with everyone else. No big fuss about obvious differences nor any need to elaborate obvious commonalities, just people getting along. All afternoon I moved through the congregation feeling very much a person, and not much a laowai.

The background roar of a thousand voices was growing louder, punctuated with staccato chants and rhythmic cheers. A light spring breeze lifted the saline, musty scent emanating from the sweaty marchers and carried it away. A crescendo of song and a sudden inrush of protesters sent a shock of excitement across the square. We stood up to cheer the cheering marchers as new recruits from all walks of life joined the growing congregation.

Banners were unfurled as line after line of new marchers hailing from diverse work units paraded by. Cardboard signs and handsome calligraphy on cloth sheets announced an outburst of new slogans, touching on themes as diverse as maternal love and occupational solidarity.

MOTHER, I LOVE FOOD BUT I LOVE JUSTICE MORE!

MOTHER, CAN YOU SEE WHO IS RIGHT, WHO IS WRONG?

WHO DARES NOT TO STAND ON THE SIDE OF THE PEOPLE?
CHINA YOUTH NEWSPAPER SUPPORTS THE STUDENTS!
THE CHINESE ACADEMY OF SCIENCE!
GIVE US BACK OUR STUDENTS!

Even service workers were marching! Service worker, or *fuwuyuan*, was an oxymoronic category that included the surly waiters, pert waitresses, somnambulant dorm staff, lazy labor-evaders and outright truculent gatekeepers who gave us much cause for argument in our daily lives. And yet here they were, beaming red-cheeked faces chanting and marching with verve, so attuned to the same master drumbeat as everyone else that they were even willing to forgo their usual midday naps.

If *fuwuyuan* were marching, then China was truly headed for big changes.

BEIJING HOTEL SUPPORTS THE STUDENTS
CAAC SUPPORTS THE STUDENTS
PALACE HOTEL WORKERS SUPPORT THE STUDENTS
XIYUAN HOTEL SUPPORTS THE STUDENTS
YOUNG TEACHERS SUPPORT THE STUDENTS
POLICE CADETS SUPPORT THE STUDENTS

The last banner elicited a hush of excitement. It was, strictly speaking, just another banner by one group of students supporting another. But if it was an indication of a widening trend, the presence of police cadets meant that some security forces were not in opposition to the demonstration. The diverse provenance and swelling number of protesters was reaching a critical mass, a level of consensus, which I thought bode well for a resolution to the crisis. To march was not going against the current but rather moving with it. It was getting incredibly mainstream, almost to the point of being unremarkable, if it were not for the fact that it was technically illegal and a deliberate slap in the face to the highest authorities.

At one point we detoured from the plaza in the thrall of people power and ambled down the unremarkable backstreets to the east of the square, looking for a respite from the constant pressing of flesh and pressure of curious eyes, only to be startled by the sight of hundreds of men in uniform, Public Security officers, Bright said. But there was no cause for alarm, as they quickly disappeared into the warren of back alleys near their headquarters. Still, the encounter was unsettling inasmuch as it was a reminder that the police, though unarmed, had not completely retreated from the streets and still had a great deal of coercive force at their disposal.

We doubled back and worked our way into the protective fold of the crowd again. It not only felt safer, it was more uplifting and beautiful than the shadowy gray alleys we had just emerged from.

Over the past few days, Communist-controlled work units, ranging from the national airlines and hotel workers to party school cadres, had joined the demonstrations. The secret police were offering no visible resistance. Was it a trap? Or were people in all walks of life drawn into the momentum of the moment keen to join in just as the fledgling movement was about to go mainstream? With the party and police showing tentative support, could the army be far behind?

As the sun dropped lower in the cloudless sky to the west, we wandered along the northeastern edge of the square, unsure of where to go or what to do next. We wended our way to the entrance steps of the Museum of the People's History, skirting the edge of the protest zone.

Again we found ourselves distinctly reluctant to leave and almost had to wrench ourselves away. The square had a distinctly Jovian gravity, like a curvature in space, a catchment basin, a people attractor.

I don't think we were alone in this feeling, for however much we lacked a firm understanding of what was being demanded, and despite whatever reservations we had about the direction in which things were going, we wanted to be at least in view of the square, indeed, had to be there, for the feeling of it, the warm communal pull, the transformative historic overtones. Something greater than the sum of its multifarious parts was at play, something was dawning, something new and unknown was being born. If we were lucky, we might witness its birth.

The Great Hall of the People was the true backdrop for such hopes. Although news crews, like provincial tourists, saw the Mao portrait hanging from Tiananmen Gate as the obligatory angle, and the geomancy of the square was riddled by a powerful north-south axis, the Great Hall was the only building with any serious resonance for the students. Mao was not yet so remote as to be reduced to a crusty founding father whose portrait hung on the square like an oil painting of a long-dead university founder in a faculty club, but it was certainly possible to turn one's back on him to consider more contemporary things.

Every one of the marches from campus to the square had gravitated to the Great Hall and tended to dawdle there, though it was continuously in use by the government and continually guarded. It was the only building on the square with any democratic function whatsoever, even if the People's Congress that met there was a rubber-stamp one.

It was at the Great Hall that Hu Yaobang's state funeral had been held, an event that drew an early wave of student protesters, three of whom made an extended symbolic plea on bended knee to meet with the premier. Li Peng ignored them, of course, while Zhao Ziyang had been busy reading the eulogy of his predecessor. There had been sporadic protests elsewhere, most safely contained on various campuses, but also, provocatively, at the Xinhua Gate entrance to the Zhongnanhai leadership compound.

The hunger strikers, for their part, clustered around the monument in the shadow of the Great Hall, and if my reckoning of how department banners were placed could be a judge, the cordoned-off space nearest the Great Hall enjoyed the pride of place, just as it had on May 4 when Beida and Shida staked out the most prestigiously located plots for their respective delegations. They looked to the Great Hall rather than Mao.

The Great Hall was now a looming silhouette as the sun dropped below it and the sky glowed orange and pink. To the east was a light wash of lunar illumination. Jenny, Bright, and I shared unspoken hopes and fears as the swarm swelled with rush-hour arrivals. We watched in wonder as the square, said to have a capacity of one million, was for all intents and purposes being completely filled in.

Each generation had, in its own way, dared to dream of a better China. So far there had been no violence and none of the strikers were gravely ill. If dialogue took place now, if a few concessions were made, the crisis might be resolved in a way that would allow for an orderly change, or so I thought, but Bright shook her head in disagreement.

We talked about what might happen next. I said the size and consensus of the crowd had already reached the critical mass necessary for people power to win the day, thinking of protests I was familiar with in places like Manila and Bangkok. The peaceful struggle, was it not all over but for the shouting? The old government would step down and a new one would take its place. A bloodless coup, reform by popular consensus!

Bright was less sanguine, but hesitated to say why.

We knew Gorbachev was being feted somewhere in town, maybe even in the Great Hall, but it seemed beside the point now. A hastily rearranged itinerary saw the controversial Russian leader welcomed at the airport and whisked off to some state guest house, avoiding the square that had embarrassingly, but surely only momentarily, slipped out of government control. The last minute rerouting of the Russian's itinerary was clumsy but still reassuring in the sense that it was back to the business of state as usual; a crackdown had not been necessary. The two big stories of the day had crossed paths but did not collide, and whatever short-term student hopes had been pinned on the Russian reformer's visit had to be rapidly revised, taking him out of the equation and putting the focus back on the protesters themselves. The crowd was the real Gorbachev of the moment.

It is near impossible to take measure of a million when you are of one with those million, so I suggested we explore the unguarded grounds of the

Museum of the Chinese Revolution, whose elevated, double-colonnaded pavilion overlooked the square. We climbed the front steps and retreated behind the towering columns of the museum façade, sauntering up more steps, testing doors, and looking for some yet-unoccupied high ground. There, before us, framed by a golden rectangle of columns, lay the shimmering, amorphous mass of Tiananmen protesters. We were close enough to hear a constant roar but not individual voices, close enough to see bobbing heads but not individual faces, yet the mosaic in motion was thriving and alive, a massive living, breathing thing. It trembled and shivered, stretched and contracted as a unitary organism.

The low western sun cast an oblique backlight on a million men and women, casting long narrow shadows from pinpoint silhouettes.

We gazed in wonder as the sun sank lower and the shadows grew longer until one million souls were swallowed up in the shade of the Great Hall of the People, reduced to undulations on a darkening, mildly turbulent sea. Hands cupped over our eyes, we could make out the purple backlit peaks of the Fragrant Hills on the molten horizon.

The reddening sun sat squat in the dusty haze above the western hills. Then, as if reluctant to set, it burst through clouds on the horizon to reveal its full fiery brightness once more before melting from sight. The sky darkened, imperceptibly at first.

And then the moon rose, almost full, looking brighter than it had in weeks.

As we talked on the museum steps, the rotund moon climbed the eastern sky in a slow parabolic ascent, a celestial ping-pong ball floating serenely over the giant game table of Tiananmen. A million people gathered peacefully in the twilight, dreaming up a new China. The weather was good, spirits were high, and it was tempting to think that the government would acquiesce to the will of the masses and make room for the new: it was not a new process, but one of regeneration.

"Remember that time? The time we came here by bicycle? Remember the moon?" I asked, recalling the square, now swollen beyond anything in experience, at its emptiest.

"You have a good memory."

"Well, what does all this lead to? What do you think will really happen?" I asked.

Jenny adjusted her position silently as Bright tried to answer. "Don't go around saying it, but this, this demonstration, it is much more serious than foreigners realize."

"What do you mean?"

"Please find another job. Journalism is dangerous in China . . . " Bright looked at the ground and paused for a minute, then said something I didn't expect.

"It looks like the government will be overthrown," she whispered.

"Are you sure?" I couldn't quite believe my ears. As fond as I was of the iconography of revolution, as fascinating as I found historical accounts, I wasn't sure I wanted to witness an overthrow. Anything and everything could happen, good and bad. Killing, burning, looting, destroying. Just hearing the word gave me the chills. "Overthrown?"

"*Tui-fan zheng-fu,*" she repeated, one syllable at a time for clarity, with a hint of impatience, as if it were obvious, as if I should have known, as if my being a naïve foreigner was somehow impeding my understanding of the real China.

MAY 17

Rising Tide of Rebellion

It's rush hour and it seems like everyone's on the road, not to work but to Tiananmen.

"Good mor-ning!" greets a chirpy voice peeking out from behind a cloth banner.

Who's that speaking English? Is she addressing me?

A young woman breaks into a fulsome, thin-lipped smile, as if pleased to discover that English, the language of textbooks and tests, actually works in the real world. Her banner announces some kind of tourism college.

"Good mor-ning to *you!*" she repeats and clarifies, eyes dancing about.

"Oh, hello."

"How do you do?" offers one of her sprite colleagues.

The English practicers turn out to be tour guides in training, friendly to a fault, though a bit unsure of themselves as demonstrators. Not for them sober banners making veiled threats against a government that refused to engage in dialogue, though they seemed to take to heart the central point of a nearby banner proclaiming WE CAN NO LONGER TOLERATE THE SILENCE.

Instead, their banners and posters, now neglected, are bland and apolitical. They carry the obligatory THE SCHOOL OF TOURISM SUPPORTS THE STUDENTS but for whose eyes are the quirky English-language poems and paens of friendship?

The tour guides in training are dressed in preppy, pastel outfits, no head-bands to muss the smooth sheen of their shampooed hair. They possess the naïve enthusiasm of latecomers to a stridently political cause, reassured by safety in numbers and a carnival atmosphere on the streets.

"Do you mind if we take a snap together?" one of the tourism students asks.

We are smiling for the camera and exchanging little jokes when I suddenly get the feeling, judging from the distracted reaction of the girl I am talking to, that someone else is watching us. I interrupt our banter to find Bright standing a few feet away, looking on with wry amusement. She had descended out of thin air, like a celestial.

"Bright, what are you doing here? I thought you were coming later."

"I saw you!" she accuses with a slightly possessive air, followed by a reassuring laugh.

"Please come with me," she whispers quietly. "I want you to meet someone special."

I wave good-bye to the now wide-eyed tourism gals, wondering who the special someone is. Am I about to be formally introduced to the boyfriend I have heard vague mention of? With the mood as bubbly and aimless as it is today, it takes a few minutes to go a short distance. At one point I reach out for her hand, but she refuses to touch, letting go with uncharacteristic brusqueness. We move forward single file in silence, slowed by merrymakers in what seems to be a funland obstacle course. When at last we reach the curb near the front gate of the Beijing Hotel, she introduces me to a handsome gray-haired man, from the looks of his well-cut Mao jacket a Communist official.

"Philip," she announces quietly, "this is my father."

I can't believe it, Bright's father! And here, in front of the Beijing Hotel of all places. "Pleased to meet you, sir."

"I have heard a lot about you," he says in a mellifluous northern voice, with a wry smile. "As a witness to history, you must tell the world what you see."

"We must go now. I will call you later!" Bright interjects, taking leave. She winks playfully, and then reaches for her father's hand.

"It was a true pleasure meeting you, sir," I call out, employing the clearest pronunciation and most faithfully reproduced tones I can muster.

I was moved. His simple words gave me confidence, not just in the possibility of a relationship with Bright, but in the possibility of a relationship with China.

As the day grew, the streets became jammed with protesters from every walk of life. Lotus emerged from the knot of people in front of the hotel over an hour late—traffic was snarled everywhere on account of the unprecedented size of the demonstration. Trailing several feet behind Lotus was Ying, a mutual friend who used to study English at a branch campus of Shida. Ying had taught Mandarin to Lotus, and in turn Lotus taught Ying everything she could about the Chinese-American world of San Francisco.

Ying, who had once taken me on a no-frills, bare-bones trip to the Manchu summer palace at Chengde with three of her classmates, struck me as being the archetypal woman of north China, plain in appearance and dress, headstrong, hardy, tomboyish, and fun.

Though no longer a student, Ying was very much caught up in the spirit of the times. One of the first complaints aired by Beijing university students was about the job allocation system. It was an open secret that students who had demonstrated in the flurry of street protests held in late 1986 and early 1987 in Hefei, Shanghai, and other cities were getting lousy job assignments. To be able to choose one's job freely was not an option for most.

Ying faced the dilemma of having to stick with a job she didn't want or face the insecurity of no job at all at a time when the labor market was all but locked up. It took guts for her to turn down her assigned job, and with it the lifelong security of a *danwei* (work unit), choosing instead the freelance life, an untested career option in a country where nearly all jobs were assigned and adhered to with cradle-to-grave thoroughness.

She liked to say she did not want to be "pinned down," and the only way she could avoid that was to live on next to nothing, which she happened to be very good at. She loved to travel, and as I knew from our grueling trip to a remote imperial retreat, and she was an extremely economical traveler, needing only a toothbrush and a train ticket to embark on an adventure.

During my three days on the road with her and her college girlfriends, I could hardly keep up with their pace of exploration, rising early each morning, replenishing the hot water thermos for all beverage needs, hiking in the hot sun from one far-flung monument to another, and recuperating at night on a wooden board bed in a cheap flophouse with no showers or private toilets. But the scenery was beautiful, and the heat and physical deprivation made the sublime otherworldliness of the art all the more memorable. I can still recall the guilty pleasure of treating the group to the best money could buy in a rural town: instant noodles, warm soda pop, and ice lollies of indeterminate color and flavor.

Ying and Lotus did not require my services as tour guide to Tiananmen; rather, they were fellow travelers enthralled by the same siren call. Without a moment's hesitation we slipped into a swiftly moving line of marchers and joined the swirl towards the holy ground. It wasn't a bold or radical thing to do, why it seemed like everyone in Beijing and their uncle was out there with us, and even the unlucky souls who could not be out in the streets found little ways to be part of it. Office workers leaned out of high windows, tossing handfuls of confetti-like bits of paper into the air. Construction crews peered down from high scaffolds, cheering and dangling banners in support.

It took a conscious effort to stay abreast of one's friends in a human stream so erratic, so ecstatic it could shift without warning. Sometimes we veered off into a cul-de-sac or got sidelined by the relentless pressing forward. One had to relinquish individual agency and be content to move in concert with everyone else to get anywhere at all while maintaining a modicum of harmony. Blindly following the lead of the people in front of us took the load of fording a path off of our shoulders, and I suppose the people behind us did the same. We bobbled north and then east, then hit a whirlpool that sent us north again and finally west. A straight line was almost never the quickest path between two points.

The expression *ren shan ren hai*, meaning "human mountain, human sea," best summed up the landscape of Tiananmen on this bright day in the middle of May. One didn't walk, one negotiated the terrain.

The crowd was now said to be a million strong, yet I was sure even more of Beijing's millions would have joined in if they could have. The strict danwei system that Ying had rejected was effective at keeping most workers in their places of work during working hours, even at a time of unprecedented demonstrations. When workers did come out, they tended to make an appearance not as individuals but as a danwei, an all or none proposition.

Ever since May 4 I had seen people in office buildings, *Xinhua News* included, cheering protesters, identifying with, even aching to be a part of the spirit coursing the streets. As the protests grew in strength, residents of tall buildings draped banners from windows and sprinkled handwritten notes; some even released low-denomination renminbi bills into the air like ticker tape in support of the parading students.

Construction workers clinging to bamboo scaffolding like birds nesting in a tree waved scraps of white cloth, whistling and shouting in solidarity. Even the high-priority nonstop work on the new western wing of the Beijing Hotel paused indefinitely in respect to the uprising in the streets. Colliding columns of foot traffic converging on the square interlaced and got tangled up, causing a jam-up. Above us, idle workers applauded and shouted militant slogans of support. Some went as far as donning makeshift armbands and headbands, putting on a show of solidarity without leaving the perimeter of the construction site.

Lotus and I joked about how we had been transported back in time to the "real" China, full of utopian zeal and workers' solidarity, the China we had grown up reading about in the glossy pages of Technicolor-tinted propaganda rags such as *China Illustrated* and *China Reconstructs*. Although our book knowledge also made us aware that the alleged revolution of culture exacted too high a price in terms of cruelty and chaos, the striking visual images we had imbibed from Chinese overseas propaganda matched many of the incredible images that were unfolding before our eyes. The normally placid streets of Beijing suddenly had the kinetic tint and hue of a revolutionary opera.

Ying was not amused. In contrast to the two wide-eyed Americans she had consented to march with, she found no solace in superficial visual comparisons with a period that brought much heartbreak to her family. As an individual struggling to break free from the confines of the Communist society, she had good reason to recoil from anything that smacked of a second Cultural Revolution. Still, there was something so infectious about the enthusiasm on the streets of Beijing that she was, for the moment, content to be part of it, even if she nursed doubts about it.

The foreground of flushed faces and bright red flags set against the background blues and grays of the cityscape was nothing if not photogenic. Rouge-cheeked kindergarten and primary school children wearing red scarves stood in front of their school waving little banners and national flags in rhythm to the rote shouts of the marchers. "*Shengyuan xuesheng, shengyuan xuesheng! Shengyuan xuesheng!*"

Headbands and armbands gave the protesters a visual unity, but it wasn't till we donned headbands distributed to us that I could fully appreciate how a simple piece of cloth could bind one psychologically to a mass of unrelated strangers. As I discovered moving in step with the arts choral group on May 4, marching is a communal activity; it requires constant attention to the people around you, and something about it makes you want to look out for those who are looking out for you.

Billowing flags mounted on long poles were rocked back and forth hypnotically as the teeming masses chanted in unison to express support of the students.

As much as Lotus and I had always wanted to understand China and mix with her people on relatively egalitarian terms, we inevitably got used to and perhaps even internalized some of the invisible walls that distinguished us. One only had to step into a walled compound or guarded building and the gate-maintenance of separate and unequal worlds went into play. Thus, there was something exhilarating about being on the street mixing with strangers under the control of no one in particular and perhaps no one at all.

Of course the grand boulevard we were coursing down had its police presence. Public Security headquarters was just around the corner, and Tiananmen Square was perhaps the most watched piece of concrete in all of China, but with an uprising of this size, those being monitored outnumbered the monitors by a liberating margin.

As we pressed closer and closer to the massively congested square, Lotus, Ying, and I were swept away by the inclusive spirit of the day. Whenever we strained to read a cursive slogan or paused to clarify something in Chinese, we would be drawn into conversation, presented with an instant set of new friends. The usual rote questions, the routine, borderline rude questions that were usually asked of strangers and foreigners, fell by the wayside. We were treated like family.

Along the meandering course to the square there must have been a dozen strangers who bestowed me with personal mementos, unpinning school pins from their vests and swapping sweaty headbands in solidarity.

The artificial walls built by Deng and his paranoid policymakers to keep foreigners on the outside looking in were being breached, as were the walls that kept Chinese from linking up with their fellow citizens. Although we were rebelling in plain sight, the ubiquitous gaze of the state had never seemed further away. There was a whiff of freedom in the air, which, however provisional, was unforgettable.

Beijing native Ying, cynical, skeptical, and bristling with annoyance at the socialist system that had nurtured her, gradually warmed up to the mood of the marchers. Despite her misgivings, she acknowledged that she had never found it easier and more appealing to meet strangers than on this day, which was a remarkable statement from someone who was quite good at talking to strangers to begin with. The status quo had been shaken up just a little bit, but this was enough to cause scales to drop from eyes and banish the suspicious habits of mind that normally governed social interactions.

The push and pull of other pilgrims continued to massage and possess us while propelling us towards the new mecca. The utter collapse of traffic control would have had tempers flaring under more normal circumstances—that perhaps being the sly intent of the lax policing—but the mood evolving here was transformative and forgiving.

Patiently plodding two steps forward, one step back led to many a serendipitous encounter. Bursts of spirited conversation alleviated the tedium. Since no one had a strict schedule to follow or exact physical location to arrive at, other than a broad plaza built to accommodate a million, the journey itself was as good as the destination. As long as you were fully surrounded by people, you had arrived. Unusual for Beijing in the late eighties, there was delight to be found in the anachronistic joy of the collective. From the look of the beaming faces, many were having the time of their lives.

"The way to go is to go with the flow," I joke, not that my fellow travelers are likely to think otherwise. I relate to Lotus and Ying how the high spirits of the revelers around us remind me of celebrating New Year's Eve at Times

Square, itself a transformative event of sorts in which habitually curt and suspicious New Yorkers can, thanks to the instant kinship of braving the bitter cold together bolstered by liquid inebriation, converge harmoniously at the midnight hour, turning the mean streets of a run-down intersection into the best block party in town.

In a similar spirit, here you had people who normally would not even exchange glances, let alone smile, chatting deliriously, reaching out in all directions at once, except this was taking place in the broad daylight without a drop of alcohol. The liberating loss of self and the paradoxical sense of invulnerability that came from facing danger as a collective made for a heady mood.

Ying admitted she was not the demonstrating type, yet she felt it essential that she be here. Lotus was definitely the demonstrating type, yet she'd never seen a demonstration like this. I continued to seek strained comparisons, such as giant rallies I had attended in Washington and New York, but the fact was this was unlike anything in my experience.

We were in no particular rush to reach the square, though the day would have been incomplete if we did not pay our respects to the hunger strike "heroes" at least once. The broad east-west boulevard was cleaved in two by a student-policed lifeline guarded with lengths of rope and hundreds of volunteers. This middle lane was kept open to allow special access, mainly for emergency vehicles, especially volunteer ambulances, in deference to rising health concerns about the food-fasters sitting it out in the center of all this delightful madness.

What little vehicular traffic there was also tended to "go with the flow" as cars, trucks, even buses were somehow commandeered for the purpose of moving protesters and pilgrims in and out of Tiananmen Square. The vehicles snaked through the people-clogged thoroughfare at mercifully low speeds, but the possibility of collision was unnerving.

As the mass of protesters reached its most audacious apogee to date, its values became increasingly Communistic and utopian. The flag waved was the red flag, the lyrics sung were youth league lyrics, the rhetoric was about people power, and the notion of social equality was implicit.

If Deng's reforms had not exactly created a two-tier system of governance, they had certainly exacerbated it. With the rich getting richer and the poor getting poorer, it was no wonder that iconic images of the supreme anticapitalist were starting to appear. Workers were waving pictures of Chairman Mao.

While escorting news crews I had heard the view put forward that what the Chinese really wanted was to be Western. There was also the condescending view that the student movement, which had capitalized on the politics of Gorbachev's presence, would crumble the moment he departed. Yet the nature of today's crowd, the biggest yet and still growing, tended to negate both lines of analysis.

Of course it was possible that today's gathering was partly in reaction to the Russian's departure, compensating for the presumed loss of the world's eye with sheer people power. Or then again, maybe all the feverish talk about Gorby reflected nothing more than the predilections of the foreign media, who found Mikhail Gorbachev more culturally comprehensible and personally attractive than the media-shy eminences grises of the Chinese politburo and the unknown kids hiding under piles of coats and blankets on the square.

However, the Chinese demonstrators I was in contact with, including those who were bumping elbows and shoulders on this red-banner day, were unlikely to be swayed either way by the posturing of orotund pundits who were shaping the Western TV narrative of events. Indeed, one reason I had the morning off was that the BBC had its eye on the ball, or thought they did, following Gorby to Shanghai, watching his every move. The limited information reach of locals, in contrast, made it easier for Beijingers to keep their gaze on Tiananmen, the navel of their beloved city.

In the late afternoon sun, we circumambulated the Monument to the People's Heroes in sedate, plodding steps. Circles within circles had coalesced around the axis of the square, rotating slowly, and not all at the same speed. The atmosphere was festive on the edges, full of anticipation in the middle, and appropriately sober on the inside, where the hunger strikers were as venerated as wizened old monks in a temple.

After two hours of harmonious perambulation we were lucky enough on the last sweep to spot an opening on a tiny lawn edged by a decorative flowerbed near the monument. I leapt for the green square of crabgrass like a runner stealing second base. For that move I could thank the advice of a high-school gym teacher back in suburban Lynbrook, Long Island. His words of advice never earned me any distinction on the playing field, but turned out to have great application when boarding overloaded buses or waiting for a table at jammed eateries in Beijing: he who hesitates is lost.

Sitting down on the grass looking up the parade of humanity provided a novel vantage point, an almost childish point of view of the impossibly complicated adult world around us. Everyone looked so tall, so purposeful, so important, and so grown-up. Look at the forest of legs, the variety of socks, stockings, shoes, and sandals. Even though we had slipped below the surface of a crowd of a million trespassers, it felt totally safe and secure to be at knee level with the rebels. So many people in motion yet so much self-restraint and tranquility!

The gathering was supposed to be a show of support for the weakened hunger strikers, but it was the location that made the journey possible. If it were an ongoing story about some hunger strikers protesting in a prison or a remote location, it might tug at people's hearts, but not at their feet.

Tiananmen was a goal unto itself. All lofty aims aside, most onlookers were mixing in to see what was going on and in doing so found little distractions and simple ways to celebrate life at Tiananmen itself, as onlookers became participants in the self-sufficient crowd. The mood of the day was expansive and cheerful in a way that belied the neurotic and morbid posturing of the so-called student leaders.

Only a small percentage of the callers who crammed into the square managed to actually get a look at the heroic hunger strikers, who were huddled together, cocooned under heavy coats, and held behind protective cordons, and what did it matter? The rest of us were content to be caught up with the natural commotion of the crowd itself. Tens of thousands could pour into this capacious architectural vessel, not unlike a flattened-out bowl or sports stadium. As in any big sporting event, the spectators were an integral part of the game. None of the assembled million were instigating a "wave" or lifting fellow spectators off the ground to pass on a bed of hands up into the stands, but there were plenty of stadium-style shouts and much outsized local pride.

A family that occupied the patch of brownish grass to our left was taking time out from this extraordinary occasion to enjoy a box-lunch picnic, as if this was just another Sunday in the park. Another group, speaking in dialect, dressed in clashing colors and motley styles, staked out space adjacent to the marble monument to snack on dried squid, bread, and soda pop. Just behind me there was a man shaving, holding a mirror to his face as if he was utterly alone, unperturbed by the hundreds who ambled by.

Here we were in the middle of the square in the middle of the city, quite possibly in the middle of a revolution, and everybody had this super-casual attitude as if it were just another day. Everyone was doing such a good job of just minding their own business, doing their own thing.

Maybe that's what made the square feel so much like a home: the Chinese adaptive genius for making oneself at home anywhere. The overworked worker's knack for taking a nap on the job, on the street, even perched on a bicycle, the enviable ability to be alone, placid and unruffled in the midst of thousands.

Some might cope by withdrawing inward, tuning out the crowd, while others were hyperaware, readily taking cues from those around them. Certain little behaviors were as contagious as yawns. Seeing a bare-chested man sunning himself was the signal for a dozen of his neighbors to strip off shirts and do the same. I was tempted to join the men in their air bath, Beijing backstreet-style, but only got as far as unbuttoning my shirt. While my half measure was probably due to a nagging sense of propriety in the company of female friends, it also reflected my inability to go all the way when it came to "going native."

The late afternoon rays beat down on treeless central Tiananmen without relief, imparting to all present the sunburned odor and communal glow of beachgoers soaking up the sun without adequate shade.

Given the intense heat, some slept under wrap, others crawled under the shade of low bushes, some collapsed comfortably into one another's laps, and still others basked on the white marble steps of the monument like seals at sea's edge.

When Ying stood up to escort Lotus to the distant underground public facilities, I tried to save a place for them by reclining on the grass. Packed in close to napping men and crying children, I took off my sunglasses and rested my arm over my eyes to block the blinding glare of the sun. Drowsy from the hypnotic murmur of so many overlapping voices, my mind wandered.

Voices at close range had the unmistakable tonal quality of Mandarin, but distant voices created a dull, muffled, and undulating tone that was never constant but never went away. I could imagine myself lying in the sand at Jones Beach, Long Island, on a crowded weekend in the summer. The coconut-scented suntan lotion on my face added to the mood, as did fiddling with my cheap pair of sunglasses.

The rise and fall of a million voices billow and break like the surf, and syncopated syllables caress my ears. There are children shrieking, vendors hawking, hustlers hustling, jokers cursing, dialect voices shouting, PA announcements echoing. Handheld transistor radios move into range and then fade, like passing satellites. The only thing missing is the squawk of seagulls.

Lying on the ground as tens of thousands of tired feet pass by is an act of faith. Hundreds of sweaty shoes, sandals, and sneakers pass within inches of my face, but none of them touch me.

The comforting rhythm and hum of a thousand singsong conversations is punctuated by the periodic intrusion of audible voices passing nearby. I expect to hear the words "Look! Laowai sleeping!" but they never come.

When I finally stand up to stretch and scan the people horizon for my long-delayed companions, my space on the grass is promptly taken and I am thrust back into an adult world. My black-haired friends spot me sooner than I do them and we rejoin the flow of humanity, going not precisely the way we want to go, but knowing the huge circular motion will eventually get us there, like circling one of the ring roads. After getting in a fleeting glimpse of the strikers—a bunch of barely visible bodies huddled under green army coats with some white-gowned medics standing by, not much to look at and we don't want to gawk—we move south, towards Qianmen.

We kick dust this way and that, pausing to rest and chat with fellow travelers, seeking a propitious tributary flow that might take us away from the square without having to go against the flood of new arrivals. Along the way, as fate propels us to meet for a second and third time marchers we bumped into earlier in the day, we exchange greetings like long-lost comrades.

The sun, which had reddened a million cheeks with its all-encompassing radiation, was now looking tired and red-cheeked itself. The first stirrings of an evening breeze teased Tiananmen, lifting evaporated sweat, ammonia, and musky underarm odors to the heavens.

"The Internationale" was on the lips of protesters throughout the day, some singing, some shouting, some solemnly pondering the lyrics, and others having a laugh. After all the tragedy descended on the head of mankind in the name of socialism this century, the Communist anthem should have been a tired, out-of-date tune if there ever was one. But it held things together, as did Beethoven's "Ode to Joy," which popped up at random points around the square, cranked out on little tape recorders and student-rigged speakers. Cui Jian's "Nothing to my Name" and Chyi Chin's "Wolf" could be heard as well. There was music in the air.

Singing songs of rebellion in the sea of the people, hands reaching for the sky, I felt today's gathering was the best yet. I felt privileged to be standing witness as one of the world's great ancient civilizations sought to rediscover itself, transform, and rejuvenate.

Bright surprised me for the second time that day when she showed up unannounced at my "expensive" hotel room for "foreigners." I was sitting on the porch talking to Lotus, who was waiting to meet Albert. When he arrived we marveled about the day's high spirits, amazed that there were still people marching to the square. When Lotus and Albert got ready to head back to the Lido, their apartment on the outskirts of town, Bright and I saw them off at the front door.

We returned to an unlit room, curtains swept wide open, the sky glowing red on one side, blue on the other. We stepped outside and took seats side by side on the balcony, gazing at the rotund moon as it rose in the eastern sky.

"The moon will be almost directly overhead some time between midnight and one tonight," I said, trying to recall the mechanics of elementary astronomy. "When the moon is full, it rises in the east at the same moment the sun sets in the west, so that's like twenty-four hours of uninterrupted light."

"The sun and moon watch over us like proud parents," Bright said with a shiver, nudging closer. "The full moon is the fifteenth day of the month of lunar calendar. It is an auspicious day. *Manyue*, the full moon, is the brightest night of the month."

The waxing moon had been good to the rebels occupying the square and it had been good to us. Each night the moon got a little bigger and glowed a little brighter than the night before. The protesters feared a nighttime attack most of all, but it seemed increasingly unlikely with the moon as celestial guardian.

A million marched today. Thousands were starving themselves to the point of collapse. But there had not been a single casualty, a remarkable testament to fortitude and restraint on all sides. The lunar illumination that lit the veranda where we talked cast its glow on Tiananmen Square, where tens of thousands tried to sleep, recite poetry, tell jokes, talk of love. The moon over Tiananmen was watching over us all.

Bright and I sit motionlessly, soaking up the night sky in silence and awe. The temperature is just right, counterpoised between the heat of day and chill of night. It is that special time of year when the sandstorms of spring are past but the blistering heat of summer has not yet arrived. The moon casts a bluish glow on the darkened cityscape.

At last Bright stands up. Time for her to leave. She pauses, as if weighing something in her mind.

"Going home now?" I ask, studying her moonlit profile for a clue as to what she is thinking.

"No," she answers, "I told my father I'm staying with a friend tonight."

"What? With who?"

"Don't ask."

MAY 18

Everyone an Emperor

No sooner had the rain and overcast gloom of the early morning lifted than, as if cued by the sun, demonstrators were out in force again, pressing toward Tiananmen on moist pavement. After a morning of leisure I was back on the job, leading BBC across the square.

The humidity was oppressive. Hot, thirsty, and exasperated by the refusal of our three trishaw drivers to bring us any closer, we lugged the weighty camera, tripod, recording equipment, and metal boxes of gear to Xinhuamen, the decorative gate marking the southern entrance to Zhongnanhai. Golden ideographs that read SERVE THE PEOPLE, done up in Mao's calligraphy, ironically served to block the people's view of opulent lakeside villas within.

We were going not to pay a visit to China's top leaders, but to look into reports about a group of radical strikers blocking the front gate.

After negotiating the last hundred yards to Xinhuamen on foot, another foreign camera crew could be seen packing up their gear. Brian's face suddenly lost all color. For a moment I thought he had fallen ill.

"Look," he screamed, "It's them. There's ITN!"

The horror of it, the horror! Back in Britain, Independent Television News (ITN) was the BBC's main rival in television news. On this historic day, ITN had just beaten the BBC to the punch. Their crew was wrapping on the radical striker story before we even started to roll. The two English crews briefly stared each other down like mad dogs in the midday sun, sizing one another up, then choosing to each go their own way rather than fight.

An almost impenetrably thick mob of spectators pressed up against tightly held ropes that marked off the strike zone. The focal point of everyone's attention was a contingent of twenty or so young men and women who had theatrically pledged to dehydrate themselves to the death. Everyone knew that death came faster to strikers who refused all liquid, and that unspoken thought heightened the drama of the spectacle.

At first glance, the strikers looked like accident victims, sprawled out on the pavement, heads bandaged, bodies covered with coats and blankets. Those with the strength to sit up had fatalistic, haggard looks, listless, immobile, and apathetic. Those napping despite the heat of the day and judgmental curiosity of the onlookers looked as unconcerned about such things as homeless winos sprawled on the curb in a stupor. The grand vermilion doorway marking the entrance to the Communist Party's citadel was a made-for-TV-news picture-perfect backdrop for the ragged human tableau below.

The cracked, white lips of the strikers told the story: these idealistic agitators were racing towards death, hoping to accelerate government acquiescence to demands for dialogue. If these men and women had strictly observed the hunger strike, they had not eaten in five days. A day ago, this elite student corps, the hunger strikers of hunger strikers, refused all water and vowed to refuse intravenous glucose or any medical assistance. Given the unbearable midday heat, the water strikers were in critical danger, unlike the food strikers, who could probably survive a week or more without irreparable self-injury.

The bold sacrifice implicit in the water strike was serious business. No sign of surreptitious snacking or drinking here. They had reportedly asked their followers to prevent the ambulance crews from taking them away until they were dead. As if prepared for that eventuality, an ambulance was permanently parked next to Xinhua gate.

Such reckless, misplaced heroism! These slow-burn spiritual kamikaze pilots were headed for a wasteful plunge into the abyss. Would such a sacrifice really make a difference? Even if it was glorious, was it worth it?

The fact that the water strikers needed no toilet facilities was a morbid reminder of how close they were to running on empty. In all likelihood the first casualty of the generally benign hunger strike would fall at Xinhua Gate and it would happen soon. Overcoming a wave of nausea, I understood why this was such a prize for competitive TV crews; it offered the implicit spectacle of death. But I wasn't happy about it. This kind of act didn't need the subtle validation that our presence might confer.

If the hunger strike on the square provoked the singing of anthems and cheers of sympathy, these far-gone water strikers in contrast provoked nothing but silent gawking and pity. They were not much to look at. The bright glare of the overcast sky drained what color their sunburned faces might have had. To heighten the indignity, they were lined up in a row like a freak show, limp bodies on view to the curious public. Though open-air, the site had assumed the dank odor of a terminal hospital ward.

Some of the strikers slept, curled up under blankets. Others propped themselves up against the giant vermilion door, staring emptily, as if without any emotional expression at all, at the enveloping crowd. Protecting the self-destructive strikers from others but not from themselves, their handlers took security with shrill seriousness. Student guards linked arms to prevent any breach of the roped-off zone.

Brian had been kind enough to invite along Lotus, who wanted to see a news crew in action. And we had enjoyed the first hour out, chronicling the arrival of new delegations including factory workers and hotel workers. But when it came to dealing with petty issues involving student security, the veteran news professional was simply out of his element. Not one to be intimidated by little rules made up on the spot by a bunch of wimpy students wearing headbands, Brian squeezed his way forward and boldly stepped over the rope barrier, then started pushing in an attempt to get past the human chain. He was shoved back and reprimanded by a row of diminutive but determined student guards. He backed off and tried the same thing from another angle. This time he was sent hurtling back with so much force that he almost got knocked over.

Lotus and I watched in dismay as he waved his press ID in the faces of those who surrounded him to contain the problem. He flailed and shouted angrily, "Let me in! Let me in, damn it! B-B-C! I'm with the BBC!"

The magic call letters didn't conjure up much cooperation this time. The students, mixing English and Chinese, implored him to leave. He ignored their halting entreaties and called on me to interpret.

"Phil? Where are you? Phil!"

"Yes, Brian."

"Now listen, will you tell this bloody moron that we just want to go in to take some pictures?"

I duly translated Brian's request, leaving out the words "bloody" and "moron." The young gatekeepers conferred briefly. Their answer was emphatic and simple. They said no.

"No? No? What do you mean, no?" cried Brian.

A neatly dressed woman standing near me offered an explanation. "No pictures are allowed," she pleaded, "Please understand. The water strikers are very weak. Nobody is allowed in."

The shoving match with the students had ended, but Brian had tenaciously remained inside the perimeter rope, so he was being watched with hawkish attention. I told the woman we didn't want to bother them and wished them luck. Then I told the crew it was a no-go.

"Bullshit!" the reporter screamed, "didn't you see that film crew, didn't you see them just leave? Phil, that was ITN!"

"Well, then, good. At least someone has pictures," I said thinking like a historian, not caring who got it as long as someone got it. My complacency was borderline insubordination from the competitive TV reporter's point of view. He was part of the BBC's corporate culture; I wasn't. The BBC-ITN rivalry meant everything to him, nothing to me.

"ITN is the bloody competition," the crew was trying to explain to me. "Phil, listen, tell the students we're from the BBC," Brian added hopefully. "Tell them if they let ITN go in, well, then, they have to let us in too."

I felt like a grammar school teacher adjudicating a playground dispute. I exchanged a few rapport-building words with a headbanded monitor who bore an air of authority. He was polite but firm, clearly irritated and unyielding.

"Brian," I said, "I don't think they want to be bothered just now."

"Damn it, Phil! Just translate!"

"I don't think they know or care who the different English TV stations are, and I can't blame them for that. In fact I'm even a little bit confused as to why every network has to step over each other's feet to get the same pictures instead of sharing them."

Brian's handsome face reddened before he turned his back on me, muttering something along the lines of "bloody useless."

The swashbuckling reporter was now trapped by student vigilantes guarding the strikers. They formed a doubly tight wall with their bodies to prevent him from getting any closer. I stepped back and made some conciliatory small talk with the some of the more relaxed student guards to our left.

"What are you doing here?" a young man inquired suspiciously.

"We are from English television BBC," I said. "We are not against you, we came to see the water strikers. We want the world to know about your struggle."

When Brian caught sight of me talking to a different group of guards, he extricated himself from the rope and, signaling the crew, ambled over to the spot where Lotus and I now stood quietly negotiating with another group of students. I had enough experience as a tour guide to know that how you discussed a problem had a lot of bearing on how it was resolved.

"There's nothing to chat about, Phil," Brian said during a pause in the ne-gotiations. "Tell the bloody fools, you just tell them they must let us in!"

"I'm not going to translate that," I said.

Bristling, Brian walked off. Perhaps he thought I was taking the "other" side, perhaps my attitude reeked of insubordination, but I felt I had a role to play, mediating the media. The BBC call letters were attracting considerable attention, none of it positive.

A student emerged from the roped-off area to confer with me. He ex-plained the need for security, and we conversed quietly.

In the student's explanation I saw a glimmer of hope. They were afraid of losing control, in regard not so much to us, but the mob of spectators press-ing in on all sides. Maybe they weren't getting the response they had hoped for. They needed cooperation and yearned for a little respect. The strikers were not fainthearted; they were the radical vanguard, engaged in a life-and-death struggle for dialogue and respect. Running through the litany of stu-dent complaints was a pent-up nationalism, so they were unlikely to bow to a bossy foreigner from some international television show. In fact, they wanted an apology.

"I apologize for the abject behavior of this Englishman," I said. "He is a good reporter, a good man, but he's tired, a bit cranky," I offered, "and I know all of you have been doing your best. Ah, it's tough, isn't it?"

"I'm glad you understand, my friend," the student spokesman explained. "Please tell that man that the strikers are very weak. People have been com-ing in here all morning. We've had enough. The water strikers are sick. They don't need pictures, they don't want to be disturbed in any way. They need to conserve energy, they need rest."

There was something deeply disconcerting and illogical here. There were young men and women threatening to kill themselves, but complaining about not getting enough rest. They were pulling a stunt to capture the at-tention of a nation yet could turn away a news crew on impulse.

And what of the fawning respect given them by their peers? Wasn't that as hollow as the generosity of the warden who gives a lavish last meal for a death-row prisoner or the Imperial Army throwing a final sake-drinking party for a kamikaze bomber? Heroic today, martyred tomorrow.

The beating down heat of the sun, the bright light, the pushing and shov-ing and the psychic helplessness of not being able to speak the language of the mob probably intensified Brian's impatience, but he was on to something when he questioned the smug, sanctimonious correctness of the student rep-resentatives. How could they claim to be protecting the strikers if they were enabling their demise by supporting the strike in the first place?

"I hope you achieve your goals, dialogue and that all, but without anyone dying," I said. "I will tell the Englishman what you told me." But before I could get back to Brian to smooth things out, I got an unsolicited invitation.

"Friend," the student spokesman said to me, "come here. You can come in and talk to the strikers, but please, no cameras. Just five minutes, okay?"

"It is not necessary," I said, more worried about Brian's reaction to seeing me on the inside than the thorny ethics of whether or not my presence was going to influence the death wish of the strikers. "It's not necessary, let them rest."

Suddenly the conversation took a refreshingly normal turn. "Your Chinese is very good," he remarked. "Where did you study?"

When I told him I had been at Shida, he cracked a smile. "You definitely must come in then, some strikers are from Political and Law, and also from Shida." The young man led me in by the hand, insisting that I step inside.

I crawled under the rope and the human chain momentarily lifted their tightly interlocked arms to let me in. As soon as I passed, the arms interlocked again. The crew, good friends who worked together on a regular basis, watched with stunned indignation.

"Can he come in, too?" I asked my student guide, feeling sorry for Brian. He was a good journalist, the first person at the BBC to befriend me. His gregarious warmth and generosity compensated for his temper.

"Yes, if he is with you," he consented.

"Brian? You can come in now," I said. "We can talk to them for five minutes, but no cameras."

"No cameras? What's the bloody point of going in if we can't take our gear?" he yelled. "Tell him that's nonsense! How come ITN could bring their cameras in?" Brian's face reddened again. He threw his hands in the air in exasperation and stomped away.

"Let's get out of here!" he yelled to the camera crew.

His words were followed by the murmur of equally indignant voices saying things about a laowai that I didn't want to hear. Lotus took it all in with her usual smiling equanimity.

I stepped forward, careful not to tread on any of the blankets and sleeping bags. Before me were sprawled a dozen limp bodies that belonged in a hospital.

A thin, handsome man with a high-cheeked, angular face caught my attention. His body was motionless and emaciated but his eyes were bright and alert. He wore a green shirt.

"You suffer. I admire your courage," I said, respectfully, lacking the chutzpah to scold him and his fellow strikers for their stupidity. Instead of telling them to go home and have some hot chicken soup, I told them a little about myself.

"My name is Jin Peili. I study Chinese. Do you know the Insider Guest House at Shida?" Not knowing whom to talk to, I addressed them as a group, but my eyes kept going back to the man with the bright eyes.

A young man in the middle of the row of fatigued bodies, smudged-up glasses dangling low off his gaunt, angular face, was the first to answer. "I am Han. Where did you learn Chinese?"

"I learned Chinese from my friends."

"Please tell others about what you see. We seek dialogue with the government."

"I understand."

"We are willing to die for our country," he whispered.

That gave me the chills, and I was unable to respond with a sensible comment. A déjà-vu refrain of "I can't believe this is happening to me" raced through my mind. This is my life, is this is really happening?

"Can you hear the cry?" Han asked. "Can you hear the cry of China?"

His plaintive call gave me a lump in the throat and I remained speechless. Seeing his arm reach upward, I took his hand in mine. The sharp-eyed student guards looked on, smiling weakly. Some strikers watched us attentively while others, though awake and conscious, stared blankly as before. I was greeted by yet another striker who asked me how long it took me to learn Chinese, a familiar and friendly question that seemed outright absurd coming from a student who wouldn't be studying anything anymore if he followed his act of sacrifice to its brutal conclusion.

I continued to field questions, the familiar set of questions a foreigner learns to deal with, like it or not, and as I spoke, I could detect a few smiles out of the corner of my eye. Maybe I said something wrong or mispronounced something with a funny accent. Even in their dismal emaciated state, they could get a kick out of hearing a laowai speak Chinese.

Did the death wish of the water strikers ennoble the student movement or darken it with disrespect for life? Did widespread popular support, the nonstop swirl of sympathizers and admirers, unwittingly put pressure on the elect heroes to do themselves in? If making jokes at my expense got them back on a more normal track of thinking, I couldn't begrudge them that.

The peer pressure was palpable on May 13 when the hunger strike began. How much greater it must be now, with a nation electrified and millions marching in their name!

There is no graceful exit from a hunger strike that does not achieve its aims. *Dui-hua* or "dialogue" was the stated aim now. But what constituted dialogue, and who was to say whether or dialogue had been achieved? The whole hunger strike struck me as a form of political poker, each side trying to bluff the other into making a concession first. I was sure at least some of the students joined the strike impulsively and I felt for them. They might have second thoughts or regrets but there was no easy way out given the immense peer pressure. It was scary.

While I was talking to Han, a delirious young man who had been propped up against the door slumped over, head hitting the ground. White-shirted medics put him on a stretcher and rushed him into the waiting ambulance. A few minutes ago, my parched throat had craved water; now I felt like throwing up. Watching the medics attend to the most recent victim of dehydration, I felt some consolation in the fact that he would be raced to the hospital along the roped-off lifeline and force-fed intravenously, diminishing the chance of death.

I asked Han if I could take his picture and he consented. An overprotective student guard was about to rip the Olympus out of my hands when Han interjected on my behalf. I thanked him and his friends and wished them success in achieving their goal. I exited the special zone with the cooperation of the hand-linked human chain and then ducked under the perimeter rope.

As I retreated into the hot sunshine, the image of the emaciated Han whispering, "Can you hear the cry of China?" was already beginning to haunt me. The more I thought about it, the more I appreciated Brian's desire to make a visual recording of the scene.

But Brian was in no mood to hear that from me now. After an arduous crossing of Chang'an Boulevard via a roundabout detour on account of the lifeline, the crew found itself stranded. The trishaw drivers had shrewdly chosen a comfortable spot in the shade because traffic was backed up in all directions.

Compounding the pressure created by the BBC's satellite deadline was the logistical problem of having to transit a crowd of several hundred thousand marchers by pedal rickshaw during the sacrosanct lunch hout. Except for the occasional ambulance rolling down the lifeline, traffic was at a virtual standstill.

When I first took a group of students on a tour of China soon after China's opening to the world, I learned that one must accept deviations in the itinerary in good cheer. Otherwise, China, with its millions of little unexpected events, would drive you crazy. With that practical philosophy in mind, I told the crew it was time to take a break. It was also my experience as a tour guide that many arguments could be avoided if people got adequate rest and nourishment. I bought bottled yogurt and orange soda for everyone, suggesting we wait a bit to see if traffic lightened up.

Maybe the loutish driver hired by the crew wasn't such an idiot after all; the tree-lined spot on the southern side of the broad boulevard offered a commanding view of the western flank of Tiananmen Square and ready access to liquid refreshment. Thanks to the trishaw tout's selfish farsightedness, we slurped bottled yogurt in the shade while a militant parade, unstoppable and impossible to speed through, monopolized the road.

Unlike the almost magical smoothness of the day spent wandering with Lotus and Ying, trying to keep on schedule with a news crew dependent on trishaws for transport created tensions. Still, Eric and Fred had made good use of little delays, scouring the crowd for interesting shots, some valiantly filmed while the trishaw was still rolling. With the trishaw hood pulled down and Fred grasping firmly onto Eric's belt, the tall cameraman was able to stand up on the moving cart, heavy camera to shoulder, to get rare tracking shots of traffic moving our way.

New, creative links were being made, reflected in the flags and slogans draped on industrial-strength trucks with factory logos packed to the brim with red-sashed workers.

WORKERS' SUPPORT BRIGADE!

WORKERS UNITED WITH STUDENTS IN SUPPORT!

But the really eye-catching, breath-stopping slogans took aim at the most powerful man in China.

XIAOPING GAODE RENREN FENFEN BU PING

"Wow! You see that, Lotus? It says Xiaoping is ruining it for all of us!"

Open-backed trucks crammed with factory workers were festooned with flags. Nearly all the banners proclaimed "*Shengyuan xuesheng*" in one form or another. It was the orthodox and politically correct way of mouthing support for the students. Quite a few posters and political cartoons were openly critical of Deng, representing a logical but politically dangerous turn of heart. But the most novel element today was the large number of Mao portraits. Militant workers proudly held portraits of Mao aloft. Mao? Where did they dig Mao up from? Was this Cultural Revolution nostalgia or an oblique way of insulting Deng, who was thrice purged under Mao?

"It's like a second Cultural Revolution!" I suggested. Lotus, who had visited China during the middle of that turbulent period, found some validity in my hyperbolic statement. The crew was unconvinced.

"The workers, the Mao posters," I said, letting the hot sun and the steamy heat get to me as the last of the puddles from the morning's rain evaporated. "This might even be the work of the old leftists, who resent the capitalist tendencies of Deng's China. Deng's the target. It's unbelievable!"

A few feet away, the trishaw drivers were involved in a noisy argument about matters far less abstract. The bald-headed tout, a bully if there ever was one, was intimidating the vendors, who he claimed had overcharged him for the price of the yogurt and orange drink. To a seasoned operator such as he, bargaining down a price was clearly a one-way street. Pay less when paying others, demand more when getting paid.

My sudden appearance quieted the argument. I asked each man present what he thought of the huge gathering around us.

"Very good," said the bald, burly driver, answering in English, sticking his thick thumb up in the air. "Like this!"

His cohort, whose suspicious darting eyes and unshaven, unkempt appearance gave him the air of a character who had just escaped from a mental hospital, turned to the lead tout for a cue, then shook his head up and down in hearty agreement. "Like this," he said, thumbs up. "Good money and no police!"

The good money was obviously a reference to us. As for the police, I guess he was right. I hadn't seen a man in uniform in days.

"Shut up, you fool!" the bald man said in reprimand to his mate.

A short distance away, the BBC guys chatted with Lotus, and through her, with my driver, a paragon of politeness in contrast to the two foul-mouthed touts who had glommed onto the crew at the hotel entrance. The lead tout, pleading lunchtime, had made it clear we were going nowhere fast, so I decided to walk around a bit.

The ground was getting dirty underfoot. The square had an air of neglect, litter everywhere, the air redolent of urine and the stench of chemical disinfectant. It smelled like a disaster. How many rotations involving how many millions of footsteps could this huge, human cyclone undergo before people got hurt, sick, or trampled?

The morning rain was the first of several bad omens for the demonstrators of Tiananmen, who had enjoyed fresh air and cooperative, sunny skies for several weeks now. The protesters' resourcefulness seemed to know no limits, however, and a fleet of buses were soon driven to the square, providing a safe, dry shelter for the weakened hunger strikers. In a way that was strangely consonant with radical Christianity, it was the weakest people who were most important; the sick, meek, and emaciated were the VIPs in this world of tables turned and temples spurned.

As the movement grew more complex, simple slogans seemed to suffice:
PEOPLE'S CRY!
PEOPLE'S VOICE!
PEOPLE'S TORMENT!

Hidden dangers abounded. The pavement-prone strikers lowered their resistance to infection, and not a few people still on their feet also were walking time bombs due to stress, long hours, poor hygiene, forced proximity to countless germs, and exposure to the elements. Rumors of a cholera outbreak were taken seriously, as were rumors that the sanitation complaints were a government ploy to get people off the square. With such a dense mass of people living in slumlike conditions with no running water, a contagious illness could reach epidemic proportions in no time.

The square was thickly carpeted with people, but with water strikers nearing death, the celebratory element was gone. Even the chants sounded rote and annoying. The movement of masses of people wasn't as fluidly cooperative as before. You couldn't walk without annoying others. Sometimes you couldn't walk at all, but had to endure being pressed against strangers, shoulder to shoulder, belly to back, stepping on and being stepped on. At one point, frustrated by the jostling movement and foul air, I stretched up on my toes to see what was causing the delay when I suddenly found myself lifted off my feet, pinned and suspended an inch or two off the ground. I gave up any thoughts of further exploration and slowly worked my way back to the rest spot.

When I got back, sweaty and disheveled, the BBC crew was biding its time in the shade of a tree. My driver was by himself, keeping a deliberate distance from the other two. He greeted me warmly, though I had hardly spoken to him, and offered me a hand as I clambered up into the passenger seat of his cart. He took a position facing me, reversing his position on his bicycle seat and leaning back on the handlebars to strike a delicate balance.

"You know much about China, don't you?" he said, using the disarming compliment "*Zhongguo tong.*"

"Sometimes I wonder. So, what do you think of all this?" I asked.

"I was in the Tiananmen incident in 1976," he said. "I know all about such demonstrations. At that time, the crowd was truly of one mind; we spoke the truth. But soon after the demonstration I got arrested. They herded us across the square and locked us up in the Worker's Park next to the Forbidden City."

"Over there?" I pointed to a tree-lined wall far in the distance.

"Yes. I was lucky, I only went to jail. Some disappeared, some were executed. The government decides life and death," he intoned with a whisper, looking around before going on. "I spent the next five years in prison. After prison I could not get a job; that is why I drive a trishaw today."

"What about the other drivers?" I asked. "Had they been political prisoners too?"

"Ha, those two jokers?" he said with disbelief. "They don't know the first thing about politics. They are nothing but common criminals."

"What kind of crimes did they commit?"

"The fat, bald one, he raped a woman. The one with the beard is a robber, he beat up someone, almost killed him," he explained. "They both just got let out of jail."

The Open Door Policy was one thing, but opening the doors to prisons was not necessarily in the interests of liberalization. It made me wonder if the square was being deliberately sowed with social deviants to whip up some trouble. Governments have done stranger things to manipulate crowds and create pretexts for ironfisted rule. Eyeing the tout and his sidekick with a new appreciation, I thought it a good idea to get the crew back to the hotel before things got really weird.

We plotted a roundabout route to the hotel, edging along a long pedestrian-choked avenue and going south to head north, essentially circling the square for expediency.

We cut close to the sidewalk in front of the Great Hall. Here crowd density was uneven, allowing for spurts of movement followed by pileups. Perhaps drawn by the symbolic power of the Great Hall, there were assorted curbside speakers addressing the sensation-hungry throngs. A man in a neat suit stood on top of an abandoned car, sharing articulate thoughts with bystanders. An older unshaven man wearing a ragged Mao jacket commanded a rapt audience of his own with boisterous nostalgia for the good old days. A few times the delay was sufficient to prompt the crew to whip out their gear. Subsequently our presence would then serve to augment public interest in whichever speaker was lucky or unlucky enough to fall under the focus of our lens.

The gray-haired soapbox orator in the tattered Mao jacket responded to the gaze of our camera by climbing up on the top of a trishaw, waving his hands at us in a ritualized, almost theatrical way, not unlike the way officials did on TV.

"Foreign friends. My greetings," his voice boomed. "Where are you from?"

"We are England television," I hollered back, responding in kind.

"I thank you for being here. You are a good friend of the Chinese people," he said, in slow, simple Chinese of the sort used for children and foreigners.

A few random bystanders cheered and clapped.

"I will take you anywhere you want to go, for free," he offered, pointing to his flimsy vehicle. "I don't want any money!"

The lead driver, who I know knew to be a dangerous criminal, moved ominously close to me to see what all the commotion was about. I tried looking the other way, but he gave me a ten-pound tap on the shoulder to command my immediate attention.

"Don't listen to that guy," he growled. "He's a lunatic!"

"How do you know?"

"Just look at that mother-effing driver preaching up there," the burly man added, poking me in the ribs. "The guy's definitely crazy!"

Eric took his eye from the viewfinder to look up, sensing trouble, but I told him to keep on filming.

"I may be . . . but . . . a common maaaan," the orator in the Mao suit said with a vibrato worthy of Martin Luther King, "but I have the dreams of an em-peh-ror!"

He repeated this refrain, priming the audience. Each time his voice reached a crescendo, he raised his arms to the sky, and those gathered round him cheered wildly.

"Our foreign friend here, right there, he can speak Chinese," he announced, pointing at me. "Tell us, friend. What is your name?"

I mumbled shyly in Chinese. He told me to shout it louder. "Jin Peili!" I said, reluctant to be drawn into his performance. It was like being tapped by a magician looking for volunteers.

"Jin Peili, I will work for you! All day! For nothing!" the man sputtered, with emphatic flourish and impeccable timing. "We want the world, the people of the world, to know about the generous spirit of the Chinese people!"

The man in the Mao jacket served up a string of platitudes with verve, plainspoken enough to find receptive listeners, compelling enough to stir the spectators gathered in our favor, though an angry racist rant delivered with similar panache might also find a ready audience.

Both the dumb foreigner treatment and the honored foreign guest routine reminded me what a cultural tightrope we walked, working such an anarchic crush. We were lightning rods for all kinds of touts and taunts.

The greedy tout insisted we move on, as if the lofty talk of volunteerism might hurt business. He coaxed our convoy of rickshaws to lurch forward before we had settled in, then picked up speed, careening this way and that. Twice the lead driver and his sidekick got in arguments with pedestrians and cyclists who had almost been knocked down. One time the bald man slapped a protestor point-blank because he had the temerity not to move out of his way fast enough.

Yet for all his impatience, the same tout also demanded frequent rest stops and cigarette breaks, all the while cooking up angles to up the fare. As a result, the unassociated cart I shared with Lotus got way ahead of the others because our driver was content to pedal slowly but steadily without a break.

We passed incoming delegations of farmers, workers, intellectuals, and merchants parading in support of the students. One key stratum of Chinese society that had not yet joined in was the military. If that happened, it would be as good as setting off a chain reaction, signaling that the overthrow was all over but for the shouting. The people would truly love an army that loved the people.

Following in the auditory wake of the path cleared by the lead cart, I couldn't help but notice the thuggish driver was quick to exploit the fact that we were foreigners for his own convenience.

"Make way for the foreign guests, you ignorant peasant!" he barked. "Get out of my way, stupid turtle!" he cursed imperiously. "Can't you see we're important?" and finally a new zinger, "Butt out of my way, buddy, I'm with the BBC!"

Things were beginning to sour a bit, and how could they not?

Then bully driver smacked another hapless bystander who had just gotten in the way of the BBC's three-cart convoy, bringing the word *laowai* to the lips of bystanders. His actions reflected badly on our crew.

"Hey, cut it out, buddy!" I yelled angrily. "Don't go hitting people and blame it on the BBC. Just do your job!" The man stopped pedaling and turned around defiantly, inviting me to a face-off. Brian's radar was in top form; he wanted to know what I'd said that got his driver so mad. I briefly explained that I was trying to rein the guy in, to stop him from hitting people.

"I'm not going an inch further," the bald tout said threateningly.

"We're in no rush," I bluffed, even though there was a satellite deadline.

"What are you two talking about?" Brian, sharp as a tack, could sense trouble in any dialect.

What it came down to was this: we would have to pay more to go faster and also pay more to go slower.

After translating about half of the conversation for Brian's benefit, we resumed our painfully slow wobble, broken by random mad dashes, all the way back to the Beijing Hotel.

Something Bright had said was still gnawing at me. If the government was being overthrown, who was overthrowing whom? What if the overthrow resulted in chaos and criminality? The problem with using the word *government* was that it wasn't a monolithic thing anymore. Maybe it never was.

At last we hit the home stretch, breaking free of the teeming masses and racing into the uncluttered hotel driveway, all but empty of people and motorized vehicles. As we glided in, I saw a reflection of our entourage with its unwelcome parallels to prerevolutionary privilege, when underpaid rickshaws carrying overweight foreigners would pull right up to the entrance of swank hotels. I had always idealized the poor rickshaw driver in my imaginative reconstructions of Chinese history, but today I had a slightly more nuanced take on the topic.

The relief of having reached our refuge, the hotel, was soured by a nasty argument that ensued the moment we disembarked.

"Three hundred in Foreign Exchange Certificates per person. I won't settle for anything less!" the tout proclaimed in feisty Mandarin, not for the benefit of my monolingual colleagues but rather to catch the attention of other drivers and doormen. He was recruiting potential allies should there erupt a disagreement, perchance an interracial rumble.

The original agreed-upon price of 100 RMB had been exorbitant enough, but now he was asking to be paid three times that in the desirable FEC money used by banks, big stores, and hotels. A hundred-dollar rickshaw ride!

"That's not the price we all agreed on!" I protested.

"What about lunch? We missed our grub. It's all your fault," the big man muttered.

Lunch in a good local restaurant cost less than 5 RMB.

Then suddenly the masterful tout switched to a loud, clear voice. "You, you laowai! Who do you think you are? Treating us Chinese like slaves!"

"Overtime," his bearded buddy piped in, "you pay overtime!"

I stepped aside to pay the veteran of Tiananmen 1976 the agreed-upon fee of one hundred, which he thanked me for and accepted without complaint. He quickly pedaled away, retreating to the anonymity of the street.

"That motherfucker, he betrayed us!" the bully grumbled to his coconspirator. I gave Lotus my room key and told the crew to grab their gear and wait inside the lobby. I carefully counted out the initially agreed-upon fare in FEC scrip for the two belligerent drivers and handed them each a crisp stack of bills.

"Only two hundred smackers?" he protested. "You must be kidding!"

"What you see is what you get!" I started to walk away.

"That's what you think, old whitey!" he said menacingly.

Instinctively, and shamelessly, I sought refuge inside the guarded hotel. For the first time I could see some merit to the cruel government policy of not permitting common Chinese in the big hotels. Among other considera-

Students consult campus wall posters for strike announcements

Arts choral group marching to the square

May Fourth marchers greeted by Beijing citizens on overpass

Staking out pride of place near Sun Yatsen's portrait

Strikers on cycle gather at Beida South Gate on May 10

"10,000 bicycles demonstration" heads for Tiananmen

Viewing the crowd from the Martyr's Monument

Yet another contingent joins the hunger strike on May 14

All-night vigil at the square

Reaching out to world media

The BBC's Brian Hanrahan and camera crew

The author consoling a hunger striker at dawn

Beijing Hotel workers support the students

On the road to Tiananmen

Jotting down notes as marchers circle the square

The Monument and Great Hall are the focus of action

Mao-era icons paraded in support of people's struggle

Factory workers join the protests by the truckload

Student "life-lines" strictly observed for safety and crowd control

On the run with rebel "commander in chief" Chai Ling

tions, the safety-conscious authorities had in place a system that protected hotel guests from annoying riffraff and street criminals.

However, those strictly segregated days were over. The same laxity that had made it possible for Bright to visit me without being questioned made it possible for these two touts to tail me inside the lobby. As Deng Xiaoping said in a different context about Western culture, when you open the door, some flies are bound to come in.

Because of the breakdown in the social order, the Beijing Hotel stopped functioning as a restricted-access refuge for foreigners and elite Chinese. People power, in both the good and bad senses of the word, was in effect, and the roguish drivers quickly exploited it. They followed me into the main lobby and then deeper into the building as I approached the elevator banks, remaining close on my trail. I got on an elevator and they got on too, just as the door was closing. I didn't get off at fourteen but rode it all the way up to the top floor, for once wishing I was being obtrusively watched by the hidden camera. I walked the length of the hallway only to hear the menacing sound of their cursing voices echoing behind me. I ducked into the emergency staircase, ran down a floor, walked down a long corridor to the elevator, and went to the second floor, where I waited in an alcove of an empty lobby.

There was no sound other than my heart pounding. An attendant looked at me suspiciously, my sunburned face wet with sweat, clothing full of dust. I had shaken off my stalkers, but it had been a close call. The idea of two hardened criminals having the run of the hotel made me nostalgic for the days when the door-watchers watched the doors.

I went up to my room to discover that Lotus was not alone, but was showing off the view from my porch to two Chinese-American friends from San Francisco. They had just arrived in Beijing from out of town and were keen to go downstairs and take a closer look at the action. For a reason that I didn't bother to explain, I declined their invitation to take a little walk right in front of the hotel. I pictured the two touts out there, frustrated and hungry for revenge, ready to cloak themselves in inflammatory nationalistic rhetoric, deviously exploiting the chaos of the streets.

So we spent the evening in. The four of us sat on the unlit porch as the sun set and the sky went to black, comparing stories, musing about the events of the day. The two newcomers had been traveling in Sichuan when they heard the incredible news that Beijing was under rebellion. They said there had been some provincial protests in support of the students.

"See? Everyone's talking about Tiananmen," Lotus said, "even thousands of miles from Beijing!" We talked about the significance of the protests and we all agreed, in a fusion of shared wishful sentiment and facile political analysis, that the spontaneous swelling of so many citizens in the streets of Beijing augured the end of the dynasty.

China was on the cusp of great change. Looking for hints and hidden signs in the swirl of people below was like trying to read submerged tea leaves moving up and down in a murky brew. We lingered on the porch for hours, studying the ebb and flow of the moonlit marchers until way past midnight.

MAY 19

◑

Breaking the Fast

The hunger strike had reached a critical stage. The weakest of the strikers were nearing death, but the government, despite a stab at public relations through an awkward televised dialogue, showed no sign of making significant concessions. Flush with the success of filling Tiananmen rim to rim with people, but unable to show any real gains, the student movement was stalling out with nowhere to go. The sweeping numbers seen in the past two days were not easily sustainable; the headcount was down.

The BBC van had made it almost halfway across the north face of the bustling square when the amateur traffic police supervising access to Tiananmen got suspicious. We were pulled over by a motley group of students, some in borrowed uniforms, others with the usual headbands, not far from the marble bridges by the entrance to the Forbidden City.

"Where is your pass?" barked one of boys in a traffic police outfit. Besides the ill-fitting uniforms and their obvious youth, the thing that most strongly suggested that the "officers" were imposters was the footwear; they wore rubber sandals and scuffed-up sports shoes.

The driver who had replaced Min, a new hire from the Great Wall Hotel, picked up on this right away. "We support the students!" he shouted felicitously.

"So what?" one of the young guards snapped. "Everybody does. You still need permission to drive here!"

I felt like I had stepped in a time warp and landed in the midst of the Cultural Revolution, when adult-hating, authority-defying Red Guards still roved the land.

"We are BBC from England. We have come to make a news report," I said, stepping into the reporter's shoes, hoping our world-renowned call letters would settle it. On this late morning outing I was out solo with a camera crew. That meant that I had to take on the reporter/producer's role of pressing for access. I could not resort to "I'm only the interpreter," when things got tough. Now I was Brian.

The unkind light of the overcast sky drained Tiananmen of its usual color just as the excess of ropeways and checkpoints were choking the flow of traffic to the square. Despite scant on-the-job experience, the self-appointed traffic cops were already jaded, doing their job with a bored authoritarian relish. There was a long slash of empty road running several hundred yards in both directions lined with townspeople on both sides; people twice the age of the students followed orders as given, either out of respect at the sight of the uniforms or indulging them for the sake of shared hopes.

Where there were no rope barriers, there existed invisible lines that few dared to cross. The bare pavement gleamed in the diffuse light of the clouded-up sun.

While the student traffic marshals huddled to argue the merits of the "England BBC" case among themselves, Eric, Fred, and I stepped out of the van, physically expressing our unwillingness to be fully beholden to kids in uniform. We stretched our legs on the edge of the forbidden zone, surveying the unexpectedly semihostile terrain. Bright, who had gone against her better judgment and come along for the ride at my urging, remained inside the van.

"You cannot step out of the car here!" shrieked a youthful voice.

"And what do you propose we do?" I snapped back.

"Go back!"

Ignoring his command, Fred, Eric, and I held our ground.

"Stop! Just wait!" ordered the student marshal.

We waited but nothing happened. Curious about what kind of deliberations the "authorities" were making in regard to our fate, I decided to walk over to their roost, a police box on a traffic island, only to find they weren't talking about us at all. Three young revolutionary traffic wardens, all female, were engaged in banter with members of the opposite sex. Each had school pins prominently tacked onto their baggy uniforms. While they gabbed, I snapped a picture, prompting a vociferous reaction.

"No pictures!"

"Why not?"

"That is the rule!"

"Whose rule?"

"Students' rule."

"We are going to the square," I said with measured firmness, thinking of Brian's argument with the water strikers, "to talk to the hunger strikers."

"You cannot go to the square," shrieked a young woman. "It is not permitted!"

"No? Well, at least can we, oh, I don't know. Hmm. Boy, you must be tired standing out here."

"No kidding!"

"Hey, why not let us set up our camera over there?" I offered. "That way we can talk to some people on the edge of the square without going inside, okay?"

The artless compromise worked. The young gatekeepers saved face, or in any case were now able to get on with their all-important chitchat, and I secured for BBC a foothold on the outskirts of the square. Still, I couldn't believe we had been refused entry to Tiananmen. The whole point of Tiananmen was that it is open to everyone, was it not? The walls, those ubiquitous Chinese walls, were getting in the way again.

We unloaded the camera gear, arranged a place to park the van, and tip-toed our way into the human labyrinth, gradually picking up speed as the amateur traffic cops, now almost out of sight, preoccupied themselves with other vehicles and questions of teenage romance. We were about halfway to the monument, well into the thick of things, when a pretty woman wearing makeup and a floral-patterned dress emerged from a thicket of people with a small entourage in tow. When I heard someone say she was a TV news announcer, I hopped over a rope and needled my way through the onlookers, all with their backs to us, to get closer. I listened intently as she fielded questions, then asked one of my own. At first she was reluctant to give me the "floor."

"Oh? You speak Chinese?" she responded coolly, in English.

"You are with CCTV?" I asked.

"Yes," she said, looking elsewhere, barely acknowledging my presence.

"We're from the BBC. Can you tell me what is happening now?"

"I've really got to run, but I can tell you this, the situation is quite grave," she said, pausing to look around nervously. "I was asked by someone in the government to deliver a message to the students."

"What is the message?"

"Zhao Ziyang is . . . " She paused, looking at her escorts. "I'm sorry, I really have to go."

In my scramble to talk to the reporter, I had swiftly hopped over a key perimeter rope guarding the central zone of the square. Once in, one was in. I waved Bright and the crew over and they were let past the rope under the auspices of my apparent authority. Because I was already inside the rope, it was assumed I had a modicum of authority. Having been seen with the famous newscaster had made a difference, too, causing my stock to surge in the eyes of those who watched foreigners and celebrities with more-than-average attention. Knowing, or giving the impression of knowing, famous people in China was useful in opening doors, revolution or not.

I talked to as many people as best I could, mostly off camera, in between the wail of sirens. Every few minutes the sirens would go screaming by, evacuating a striker who had fainted or tending to some other small emergency. Over two thousand strikers had been taken to the hospital, I was told, and many of them had already returned to the square, only to willfully weaken themselves again. The best news I could gather was that none had yet perished, but it was only a matter of days, if not hours, before some limp, dehydrated body would give the movement its first martyr. Popular support for the hunger strikers had been enthusiastic, and much pent-up energy had been released, but to what effect? The strikers clearly had the government worried, but there was never any question about who was running China.

From the steamy ports of Hainan Island to the forbidding Himalayas and on to the Yellow Sea, from the windswept grasslands of the north to the tropical jungles of Yunnan, the Communist Party and the PLA reigned supreme. What could a bunch of students possibly hope to do?

The televised meeting yesterday between Li Peng and a group of students, including Wang Dan and Wuerkaixi, was a fascinating exchange but gave no reason for hope. Li Peng had come off as being cold and condescending, but the students, Wuerkaixi from Shida in particular, had been unsuitably brash and insolent. What amazed most people was that such an encounter took place at all, broadcast on national television no less. CCTV news reports on leaders were typically edited, voiced-over, and sanitized; one almost never heard actual dialogue taking place. Li Peng looked ill at ease while engaging in an unexpectedly real and unscripted dialogue with campus hotheads, who were, as he pointed out, "younger than my own children."

Rumors of troops coming in from the provinces were cause for some alarm, but few expected the PLA to attack the city. After all, it was the capital of China! The Chinese army was not incapable of turning its guns on the people—in the past few years numerous Tibetans had been shot dead in the streets of Lhasa, but given the racially tinged, heavy-handed treatment of non-Han peoples, many would argue that that was a special case.

When I visited Tibet in 1986, the contrast between the khaki-clad Han Chinese troops and the maroon-robed Tibetans reeked of cultural clash. There were ethnic tensions between Tibetan merchants and migrants from Sichuan, and more than once I was reprimanded by militant, long-haired Tibetans for speaking Chinese, the language of the oppressors. The construction of unsightly PLA barracks smack in front of the sublime heights of the majestic Potala Palace suggested a city under an army of occupation. But in Beijing, such open contempt between the army and the citizenry was still almost inconceivable. After all, as some of the Tiananmen "peace" posters proclaimed, with unintentional but implicit racialism, "Chinese don't kill Chinese."

Tear gas, batons, and fists might be called into action, with the PLA or police roughing up a few people to disperse the crowd, but it was hard to imagine things getting worse than that. Thus, the rumors and sightings of troops arriving in Beijing, while not good news, were not exactly terrifying either. If it came down to soldiers pushing the people off the square in a colossal shoving match, then the people still had the edge in terms of collective body weight.

Even so, how could this student movement, disciplined and enthusiastic as it was, possibly overthrow the government? No matter what was happening in Beijing, China was so vast that most of the country would continue to function as normal. The students had undreamed-of influence for a few fleeting days, but it was worth keeping in mind that their power on the ground was limited to a big patch of pavement. The government was losing prestige, but it still ran the country. It took Mao and his revolutionary bandits many decades to gain the support of China's vast countryside, a bloody struggle greatly aided by the Kuomintang's ineptitude and the harshness of the Japanese invasion. The students had only been at it for a few weeks with no weapons other than the power of their ideas, raw emotion, and a friendly wink from the Western media.

While the ringleaders at Tiananmen had no serious democratic claim to speak for "the people" or to lead "the people," they did effectively question the government's lack of democratic authority to do the same. It was more of a power play within a Communist society than anything recognizably democratic. The main power enjoyed by the students was, appropriately enough, in the realm of ideas. Fresh ideas and new cultural trends injected into the public debate by the students might well induce change in Chinese society, much as had happened in the creative outburst of May 4, 1919.

What little organization the students possessed was problematic as well. Student organization was top-down hierarchical, those who claimed to speak for others were often overbearing, and they had a fledgling security system to enforce the organization. They hoarded classified information, held secretive meetings, and issued propaganda designed to support the "student" worldview. The hunger strikers' demand for dialogue displaced calls for "freedom of the press," the rallying cry earlier in the month, while the daunting logistics of occupying the square led to limits on press access and information flow. Bound by discipline not to reveal secrets, especially to foreigners, students hewed to a "party line" not unlike that of their elders. From time to time they would stage a press conference to publicize the latest official position.

The new BBC driver understood well the new law of the road. He had hitched a red banner saying "We Support the Students" to the radio antenna of the van and wrote a similar message on a cardboard sign that was wedged under the wiper on the windshield. He was not exactly a convert to the cause—he quickly took prostudent signs down the minute we were out of student-controlled areas—leading me to ask him what he thought of the students.

"I hate those conceited little student guards," he told me, with a satisfied laugh, "but when they see the sign they wave me right through!"

In the last day or two, students had been put on a pedestal that would be laughable were it not for the mortality of the hunger strikers in their midst. Beijing's bend-with-the-wind types, bent by a steady diet of political campaigns since childhood, were quick to adopt the new orthodoxy. Any fool could make a bid for instant acceptance by spouting the new jargon. Our new driver was better at negotiating people traffic than Min, in part because he was a better liar. Not that Min was a paragon of truthfulness. Min had tried in his own inept way to get out of trouble by saying what he thought the hunger strikers wanted to hear. "We are bringing food to the students!" was the artless ruse he came up with the day the occupation of Tiananmen began.

Outward compliance often counts more than inward conviction in such situations. Did the Chinese people not see the tragic implications of fooling others and fooling themselves by just going through the motions? Letting a "democratic" slogan such as "support the students" snowball without resistance until it achieved a kind of hegemonic orthodoxy might give the movement rhetorical unity, but how was that different from screaming, "Long live Chairman Mao"?

The word "student" was suffering from hyperinflation. It was hard to do anything around Tiananmen without getting the approval of someone who had no qualifications other than a red headband and a school pin.

Who were these "students" anyway but young people nurtured by the state, a tender elite who had not yet worked a single day in their lives? And what were they in danger of becoming? The new Red Guards! In the Cultural Revolution, donning a red armband gave young people the right to terrorize their elders. Teachers, parents, and party officials were hounded, sometimes to their death, by the young and ignorant. Afraid to disagree, millions pretended to support Mao's disastrous policies during the Great Leap Forward and the Cultural Revolution. Could such madness happen again? It was enough to give me a sense of pity for the embattled government.

Bright, who was uncomfortable moving in the company of journalists, went to look for her friends. I agreed to meet her later, then joined Eric and Fred in lugging the gear across the square, wary of "young Nazis" ready to pounce on us in the name of the students, while hoping to get deep enough into the now heavily segmented square to score some good visuals of the hunger strike.

Row after row of big, boxy buses had been parked on the north side of the monument, creating an impromptu trailer park for the starving strikers, grouped, as ever, by university affiliation. The area defined by the buses had the look and smell of a refugee camp. Doctors and nurses administered first aid from tents interspersed throughout the lot. A steady wail of sirens assured one that the sick and the unconscious were being attended to. Supplies of glucose, intravenous drip equipment, and big bottles of medicine were stacked inside a makeshift pharmacy. Boiled drinking water was stored in plastic Coke bottles, jars, and vacuum flasks.

Damp sleeping bags and blankets were draped out on the roofs of buses for an airing out. A student willing to show me around explained to me how the buses were lined up in such a way as to enhance security, creating narrow, restricted alleys between them.

Near the center of the square, a woman with the charismatic élan of a stage actress was singing patriotic songs at the top of her lungs to the accompaniment of a single accordion. This was precisely the kind of stuff that looks good on television, so we followed her from bus to bus. This gave us a chance to peek inside several buses, something that would have been difficult to arrange otherwise. Security was tight in the wake of visits from China's top leaders. Both Zhao Ziyang and Li Peng had visited strikers on these buses this morning, perhaps keeping an eye on each other as much as greeting the strikers. The mere presence of a foreign film crew was not enough to impress anyone anymore.

Bright found me and took me to see Lily, who was still on strike. The student security guards, understanding us all to be friends from Shida, were gracious enough to allow us to talk with her, but she made it clear she could not be interviewed. According to discipline, Lily had to stay with her group. No one was supposed to talk to the press except the designated spokespeople, and then they were guided by rules of what constituted official student policy. There were all kinds of instant and arbitrary rules for visitation, so we could not chat for long. Lily had lost some weight and was looking pretty grim and parch-mouthed, but I was comforted by the thought that she wasn't on a strict zero-calorie diet.

A few days before, we found her in the hunger-strike zone quietly nibbling on a chocolate bar. I asked her if chocolate was permitted during the hunger strike and it was her impression that it was. In any case, she had made no secret of it; she had chocolate smeared above her lips. But even with the high-calorie chocolate intake we were worried about her and quietly expressed the hope that she wouldn't persist. What's the point of winning a symbolic victory only to lose a life? Although the hunger strike was having a tremendous impact, galvanizing the sympathy of an entire nation, a good motherland should not consume its young.

Lily wasn't the only striker unavailable to our camera. With the crew in tow, I was shooed away from each and every bus the moment I tried to do an interview. The fact that the BBC wanted interviews in English further complicated the search. A few times I managed to find someone at least tangentially related to the strike, a volunteer or whatever, quite willing to talk and adequately articulate, but who would suddenly balk when I explained that they would have to talk to me in English.

At last I found a young striker willing to say a few words in the lingua franca of the Western world. Standing on the steps of his bus, he hungrily finished the cigarette lodged between his thin, parched lips, then coolly flicked the butt away. Recent weight loss, a skinny frame, and the untended whiskers on his face made him look twice his age

"How do you feel?" I asked for openers, wondering if the nicotine helped stave off hunger.

"We, uh, no. We want dialogue to government." His English had been more impressive off camera.

"Yes and you must be very tired and weak. Where do you sleep?"

"Sleep?" he asked as if he were trying to remember how to put an English sentence together. "We sleep on bus."

"I see some sleeping bags on the roof, does anyone sleep up there?"

"I don't understand."

"That's okay, um, let's see, where is the toilet around here?" I asked, repeating the question in Chinese.

"Behind bus," he said. He pointed to a blanket that was rigged up to block the back seat of the bus from view.

Since the strikers had presumably consumed nothing but water for days, the jerry-rigged urinal did not leave much of a stench. The hunger strikers were spared from having to trek to Tiananmen's inconvenient but serviceable underground public toilets.

"Did you see Zhao Ziyang when he came here this morning?" I asked.

"Not really." He switched into Chinese to explain that Zhao had boarded a different bus, but his friend had seen him and gotten his signature.

"You have many signatures on your shirt," I said, continuing in Chinese. "What is that all about?"

"To remember my friends," he said, muttering something in Chinese while groping around for something in his pocket. He produced a pen and asked me in to sign his cap.

"Phil?" interrupted Eric, peering up from behind the camera. "Are we doing an interview or what?"

The cameraman was not just puzzled to see me offering my autograph in the middle of an interview, he was also nudging me, reminding me to keep the conversation in English. I indicated that he should keep rolling.

"Okay. So, where were we? Let's keep this in English, please."

"I have to . . . " broke in a sweet female voice just off camera.

Standing behind the English-speaking striker towards the back of the bus was a pretty woman with long hair wearing an airy cotton dress. She clutched a Coke bottle in one hand and a bouquet of flowers in the other. She looked like someone who had gotten on the bus to Woodstock and ended up at Tiananmen by mistake.

"Are you allowed to drink that stuff?" I asked, pointing to the red-wrapped plastic bottle in her hand.

"I eat Coca-Cola every day," she said in English, pausing to take a swig of the bubbleless brew, "but I eat no food."

The starving students had taken to swigging the flavored sugar water from Atlanta in their ascetic battle for the hearts and minds of the Chinese people. No wonder journalists, not to mention ordinary citizens, were kept at a distance.

"My friend," the young man explained, "He, she, ah, Institute of Minority."

"Phil. You can't interview two people at the same time," Eric said, flashing a look of frustration as the interview fell apart. "Will you tell her to get out of the shot?"

"I am talking to someone else now," I duly scolded her. "Please move back, will you?"

She just kept looking at me.

"Back, please, will you? I will talk to you later."

To my chagrin, our featured English speaker was puffing on a new ciga-rette. It wasn't just the noxious smoke that bothered me; the cigarette also caused the interview to have a visual continuity problem, cigarette in mouth for some quotes, not others.

"Okay Phil, I think we got enough here," Eric abruptly announced. Then the Woodstock waif stepped forward with a bounce, smiling in recognition.

"You're Jin Peili? Am I right?" she asked. "Remember party with Zhou Duo?"

"Zhou Duo, um oh, yes . . . " I was stalling for time. I couldn't remember this flower child, but I remembered Zhou Duo very clearly. A prominent in-tellectual who dabbled in business but preferred talking about the issues, he had a hosted a salon-style dinner party at his house a few years ago. Most of the talk was highbrow—politics, philosophy, and ideology—a cultural salon of sorts.

At the party, I remember meeting a slightly plump, round-cheeked young woman from the Minorities Institute who could speak passable Thai. Could this be her?

"*Suay mak!*" I said, testing the waters. I told her she was beautiful in Thai. Not exactly a traditional greeting, but it worked because she broke into a shy smile.

"*Phood thai dai mai khrap?*" I continued, "You speak Thai, don't you?"

"*Kha! Sawatdee kha, chue meo, kha,*" she said, greeting me in practiced standard Thai, adding that her nickname was Meo, meaning cat. She pressed her hands together in a traditional *wai* to greet me. Meo was not Thai but she was from the Dai minority in Yunnan Province and could speak a dialect that allowed for some mutual comprehension. Her fellow hunger strikers hovered close to us, watching with rapt incomprehension.

"*Nong Meo,* at first I did not recognize you. You have become so thin!"

"It is so good to see you!" she smiled warmly. I could see Eric folding the tripod and Fred packing up the sound gear, getting ready to go.

"I want to see you again, how can I get in touch?"

"I have no address, you can find me on the bus 1056."

"But what about your home address?"

"Today is day seven of the hunger strike; I will stay here till I die."

Her words shocked me. If this hunger strike continued, a decision wholly in the hands of other people, she might not live another week. I reached out and hugged her. She reciprocated, holding me tightly.

Why did someone so young, with so much promise, have to face a grueling death from starvation? What madness politics is, what it puts people through. I let go and said good-bye. I stepped off the bus and ran, eyes unable to see clearly, as I strove to catch up with the others.

"Your friend is very beautiful," Eric said, trying to show he wasn't angry as we lumbered back to the van waiting on the other side of the ropes. Just then there was a loud crackle and hiss. The student PA system was being jacked up to full volume.

"Please get off the buses and report to your group leader, please get off the buses and . . . "

It seemed something important was about to happen, so I asked the crew if they could wait long enough to give me a chance to see what was going on.

I asked around and the answers I got were as different as people's faces— a party-line explanation had not been settled on yet. Reporting was a bit like asking for directions; one needed to ask the same question repeatedly in order not to be steered in the wrong direction.

Why are the buses being evacuated, where are the hunger strikers going?

"Nothing's happening, who are you?"

"It's the announcement for the daily meeting."

"It's nothing special, everyone has to get off the buses for bus cleaning hour."

"A new strategy is to be declared."

"There will be an important announcement at four."

Unsure of whom to believe, I convinced the crew it was worth waiting till four to find out, although we were plenty hungry and tired by then. We set up the camera and filmed the tragicomic scene of hunger strikers exiting their buses in disheveled states of wobbly infirmity. Group leaders barked commands into battery-operated megaphones. The limp and hobbling strikers, some of whom could barely stand without assistance, were lined up in neat parallel rows as if they were army recruits about to be inducted into boot camp. A middle-aged man standing near us was being besieged with questions. I pressed closer to find out what was being said.

"The students do not aim to topple the government," he was explaining as the clutch of listeners pulled in more closely around him. "Second of all, the hunger strike has seriously weakened its members. There will be a new strategy to deal with the government's threat of violence. Finally, the hunger strike will end at 6:30 today."

I wanted to find out who the man was, but he was whisked away in a flash by student handlers, with easily a dozen people chasing after him. Students addressed him respectfully as "teacher," but that didn't necessarily mean he was a professor. My guess was that he was with the Academy of Social Sciences, one of those scholars who served as a bridge between the government and students.

Another "teacher" who had been standing near me while the first man spoke breathlessly related that someone from CCTV had told him that Communist Party chief Zhao Ziyang, who had broken ranks with the leadership by openly showing support of the students, was now out of power.

If true, that was big news. The man added that the square could be attacked at any time now and pointed out that the students, weak and sick as they were, could no longer offer effective resistance.

I heard others argue that the strike should continue. Surprisingly, some of these voices came from the strikers themselves, which just goes to show how people can get bent on a particular course of action and how hard it can be to snap out of. Despite their discomfort and debilitating hunger, they had become national heroes. They were "our students," the good soldiers of a good historic cause. If and when the strike ended, they would have food in their bellies and could be nursed back to health, but the movement would lose its soul and they would be regular nobodies again.

So who was calling the shots around here? The student leaders were clearly in charge of the strikers, but who was in charge of the student leaders?

For the sake of friends like Meo and Lily, I was hugely relieved to see the hunger strike come to a close. As I watched the sickly supplicants accept their rations of warm orange drink and bread, I said a prayer of thanks that nobody had perished.

A doctor made the rounds, cautioning the strikers to first consume liquids and not to overeat. Tea and soup were the foods he recommended. That was good advice in theory, but neither was available on the square, so it came down to a break-the-fast of lukewarm orange drink and sweet rolls unloaded out of blue plastic crates. It was touching to watch these young heroes nibble, then wolf down their first meal in a week. Somewhere in that hungry gang of hunger strikers were Lily, Meo, and other friends. I was content to know that bus number 1056 would not be anyone's terminal address.

As relieved as I was, I had to admit that the moment the hunger strike ended a flame was extinguished at the center of Tiananmen. The hunger strike of the Chinese students, like the acts of self-denial of Mahatma Gandhi, captured the people's imagination but set a terrifyingly high standard. How much are you willing to suffer for your country? What better way to show selflessness in a land where "Have you eaten?" is a standard greeting than to willfully deprive yourself of food? The collective act of self-sacrifice had served to purify the movement, to distinguish it from ordinary power-grabbing politics. For a few extraordinary days, Tiananmen had assumed the quasisacred aura of a sacrificial altar.

Had Zhao really been pushed out of power? Zhao's early morning appearance at the square was a tardy show of support, but the students I met were moved by his gesture. Some even asked for his signature. Whatever Zhao's game was, whether it was a genuine show of support for the idealistic uprising or a last-minute attempt to shore up his own crumbling power base, he had not been able to turn things around.

From what the second "teacher" had been saying, there was a partisan quality to the movement, at least behind the scenes. Though both Li Peng and Zhao had respectively met with students, only one had any support from the students. If tacit support for Zhao in return for Zhao's tacit support for those who supported him was part of the equation, his downfall called for a new formula.

Zhao had told the strikers he was too late, yet his timing was propitious in a way. Word leaked to the street of his downfall caused the hunger strike to end. As to who was calling the shots, I could not determine, but the outcome was reasonably good. It was a miracle that, in a strike as large as this one, not a single striker had succumbed yet. And now no one would; it was over.

The rocky road of Chinese revolutionary history was littered with stirring examples of self-sacrifice in the name of the collective, often to the point of martyrdom, yet this unexpected twist was a testament to how much things had changed in the thirteen years since Mao's death, how "normal" China had become, how much it had recovered from the wounding mass hypnosis of the Cultural Revolution. This time around the "heroic" exhortation to self-sacrifice was tempered with a healthy dose of selfishness. Chocolate was okay; milk was better. Coca-Cola was not out of the question. The restoration of individual dignity was tentative and incomplete, but it found expression here in little acts of self-preservation along with the larger solicitous concern for the failing health of the young heroes.

What could well have become a serial, suicidal disaster ended on an upbeat humanitarian note. The gripping dramatics of withering away in public paradoxically imparted a life-affirming aura to the movement. But what now would sustain the spirit and the unity, what now could possibly recapture the lost urgency and focus of the hunger strike?

What was the next logical move on the giant chessboard of Tiananmen?

PART III

WANING MOON

◑

Martial Law

An ear-piercing whine made me shoot out of bed faster than a bad dream. Sweaty sheets discarded on the floor, I looked out the window in time to see five green helicopters swoosh past my balcony. The flyby had the unreal look of a special-effects scene in a war movie, almost close enough to reach out and touch.

I ran out to the porch. Hurtling westward in formation above Chang'an Boulevard, flying nearly eye level to the fourteenth floor, the whirling metallic beasts sliced through the air over the heads of the antlike trail of marchers, causing commotion and scurrying below.

The student strikers may have held the ground, but the sky was up for grabs. Buzzing the crowd in formation with a few loops around Tiananmen was the government's way of saying they were in control of the square even though they weren't. Tiananmen was still a liberated zone.

From my balcony I could see the helicopters hover and circle over the square like a pack of metallic dragonflies. What in the world was going on? Was Tiananmen under attack? Was this it? I looked at the big, shiny alarm clock that Bright had lent to me. The clock said 9:30. I called the BBC office, but they hadn't heard anything about any helicopters. I called *Newsweek* and got the same response.

I flipped on the TV to get a second opinion on what I had just seen with my own eyes. A few minutes later CCTV made an announcement saying martial law was now officially in effect. Last night they had made repetitive announcements about martial law on TV and on the radio, but it had no visible effect except to make the mass of protesters bigger and angrier. Now it was official, but other than the helicopters, the view outside looked pretty much the same.

The streets were starting to fill up with the usual morning tide of marchers, but they had never really emptied during an extraordinary night of ceaseless marching and shouting. The dominant refrain, clearly audible even at this height, was, "Down with Li Peng!"

There was a familiar knock on the door. Bright was back!

Martial law was supposedly in effect, but the instant I saw her smile I knew everything was more or less okay.

"How'd you get here?"

"I flew!" she said, thrusting her arms outward as if she were a bird. She was in a mood that defied the doom and gloom outside.

"You didn't see the helicopters?" I asked. I found myself wishing it had been a dream, after all.

"Oh, them?" she said nonchalantly. "They're just dropping leaflets about martial law, that's all."

"That's all?" I was relieved and disappointed at the same time. What did she mean, "that's all"?

With the pressure building up like this, I was tempted to think that the sooner things came to a head, the better it would be for everyone in the long run.

Thanks to CCTV we knew all about martial law. That's why everyone was up all night, running around so defiantly, part last hurrah, part mobilization.

So far it didn't amount to much. Were the helicopters just an intimidating reminder for everyone to just pack up and leave? At best they were aerial shepherds, herding the students on their way, but wasn't it a little redundant to repeat an announcement already made ad nauseam with helicopter-dropped leaflets? Then again, the target audience did not have TV sets to pick up the news, not on the square anyway.

In a way it was a media war from the start. The students had taken to the streets because they could not vent their thoughts in the state-controlled media, epitomized by the *People's Daily*. Now the government, even with its mighty media monopoly, had to go to the streets to get its message to the media-deprived students, who used newspapers, if they bothered to read them at all, as things to sit down on to lessen the chill of dusty flagstones. Students instead relied on chants and word of mouth, brush-pen manifestos and hand-painted slogans, low-tech mimeographs and megaphones to say things the government media wouldn't countenance.

If the media power was asymmetrical, there were compensations. Obvious underdogs, charming when they had to be, the students had already won the public relations battle for the hearts and minds of the foreign press; Li Peng and his men didn't stand a chance. This development gave students media reach that in some ways exceeded that of the government; the high-tech, high-production coverage they were getting from foreign TV crews like the one I worked for gave them instant international renown.

But I still couldn't figure out the lackadaisical implementation of martial law. The use of army helicopters to drop paper leaflets was intimidating or comic, depending on how one looked at it.

"Last night they said martial law goes into effect the day after the announcement, right?" I asked. "Like at ten a.m. or something. Well that's now. So? So are we under martial law?"

"No, actually it starts tonight," Bright explained. "That's why I came over now. It is serious; if you are discovered working for BBC without a journalist visa, you can be arrested, even kicked out of China."

What protection did I have? I was not an accredited journalist and didn't even have a paper contract with the BBC. As an American working for a British company, I fit the profile of individuals who had been expelled from China recently, like the American reporter who got kicked out of China while working for Agence-France Press.

Bright had asked me to bring this up with the BBC and asked me again if I had.

"Well, I asked Mark, the producer, and he said not to worry; he would be the judge of what was safe and what was not."

"What does he know?" she said.

She hardly needed to give me advice; she was already my bellwether. Unwittingly she helped me see the direction of things and put things in a larger perspective. She had influenced my decision to march with the students in early May, and had illuminated some of the pitfalls of working for foreign media.

She had a point, but I didn't want to quit, even though my conversation with BBC had hardly been reassuring. When I had pressed to be involved in discussions involving the safety precautions and suitability of assignments, the BBC producer raised his eyebrows with incredulity. He then made a concession, designed as much to help the BBC get off the hook, I suspect, as to protect me. He said I should not carry the tripod or camera gear since that would provide incriminating evidence of the BBC having hired a nonaccredited freelancer.

Bright and I went out on the porch. The helicopter buzz had the effect of agitating the street marchers to a new level of stridency. If anything, traffic to the square was on the upswing. The air resounded with a variation of an old chant:

"*Dadao li peng! Gankuai xiatai, renmin wansui!*"

"Down Li Peng! Step down quickly! Long live the people!"

I was aching to know what was going on at the square. Was it swelling with spectators as students packed up and marched home?

"Look, here they come again, let's count how many this time!" Bright chirped excitedly. She got carried away with childish enthusiasm every time the "Flying Tigers" motorcycle brigade roared by.

Motorcycles, being the speedy, noisy machines that they are, were, according to my Long Island mentality, not to be admired—they conjured up images of Hell's Angels and traffic accidents. But in this context, the revving and roaring, even the trail of exhaust of the hot engines, was life-affirming and reassuring.

The motorcyclists provided up-to-the-minute information about events around the city, a dramatic innovation in the ever-evolving media tug of war, an answer to the helicopters or perhaps, circularly, the helicopters were in answer to them. They were the protesters' early warning system in case of attack, the vanguard, should a crackdown be set into motion, because they patrolled the dangerous outside perimeter of people-controlled Beijing.

Bright explained that the "*Fei Hu*" circled the old city clockwise along Second Ring Road, much like the path we had taken in the bicycle demonstration. Each time they cruised by the hotel and the square, a slight detour on the southern link of their journey, it was a sign that all was well.

"Sixty seven, sixty eight, sixty nine . . . " Bright counted out loud like a schoolgirl. "I counted sixty nine, how many did you count?"

Although I wasn't counting, I shared her joy in watching the Flying Tigers roar by in such large packs. They circled Beijing as sentinels, on the lookout for trouble, intrepid representatives of a besieged population, like U.S. General Chennault's original Flying Tigers, American pilots who came to the rescue of China before the formal outbreak of war with Japan. I liked the comparison, not least because it was a reminder that Chinese and Americans had once been comrades in arms.

A workers' brigade followed on foot and bicycle, filling in the wake left by the Flying Tigers, almost matching the noise of roaring mufflers with vociferous militant shouts.

"*Dadao Li Peng!*" "Down with Li Peng!"

"*Dadao Li Peng, dadao Li Peng, dadao Li Peng, dadao Li Peng!*"

Bright surprised me by joining in from the balcony, adding her voice to the cacophony of thousands below.

The tempo and pitch of the repetitive, catchy "*Dadao Li Peng*" slogan surged until it sounded like nonsense syllables. The rhythmic, hypnotic cadence reminded me of a cross between a Balinese monkey dance chant and John Lennon's ditty, "number nine, number nine, number nine."

"*Bupaliuxue, bupazuolao!*" "Don't be afraid to spill blood, don't be afraid of prison!"

Another rhythmic formula, but one I found considerably less agreeable. Why talk about spilling blood? What kind of bravado was that?

Eric and Fred stopped by my room to get an update and to tell me that the BBC brass were all stuck in the Great Wall Sheraton due to the citywide disruption of traffic.

At one o'clock, we heard a new slogan being whipped up with enthusiasm. "*Fandui junguan, fandui jieyan!*" The angry protesters were screaming, "Oppose curfew, oppose martial law!"

Bright's excited response to the rebellious currents below startled me.

One day she tells me the government is going to be overthrown, the next day she advises that I quit the BBC to avoid arrest. So what's with martial law? It's serious, she says, but the hour of implementation keeps changing. It's dangerous, she says, and she's out on the porch shouting slogans in solidarity with the radical marchers below.

Was it possible to hate Li Peng and like martial law?

My friend Xiaoping, whose name was the source of gentle joking as it was written with the same ideographs as that of the top leader, gave me some advice over the phone. She took martial law at face value, saying I was too involved already, didn't have a clue as to what was really going on, and it was high time I quit hanging out with the activists. She had been a wonderful host during my 1983 visit to Beijing and I didn't want to disappoint her. But her words about disruptions to traffic and ensuing chaos echoed almost exactly things I was hearing on CCTV, so I chose to ignore her good advice.

After helping the BBC with a news update, Bright and I took a slow walk down Chang'an, lagging behind the energetic marchers but gravitating towards the square just the same. The protests had been going on so long that we felt at ease, even in the jet stream of militant marchers, free from harm, free to drift wherever the currents would take us.

My trusted companion was in a mood alternately pensive and attentive, and gradually she conveyed a sense that she was more worried than she had cared to reveal upon greeting.

When we at last went to the bicycle parking lot, she let the aluminum key dangle in hand, saying she had to go, but not unlocking her bike. She said she was worried and that I'd better stay away from the BBC. I told her I appreciated her coming to see me, but I didn't like the idea of her biking around town during the uncertain situation of martial law.

"You sound just like my father," she said.

"You should listen to your father," I said, inwardly pleased at the comparison.

"But if I listen to him, I have to stay at home, because it's martial law. And that means, maybe it means I can't see you."

We faced each other for a fleeting eternity in the bicycle parking lot, the air resounding with slogans and shouts, as marchers opposing martial law marched in and out of Tiananmen. There were so many things I wanted to say but it didn't seem like the time to say them. It was not simply because we were surrounded by hundreds, even thousands of people; we were used to that. It was something deeper, something inside. She too seemed at a loss for words.

She turned away shyly, not letting me see her face until she had wiped her cheeks. She unlocked her bicycle, mounted her bike, and waved good-bye. I waved as she merged with the brisk traffic of marching protesters and watched her sail away until she disappeared, swallowed up by the multitude of fellow citizens unknown.

◐

Provincial Vagabonds

The moon was on the wane, lopsided and losing light. Two days after the rebound in populist defiance that came in lull after the hunger strike, spurred on by the declaration of martial law, headcounts were dwindling and the mood on the square transmuted yet again; it was edgier in some quarters but had slackened off in others. Was Tiananmen the last stand or the last stop before going home for a good shower and a change of clothes?

The tenuous floating community was fragmenting rapidly. No one dominated, not even Beijing University students, who were traditionally more equal than others. The monument was still the center of action, but the museum steps directly to the east were taking on new significance as the provincial students demanded equal voice. There were worker groups, artist groups, college groups, and foreign journalists staking out portions of the square, each holding their own separate vigils, each for their own reasons.

No single slogan prevailed. No one "in" group could convince everyone else to follow.

After keeping low for two days, Bright was back. Tape recorder in hand, she and I walked around the square, going from group to group to record songs and speeches. The Communist classic "The Internationale" was still number one on Tiananmen's charts, though recordings of Cui Jian's signature anthem were gaining ground. No government slogan could come closer to expressing the angst of Chinese youth than the idiomatic refrain "nothing to my name," especially to those devoted protesters who slept under an open sky.

Hou Dejian had not been involved in the student protests when I had dinner with him in early May at the home of Gladys and Xianyi Yang, two well-known translators of Chinese literature. If anything, he was more dismissive of the youthful idealism than the elderly Yangs. But he listened to my account of the May 4 rally with great interest and wondered out loud if there was a role for someone like him to play.

Up until now, both of these thirtyish musicians had kept their distance from the college-aged strikers at Tiananmen, but in a way their physical presence didn't matter, because their recorded music had preceded them and was played in their absence.

As Bright and I wandered the square looking for music, a circle of fifty or so students from Nankai University were having a sing-along to the accompaniment of a tinny guitar. We moved closer in to watch and in no time we were invited to join the widening circle and participate. The Nankai delegation, who had arrived by train from the nearby port city of Tianjin a few days before, were now living on the square. Like other newcomers, they were more energetic than the Beijing veterans. We watched with amusement as each person was asked to perform a song on demand until all eyes turned to me. Egged on by a manipulative and insistent round of applause, I tentatively stood up.

"Sing! Sing!" student voices shouted. I was being put on the spot, but being put on the spot was the whole point of such a gathering, and I didn't see any way out of it, so I complied, making up a little ditty to the tune of Mao's anthem "Dongfanghong."

> The East is red, the sun is risin',
> the Chinese students on the horizon,
> um, let's see, doing good things,
> for the, the good . . . of the peo-ple.

I was not at all pleased with my performance. Despite howls of enthusiasm prompted by the sight of the laowai singing in Chinese, I should have just said no. But I had been drawn in and succumbed to peer pressure of people I didn't even know, just sucked in. And though I happened to support the students, generally, it would have been very hard to disagree with them if I didn't. If it could happen to me, an outsider, how much harder it must be for Chinese to say no. Or so I thought. When it came to Bright's turn, she was clever enough to say we had an appointment elsewhere.

After cutting west across the square we found another node of excitement. A fast-talking comedian was doing a parody of the Chinese leadership, reminiscent of Black Horse's performance earlier in the month. The speaker announced the founding of *"Liumang Daxue"* or "Hooligans' University." The Communist leaders were given academic titles such as "Dean of Dishonesty" or "Doctor of Corruption." The silver-tongued emcee agreed to let me tape him, but he insisted on no photos.

We paused for a cool drink at one of the many vending stands doing a brisk business near Tiananmen's tent city. Row after row of bottled orange pop, which came in varying hues, was artfully presented on huge slabs of ice flecked with pieces of straw. We enjoyed a delicious *jianbing* pancake and an iced drink for lunch. That fact that we could eat a passable meal on the square was an indication of how much the empty urban space had been transformed by the student squatters.

If creature comforts had improved, the political situation was deteriorating. Activists increasingly shielded their faces or waved angrily if a camera was pointed in their direction. Others didn't get mad, they got even, coolly taking aim and clicking at whoever had the temerity to take pictures of them, including men with heavy cameras who appeared not to be students at all.

The government loudspeakers mounted on poles around the square were back in action, blaring out ominous martial law commands, drowning out the student announcements of lower audio fidelity. An unseen government spokesman was droning on to the effect that PLA troops were entering Beijing to restore order.

"The PLA is on the side of the people, they will not hurt anyone."

I asked a few students what they thought of the martial law announcements.

"The government is devious!" one said.

"It's all lies, lies, don't believe them!" said another.

"Never, never trust them!" hissed a third.

A taped message stipulating martial law restrictions, recorded in a honeyed but menacing voice, played repeatedly on government-controlled speakers, echoing spookily on all sides of the square—not that anyone seemed to pay it much attention.

A cardboard sign a short distance from where we stood had different ideas about martial law.

JUNDUI JINCHENG, XIANZHAO LI PENG! (When the troops enter the city, they should catch Li Peng first!)

DENG XIAOPING, GO BACK TO SICHUAN!

DENG, YOU ARE BETTER OFF PLAYING BRIDGE!

LI PENG SHOULD BE KICKED OUT OF THE PARTY!

LI PENG MY SON, YOU PUT ME TO SHAME!

The last paired couplet was written above a portrait of the late premier Zhou Enlai. Even as the new generation reevaluated the Communist creed of their elders, Zhou Enlai remained a most highly respected personage, surpassing Mao in the minds of many. How then to make sense of the fact that Li Peng was the adopted son of the wise and venerated Zhou? Was the unpopular premier a chip off the old block or a son who had failed to emulate the best in his stepfather?

Recently workers had been chanting slogans and carrying signs advocating violence. While these slogans could be "spontaneous" expressions of mounting anger and frustration, they could also be part of a calculated campaign to discredit the peaceful movement. Any indication of readiness to use violence on the part of the demonstrators would give the martial law authorities the excuse they needed to crack down.

Thus it was disquieting to see a sign that said DIAOSI LI PENG!

Did they really want to say Li Peng must be hung? This disturbing phrase robbed a small corner of the movement of its moral, nonviolent stance. If it came down to gun-for-gun, eye-for-eye violence and retribution, the rebels did not stand a chance. Perhaps the disconcerting slogan was an intentional allusion to a well-known episode in Chinese history in which bloodthirsty rebels frightened the unpopular Ming Emperor Chongzhen out of the Imperial Palace in 1644. Rather than submit to their justice, the despairing emperor hung himself from a tree on Coal Hill in view of his opulent enclave, the Forbidden City. If the historical allusion was intentional, the message was: The end of the dynasty is here; get ready for some old-fashioned people's justice.

The protesters' slogans were on the one hand increasingly strident and mean-spirited. On the other hand, the all-purpose word democracy was gaining currency, though democracy itself was, if anything, on the retreat. Still, "Minzhu!" came closer to replacing the now out-of-date "We support the students!" than any other cry.

Later in the afternoon I took one of the BBC crews around the square. The most engaging chat I had was with a young student I had first met playing basketball at the Sports Institute. Crazy Zhang, as I liked to call him, was youthful, muscular, overconfident and a bit of a ham. Today he proudly toted an authentic-looking khaki-colored soldier's cap decorated with a bright red headband.

Asked about the army cap, he boasted that he got it from a "soldier who surrendered to the students."

"What do the other students think about it?"

"I don't care what those mothers think as long as I like it!" he answered with a gruff laugh.

Crazy Zhang seemed to emulate the bravado and derring-do bearing of the legendary Zhang Fei of Three Kingdoms lore. It had to be a put-on.

"So, like where's Wuerkaixi today?" I asked.

"I haven't seen that dude around today, but he's about."

"So, what's going on?"

"The government wants to crack down on the students. Ha!" he sneered. "If they dare do that we will fight back. But I am confident. After all the army will support us." Crazy Zhang flashed his trademark grin and then adjusted his oversized army cap.

"What makes you so sure?"

"Nie Rongzhen, Xu Xiangqian, Zhang Aiping—all PLA military generals— they said they will oppose any attempt to use the army against the people. They are on our side."

"How do you know that?"

"We have our sources," Zhang said smugly. "The old generals, they're great! They called on Deng not to use the army against students. If anyone tries to hurt us, they will kill them."

"So, do think there will be fighting?"

"Blood may flow, but this is for freedom and democracy. We must sacrifice for tomorrow."

The mention of blood was troubling, but I chalked it up to youthful bravado. After all, there was some hope for a peaceful denouement if the respected senior cadres he mentioned really opposed using force against the people. For the sake of all of us I hoped he was right.

We traipsed across the stained and litter-strewn square like electronic beachcombers looking for treasure at low tide. There was talk of a united general strike, but there was also divisive talk. Some were calling for a preemptive withdrawal from the square to avoid conflict. Others, like Crazy Zhang, were confident, cocky, and militant. The chessboard was thinning out, the game becoming more treacherous. Did the students have the pieces and strategy necessary to keep the government in check?

During an evening tour of the square, the crew took a break in front of the history museum, parking the van near the camp of the provincial students. The protesters around us didn't seem to mind our presence, though it was hard to enjoy the hotel-bought drinks we had kept stored in an icebox in the van in the midst of so many undernourished, homeless students from the countryside.

Then I noticed a young man in dusty clothes staring at me through thick black-rimmed glasses, eyeing the Coke I had in my hand. He had a wiry build and sported a flattop crew cut that made him look more a police cadet than student. He had a wide-eyed but vulnerable expression on his face, as if he wanted to talk but was afraid. I offered him a can of soda from the BBC icebox.

"Thank you, man!" he said nervously in English. He smiled like a baby who had just gotten his bottle, then he downed the soda so fast I felt sorry for him.

"Here you go, friend," I said, tossing him another.

"Do you know about the fighting outside the city?" he asked, face drawn with earnest tension until he burped.

"What? Fighting? Tell me about it."

"The troops starting beating the common people," he said, rushing into a description of the incident.

"How do you know about this?"

"I was there!" he said authoritatively. "Do you want to know about it? Are you a reporter?"

"Sort of. An interpreter. A freelancer, actually. For the BBC. That's the crew," I said, pointing to the tailgate party.

"Nice vehicle. What model is that?" he asked.

"I don't have the slightest idea," I answered honestly. He looked me over from head to toe as if to say "How could you not know what model of car you have?"

"I'm Wang Li," he said. "I'm from Xian. I give you this information." He handed me some scribbled ideographs on a crumpled sheet of paper.

"Listen, little Wang, you can call me Jin, *jin* as in gold. Jin Peili."

Taking a closer look at his notes, I could barely make out his writing, but there was a list of some place names, times, and dates.

"Thanks for the information, but the BBC does not usually have the time for a specific incident recorded in detail such as this."

"But isn't this news?"

"It may be," I said. "But TV news is, um, different. There's a lot of information that never makes it on air." He looked as disappointed as a puppy that had just returned a stick that its owner didn't want to throw anymore.

"This might be useful for a newspaper, but TV news is, well, forget it."

"Do you want more information?" he asked.

"Sure, let's keep in touch," I said, not sure if I meant it or not. I had met too many unusual characters lately, and some of them were so weird I had lost confidence in the cliché that a stranger was a friend I hadn't met yet.

"Okay, I tell you what," I said, trying not to sound too encouraging, "if you have some interesting news, you can call me at the Beijing Hotel. My room number is 1413. And how can I get in touch with you?"

"I am always here, on Tiananmen Square, with the provincial students," he said. "Just ask for Wang Li from Xian."

Later that evening he telephoned my room, waking me up.

"I'm Wang Li," a hoarse voice said. "I met you on the square. I have something very important to tell you."

"What time is it now?"

"12:15. I'm in the lobby coffee shop waiting for you."

"Okay, okay, I'll be right down."

Coffee shop? At this time of night? Not in the Beijing Hotel. This place closes down early. So what does he want? Food I can offer him, a place to stay? Well. Anticipating his request, I open the refrigerator and stuff all the food and drink I can squeeze in into my shoulder bag.

The lobby was dark and forbidding. The red carpet was inky, almost black. There were no attendants anywhere in sight. When I passed the decorative screen that was designed to keep ghosts out of the lobby I could see some people sitting in the empty coffee lounge. Four young men, no, it was three men and a woman sitting around a low round table masked in shadows. At an adjacent table I could see the silhouette of two young men. One of them leapt up and waved me over excitedly. It was Wang Li.

"*Jin, ni hao*," Wang Li said, approaching me with outstretched hands. "This is my friend Hu, he is also a student from Xian," he said. Hu and I said hello and shook hands while Wang Li fumbled nervously in his pockets for something. "Here are our student ID cards, I want you to trust us."

I scanned the cards briefly in the dim light and gave them back. I put the fruit juice and snacks on the table and took a seat.

"Jin, there is so much I have to tell you," Wang Li said, as if we were old friends.

"Have something to drink first," I insisted. He gave me a jagged piece of paper with notes scribbled on it. I couldn't help but notice that the coffee shop menu that lay open on the table was missing half a page whose jagged edges matched exactly the piece of paper he had just handed me.

Written in the coffee-stained margins next to "chilled lychees in syrup" and "yoghurt with honey" were scribbled the words "Liuliqiao, army troops, 70 civilians receive injury, tomorrow huge demonstration in protest."

Wang Li and Hu gulped down the juice and ravaged the snacks as if they had just ended a private hunger strike. While they ate, I looked at the other table, where a group of four young people were talking in low whispers next to the ornate ghost screen that blocked view from the entrance.

"Listen, troops have arrived northeast of Beijing. There are thousands of soldiers, tanks, and I heard there are trucks full of ammunition."

"How do you know?"

"We were there," he said. And then, anticipating further questions, he said, "We know a journalist needs evidence, so we want to go back and take pictures."

"Isn't that kind of risky?"

"No, we must do it, Jin. Can I borrow your camera?" He read the doubt on my face. "You can keep my ID card until I return with the camera."

"No, no, that's not necessary. I trust you." I said, using the immortal words of someone about to be conned, but actually I didn't trust him. If anything, his offer of the ID made me a little suspicious. If he were really a student why was he flashing his ID around? No one else did that.

"Thank you," he said, looking greatly relieved. "You are a friend."

"Where have you been sleeping?"

"On the square," he said.

"What about tonight?"

"No sleep. We will be out all night looking for troops."

"You have to get some sleep some time." I didn't have that kind of stamina or drive. I started to admire this guy's dedication to the cause.

"I'll tell you what, tomorrow you can shower and nap in my room if you want, okay?"

Even as the words left my mouth I wasn't sure why I made the offer, but it got me off the hook tonight. And I did feel for these ragamuffins. And we shared something in common; we were interested in finding out what was going on, but we weren't journalists. I couldn't forget how I was almost reduced to sleeping on the streets during the early vigils at Tiananmen.

"Can you give me some film, too?" he asked, revealing sharper bargaining skills as my skepticism softened.

"Yeah, okay. By the way," I asked, pointing to the figures in the shadows about twenty feet away, "who are those people sitting at the table over there?"

"They're our student leaders. That's Wang Dan, Wuerkaixi, Chai Ling, and Feng Congde."

"The student leaders?" I asked in disbelief. Wasn't this a government hotel?

We got up to leave. I walked past the other table to get a closer look. The quiet conference in progress momentarily went silent as we walked by. On the way out, I gave my camera to Wang Li, not sure if I'd see it or him again. Even so I felt a pang of guilt. Was it right for me to encourage him to go running after troops?

And what were the student leaders doing in the Beijing Hotel in the middle of the night? Was someone protecting them, did they have a powerful benefactor in the building? It was close to Tiananmen Square, and in a way, it was a good hideout. After all, who would expect to find them here? Like Shanghai in the thirties, where the underground Communists frequented the same bars, brothels, and hotels as the anti-Communist city bosses, Beijing was becoming a city of shadowy intrigue.

MAY 23

◑

Egg on the Face of Mao

Three days into martial law, the mood got nastier. It was getting tougher to do street interviews and I felt obliged to tell potential interviewees that we were doing unauthorized interviews and anything political that they said might get them into trouble. I don't think the BBC would have been happy if they knew I was sabotaging their interviews with my version of interviewee Miranda rights, but it seemed only fair. However, in my eagerness to strike up rapport and exchange information rather than just extract it, I probably talked too much. Chinese grow up with the habit of guarding information and not revealing any more than necessary.

"You shouldn't tell people you support the students!" Bright had scolded.

"All I said was that I thought the demonstrations were patriotic."

"That is supporting the students," she said. "You are not being careful enough."

"So, what's wrong with supporting the students? You do, don't you?"

Bright was not interested in lecturing me on journalistic ethics or the importance of being neutral. Her concern was practical. First, it was martial law and foreigners were forbidden to get involved, and second, "You don't know who you are talking to. Some of those people are informers. They come up to a news crew and act as if they are your friends," she explained. "Please. Especially at a time like this, you can't trust everyone."

"But you have to trust some people."

"You don't have to say anything," she emphasized, echoing a caution that was not in evidence when the demonstrations were at high tide. "I'm getting worried about you."

She was sounding more like my conservative friend Yao Xiaoping, who liked to tell me I didn't know what was going on. Stung by the criticism while inwardly recognizing that it was not without foundation, I decided to be more on guard. Inevitably, there were ordinary Chinese people who were happy that I could speak their language, and they wanted to know what I thought, what Americans thought, what the world thought about this historic moment. Yet the most prudent thing to do was to prepare a ready-made answer, the implications of which hurt me a little.

"This is an internal matter of the Chinese people; it is up to you to decide," I would endeavor to say from now on. "It's hard for us foreigners to understand."

I felt guilty for willfully adding my own brick to the wall of racial inscrutability, the age-old "we" and "them" dichotomy, even if only for temporary tactical reasons. As the risk inherent in talking politics with strangers increased, it seemed a good idea to save my political discussions for those whose acquaintance I had already made. After work, I invited Wang Li back to my room for a chance to rest and take a much-needed shower.

For a student who had been living by his wits on the mean streets of Beijing, he had surprisingly discriminating tastes. He took one look at the brittle bar of soap supplied by the Beijing Hotel and threw it on the tiled floor.

"Jin, this hotel soap is a joke!" he said with a superior air. "I have better soap. Let's use this." He pulled out a new bar of Camay soap from his bag.

"Sure, go ahead, take your shower first!" I said, curious about why a man who traveled with no luggage would be carrying a big bar of soap. Well, maybe he didn't know that Western-style hotels offered complimentary soap, I thought as I sat down to watch the CCTV news.

Wang Li monopolized the shower for almost an hour, his first chance to wash thoroughly since he arrived in Beijing. When it came to my turn, however, the bathroom was like a steam room, flooded with an inch-deep puddle of water on the tiled floor. He had neglected to pull the shower curtain and every one of the towels was soaking wet. Apparently the Camay connoisseur didn't know what a shower curtain was for.

The seemingly nonsensical words "Chairman Mao's portrait was attacked!" rang in the air the moment we stepped outside for an evening walk. In a blink we ran down to Tiananmen Square. Sure enough, old Mao had been defaced and disgraced. The famous visage was pockmarked with splotches of colored paint. A nervous swarm assembled to stare at the damaged icon. A few years back, such an act would have meant certain death. But nobody was sure what it meant in China today, let alone in the middle of an uprising.

We watched as a work crew with a huge crane arrived on the scene. As day yielded to night, the Tiananmen rostrum took on an unearthly glow. The lamps that normally illuminated the Mao portrait paled under the emergency crew spotlights and the incessant flashes of excited cameramen. Tiananmen, a veritable film set.

Who would have known there was a spare portrait, waiting and ready? Thirteen years after his death and nearly a decade after his wife was arrested, tried, and given a suspended death penalty, Mao's soft, doughy visage still commanded great reverence. Nearly every person I ever asked in China told me they thought Mao was good-looking. Many non-Chinese would agree if they saw photos of the dashing young revolutionary dating to the 1920s, but the Mao of the Mao portrait fame was more homely than handsome. Still, after a decade of dismantling the Mao personality cult—his statue had been wrapped in tarps and unceremoniously taken down in the middle of the night two years ago at Shida—the portrait at Tiananmen was deeply respected and almost sacrosanct.

As I forded westward through the mass of people assembled underneath the colossal portrait, I wondered what the cunning old fox would have made of the protests. Would he take the side of the radical students to smash his rivals, sealing their fate by appearing on the rostrum of Tiananmen, taking a symbolic headband from a hunger striker? He had the pluck, he had the nerve, and he thrived on chaos, unlike the clay-footed bureaucrats in charge of things today.

Was the knee-jerk nationalism of the students wearing thin? On May 4 they hounded a photographer to get off the frame of Sun Yatsen; what would they make of this?

The defacing of Mao did not precipitate student support. In a fit of self-preservation, student vigilantes apprehended three suspects and turned them over to the police, a hypocritical gesture since the students had been knocking down other myths and other icons on a daily basis. The spirit-dampening effect of martial law was beginning to have some effect. Perhaps the quick but callous response of the Beijing students to this crisis helped them buy more time. What sort of provocation would test them next? What would it take to turn the people of Beijing against the demonstrators who they affectionately called "our students"?

One of "our students" was in my room. After I treated him to a big meal, he had asked if he could take a nap, getting his foot in the door. In preparation for his nap, he cleared a little corner of the room for his modest earthly possessions: a pair of shoes and a small vinyl bag with two or three articles of clothing. After a week on the square living by his wits alone he was now sleeping on a full stomach in a real bed, snoring happily.

The new driver of the BBC van and I hit it off well enough that he offered me a free ride back to campus to get a change of clothes and I took him up on it. The university grounds were quiet and the air was noticeably fresher than downtown.

"Going to the square? We need a ride!" a group of young protesters loitering in the university district shouted to the van as we headed back downtown.

"I have a passenger, you must ask him," the driver answered, thoughtfully deferring the decision to me.

"Sure, come on in!" I said opening the sliding door before the van came to a halt. "Next stop, Tiananmen!"

The rowdy boys clambered in noisily and excitedly. "Thanks, it's a long way to walk."

"Hey, laowai, I mean, hey brother, haven't I seen you on the square?" one of the young men behind me shouted.

"You're a friend of Little Zhang, aren't you?" asked another.

"You mean the bodyguard?" I asked.

"Yeah, he's crazy, isn't he?" That's when I knew we were talking about the same person.

"Well, you know, we are from the Sports Institute," one of them explained. "We sportsmen are stronger than most, you see, so a lot of us work for student security."

Picking up the student hitchhikers turned out to be a good move, for we encountered half a dozen civilian-student–manned roadblocks during the long drive back into town. Rebel street vigilantes had only to poke their heads in the rolled-down window to get a whiff of the rebel power inside the van. Thanks to the headbands, the boisterous display of school spirit and exchange of rote slogans on the part of the gregarious athlete activists, we were given not only unfettered passage, but free advice about other barricades and reported troop movements. After exchanging expressions of solidarity, we were waved on like comrades. It wasn't about democracy, it wasn't about the hunger strike, it wasn't even about the students. It was about every uprising that China had ever had, it was the theme of every revolution everywhere.

"*Renmin Wansui!*" the volunteer guards shouted. "Long live the People!"

"Long live the People!" we shouted back. "Long live the People!"

MAY 24

◗

Tiananmen Headquarters

Gaining entry to the broadcast tent, nestled next to the monument in the center of occupied Tiananmen, was not easy. The tent was where the student leaders, now led by Chai Ling, mapped out strategies and made their broadcasts. Given the intense ad hoc security arrangements, entry was, in theory, invitation only, an honor of sorts. It was ground zero of the student command, the sanctum sanctorum, the general headquarters, the new Zhongnanhai, and it was closed to the public, even those ardent and selfless supporters encamped on the square who spent their days in a sweat and nights in a shiver, protecting the student command center with their bodies.

Once inside, however, I felt a bit like I'd just peeked behind the curtain at the Wizard of Oz. This was it? This was the projection booth responsible for the amazing, rainbow-hued phantasmagoria outside that only days before involved the choreography of a million obedient souls?

The inner sanctum itself was slummy-looking, a modest patchwork of canvas and tarps mounted on poles nestled up against an angular recess in the marble pedestal of the Martyrs' Monument, but its centrality was not to be underestimated. Spending the afternoon inside the tent gave me a vivid sense of how hierarchical things were getting, how overwhelming the scale was becoming, how raw and apparently arbitrary was the power that emanated from this ad hoc command center in the heart of Tiananmen Square. The most obvious trapping of power, with parallels to both gang organizations and legitimate governments, could be seen in the plethora of security guards who controlled access and watched my every move. The broadcast tent was not much to look at, but crucial decisions hammered out here were disseminated to tens of thousands by loudspeaker, printed handouts, and word of mouth.

A portable generator rigged up just north of the tent sputtered and growled, supplying power for announcements, radio, and lights. Matching signs announced NO SMOKING and NO PHOTOS, as if the two prohibitions were somehow related. The smoking ban was judicious as there were containers of kerosene stored adjacent to the flammable tent. Despite the sensible warning there were a few rules-are-for-other-people types smoking away in defiance of their own edict. I pulled out my camera to see if perhaps the rules were not being enforced. I was sternly and unambiguously instructed not to take pictures and had to put it away. While waiting for permission to enter, I had to stand around conspicuously in front of the tent on a rarified patch of empty pavement with a thousand eyes on my back. The strictly guarded sterile zone in front of the tent, roped off and maintained despite the press of the crowd and inevitable shoving matches, was like a square within the square, an empty ceremonial space imbued with symbolic power. It was the undemocratic center command of the democracy movement, shrouded in security and secrecy, riddled with intrigue and infighting.

Then, with a silent hush as if an imperial audience were about to begin, a series of student bodyguards waved me on, ushering me into the "studio," the China Broadcast Station of the Tiananmen nation. Stooping to step inside the low-slung tent, the first thing that caught my eye was a portrait of Mao displayed next to decks of electronic broadcasting equipment. The painted likeness of Mao was based on a well-known photograph of the great leader as a young revolutionary. In the spirit of the tacky personality cult of the Cultural Revolution era, it portrayed the handsome demigod against a solid red background. Were the students closet Maoists? Or was it some kind of inside joke? A good-luck totem, perhaps?

The portrait was hung respectfully in the center of the tent, much as it might have been had these students been Red Guards making revolution in 1966. If the kitschy painting was a period piece from the 1960s, then the painted plate was at least as old as the students who had put it up in the tent for inspiration.

"So why do you have a picture of Mao up there?" I asked a bodyguard.

"Oh, Mao? We just put him there just for the fun of it. It's our way of showing our discontent with Deng," he said with a jocular laugh. "But China does need a great leader."

Maybe there was a yearning for a great leader. I heard similar sentiments during Gorbachev's visit and I had seen ample evidence of "sixties nostalgia" in the use of Mao and Zhou portraits during the big demonstrations last week. In a way, the humble broadcast tent was this generation's equivalent of the homely Yan'an caves that once housed Mao and the fledgling revolutionary leadership.

A bare lightbulb illuminated the cluttered interior of the lean-to tent that was nestled comfortably in an indented corner of the monument at ground level, where the white marble facade met the gray stone pedestal of the monument. The south and east walls of the shelter were composed of canvas. The sturdy north and west sides utilized the fastness of the marble monument itself. The stone-slab pedestal of the monument, which rose about four feet off the ground, was wider than the decorative marble structure that it supported. This created a ledge that gave the tent instant bookshelves, filled with bric-a-brac worthy of a home. The ledge was cluttered with assorted odds and ends ranging from a bouquet of flowers in an empty Coke bottle to packets of medicine, printing supplies, crumpled paper, and piles of hand-printed reports.

Two banks of brand new amplifiers were stacked four or five high, nestled against the marble wall. The amps looked like store-bought stereo equipment. They were plugged into a socket mounted on the wall that led to the generator in a tangle of wires. The student announcers, squeezed next to each other on a narrow cot against the marble wall, handed back and forth a bouquet of microphones strapped together with tape. They spoke stridently, in that kind of orthodox radio voice, not half as gentle and mellifluous as Shen Baoqing from China Radio. What, would their political team also take issue with "dark, night images" of Tiananmen?

But I didn't ask any questions. A woman and two men, both of whom looked to be around my age, sat on the cot going over scripts for the next announcement. Sitting next to the radio equipment was yet another woman who also looked to be in her early thirties. So this was a bit more than a student movement. But who was she? It was possible she was merely a graduate student or a sympathetic faculty advisor, but it struck me as possible that she might be a link to someone high up in the government.

The broadcast tent propaganda crew were preoccupied with writing, editing, and reading "official" announcements, but every once in a while one of them smiled or otherwise acknowledged my presence. One of them kindly suggested I could take a nap, offering genuine make-yourself-at-home hospitality in spite of the tense and cramped work conditions. Although I seriously doubted that I could sleep in the middle of such hubbub, with tens of thousands more milling around outside, the air was hot and stuffy and I was tempted by the offer. After politely refusing to monopolize the cot and displace others, I settled for an open space on the cot that lined the east wall of this makeshift studio. Given the womblike embrace of the tent, I felt safe and secure, even though I was surrounded by thousands of what the government now characterized as "thugs and rioters" in the middle of an illegal encampment in a city under siege.

MAY 26

◑

Radical Camp

On May 26, I got another glimpse of student command central when Shida graduate student Chai Ling was at the height of her power. She was holding court in the broadcast tent, the ideological hothouse of student-occupied Tiananmen Square. It wasn't easy getting in. I had to pass three rings of student security to secure an "audience."

The BBC had yet to give me any kind of ID, so I learned to talk my way into things. My only press pass was my wit, which worked okay because I liked to talk and could do so in Chinese. There were times when the well-known call letters BBC did not suffice to gain entry, while merely saying I was looking for a friend from Shida might do the trick. The closer I got to the student center, the higher the likelihood I'd run into someone who'd seen me before, which also helped expedite entry. I could remember most of the faces if not names of the hundreds I'd spoken to in the last few weeks, so overall I had a high degree of mobility on the cordoned-off, student-controlled square.

As a provincial student leader, self-appointed or otherwise, Wang Li expected and obtained a certain amount of access to the Beijing student command center at the broadcast tent. What Wang Li lacked in social cachet as an unknown provincial student from Xian I think he started to make up for by speaking on behalf of the BBC, since he was staying in my room and doing errands for BBC, and knew he could impress fellow students with his important international connections. Student security guards were vigilant about keeping ordinary Chinese away from their "leaders," but by claiming to be a student leader or media person, many of the petty controls could be circumvented.

186

Wang Li put in a word for me with the provincial students, but they seemed terribly disorganized and no interviews or memorable conversations came out of that effort. After jointly touring the provincial student outpost near the museum, we cut west and headed towards the broadcast tent in the center of the square. The amateur security got woollier and woollier as we pushed towards the center, so we temporarily split up when he got permission to enter a controlled area that I couldn't enter. Wang Li rushed ahead on his own to see if he could find a student leader willing to talk to me. In the meantime, I decided to wing it, slowly working my way past various student gatekeepers until I ran into a familiar face from the Sports Institute.

"Hey Jin," yelled a boisterous baritone, "what are you doing here? Good to see you, come over here!" It was Crazy Zhang.

When he got within arm's length he gave me a few friendly punches that actually hurt. He wasn't called crazy for no reason. The last time I saw him he was wearing a khaki green cap with a red headband around it.

"Go fight someone else!" I shoved him back.

"Better not try anything or I'll have to throw you out of here," he said with a straight face.

The smart-aleck muscle man grabbed me by the arm and led me up the north steps of the monument's marble base past a guarded security rope. He directed me to descend the steps on the east side of the monument to a roped-off area from which it was possible to enter the broadcast tent. When I got inside that zone, I found Wang Li standing outside the tent. He waved me over with his usual sense of urgency.

"I'll leave you here," said Zhang, this time with a gentle pat on the back instead of a threatening punch. "See you later."

Wang Li ran over excitedly, barely avoiding a confrontation with the solidly built Zhang.

"Jin!"

"What is it?" I asked.

"Come now!" he said excitedly, "Chai Ling, she wants to talk to you."

"Chai Ling? Where is she?"

"By the tent," he shouted. Since we were both already inside the innermost perimeter, it was just a matter of turning the corner of the monument to reach the entrance of the broadcast tent.

There she was, the queen bee in the middle of a humming hive. She was petite and pert, wearing a loose-fitting white sports shirt with sunglasses hanging on her collar. She smiled in greeting when she saw me approach, but didn't say anything. There were people on her left and people on her right and from the looks of it they all wanted a piece of her. There were excited discussions about some pressing matter or another, but I couldn't hear very well because a noisy diesel generator was roaring just a few feet away. Just as I was about to ask her a question, she was called away, disappearing for a few minutes into the shadows of the truck-sized tent.

The petite, bronze-faced leader popped in and out of the broadcast tent a half a dozen times in as many minutes while attending to the minutiae of running the tent city of Tiananmen Square. Behind a well-secured safety rope was yet another group of student supplicants bearing urgent requests. There was that precious patch of empty ground in front of the broadcast tent where I thought I might hold a quick interview, if one didn't mind the hundreds of onlookers just a few feet away on the other side of the rope. I could already feel the heat of open-mouthed stares building up. Who is the laowai and what is he doing on the inside?

This was the command center, where strategic decisions were made and announcements broadcast to a mere tens of thousands on a slow day like today, or perhaps a million during the high tide of the movement. With crowds that size, it was unimaginable to have no governing structure, so the idea of student leaders fit the bill, even if their powers were largely imaginary.

Deep in the throng of wannabes who did not have permission to enter the command center were three familiar white faces: Eric, Fred, and Brian. Being good journalists, they didn't take no for an answer. They wanted in.

When the usual "We're BBC!" didn't work its charm, they started pointing to me, as much a ruse to slip in as a bid to get my attention. They were turned back, however, and there wasn't much I could do about it. To make matters worse, a student warden asked me to translate, leaving it to me to say, "It is not allowed to go inside the rope without special permission."

Rather than say that, I just hinted to the crew that I was working on it and went back to the leadership tent to see if I could arrange something. I stood around, baking in the heat of the sun and soaking up unwanted glances, until Chai Ling finally walked over and offered me her hand.

"*Ni hao*," she said, stepping forward to greet me.

"*Ni hao.* You're at Shida, right?"

"Yes, graduate student, educational psychology."

"Do you know the service building? You know, the Insider Guest House above the campus store . . . "

"I know that building. You speak Chinese very well."

We were interrupted by a young man who whispered to Chai Ling a flurry of messages and handed her some hand-scribbled notes on onionskin paper. The exchange went on for a few minutes, then the young man withdrew back into the tent. She turned around to resume our chat, apologizing with a weak smile. She was sunburned and looked tired. I started to have my doubts about arranging an interview.

"Maybe I can talk to you somewhere else, some other time."

"Now is fine, but I only have a few minutes."

"Is it okay for them, um, you see my BBC friends, over there, for them to come in here? We can set up the camera right here."

"You can do that," she replied. Wang Li heard the word and went to give the crew a thumbs-up. When Chai Ling got called aside to attend to some business, I helped the crew get inside the rope.

"What's going on, Phil?" Brian asked impatiently.

I explained that one of the top student leaders had agreed to talk to us.

"Why don't we set it up over here?" I pointed to the "front gate" of the tent and Eric and Fred went to work. Held back by a human chain of interlocked arms, student guards, and rope, the curious throng strained to get a glimpse of news in the making. It was a relief to have student security handling crowd control this time around.

But allowing a foreign news crew to enter the "VIP" zone just added to the air of intrigue. Several Europeans with cameras tried to sneak into the command center by following on the coattails of the BBC crew, but they were all stopped by truculent student guards and turned back. Some of them started to make a scene, yelling angrily in English. Making a pretense of protocol and to indulge student illusions of control, journalists had in recent days gotten into the habit of flashing any old ID cards before walking into student-controlled areas loaded with cameras and recording equipment. But that gambit didn't work this time.

"Vie kant vee go in?" pleaded one of the Europeans.

"Vee also are from zee press!" his companion added.

"Vie you let zem in?" the first man complained. "It is not fair is it?"

Unlike our tension-fraught visit to the water strikers last week, this time the BBC was on the inside and our "competition" was left dangling on the other side of the ropes. As for my colleagues, who knew very well what it was like to be excluded, I could detect not an ounce of sympathy for those left on the outside.

Foreign newsmen at Tiananmen were generally supportive of the democratic tide but not one another. By now even student media handlers like Wang Li knew the value of exclusive access, and the access game worked both ways. Some journalists had been to Tiananmen every day, and not without justification could they feel indignant at being refused access or having to settle for reduced access.

After some heated deliberation, the student guards agreed to allow a single photographer to come in, but not the two complainers with video gear. Instead, a photographer from *Vogue*, French edition, was escorted in and immediately started snapping pictures. At one point he turned to me to ask some questions about Chai Ling. He said he was working on a story titled "Role Model for a Generation of Women."

By the time the BBC had set up the camera, Chai Ling was back. The generation/gender role model and I did a short preinterview chat while the French photographer did his thing. She and I talked about the relative merits of Shida and Beida. She liked both campuses, but she had joined Beida's hunger-strike committee because she had more friends there.

Eric gave the signal that the Beeb was ready to roll. I had suggested to Chai Ling that we do an informal interview, hoping we could get a few candid comments on tape without a formal setup, but Brian had different ideas.

"Move out of the way, Phil!" he said, nudging me to the side to take a stand between the two of us.

"What do you mean?" I said, trying to regain my footing. "I'm talking to her."

"I do the talking, Phil!" he said. "Okay Eric, start rolling."

I stepped back dejected but not defeated. I watched Brian talk, then gesticulate, then resort to primitive pantomime, as Chai Ling was not able or willing to converse in English. Seemingly oblivious to the language gap, he went on doing this for a few minutes, getting lots of puzzled looks but no words in response. Chai Ling looked at me, then at him, and back at me again. Brian threw up his hands in frustration and walked away.

"Turn off the camera!" he instructed Eric, then turned to me. "Listen, will you? We need someone who speaks English."

While the BBC reporter paced about impatiently, apparently looking for another interview, Chai Ling resumed talking to me with rapid-fire delivery, telling me things I hadn't even asked about. She started to give a very emotional account of her involvement in the movement. I don't think she knew much about video recording and perhaps she did not care, because the camera was not rolling. It wasn't even mounted on the tripod anymore. I detected pain in her expression and listened intently, trying not to be distracted by the mumbling and grumbling behind me to the right. She kept on talking and I kept on listening.

Out of the corner of my eye I could sense the crew was busy, probably packing up, but I did not break eye contact because I wanted hear what this intense young woman had to say. There was something dark and troubling in her countenance.

She continued to pour her heart out. After a few minutes, I realized that the film crew had not in any case just stepped back to change tapes or put in a new battery. Going, going, gone. They wrapped in a huff and disappeared without saying a word.

Chai Ling and I shared the mutual embarrassment of having an interview fall apart even as we spoke, leading us both to shrug our shoulders and laugh.

She continued talking politics, in a low voice but with great energy and emotion, telling me the student movement had come to a crucial turning point. The future was full of uncertainty. There were serious conflicts between rival student groups. The Beijing students were tired but tempered from weeks of demos and the hunger strike. It was the provincial students, relatively late arrivals, who were pushing for action. Chai Ling said there was a plot to destroy the movement and she didn't know who to trust anymore. She spoke of betrayal, of fear, and of her sense of responsibility as a leader. We were interrupted again, this time by a student messenger. Upon the receipt of some urgent communiqué, she turned to me and said she had to go, asking how to get in touch.

"*Bei-jing Fan-dian*, 1413," I said, giving her my room number at the hotel.

"I want to talk more," she said with a soft-spoken intensity. "Can I trust you?"

I waited for her to say more, trying to understand.

"I want to run away . . . " she said.

"What?"

"It is getting very dangerous!"

"Yes, you should be more careful," I said. "But what did you say, run away?"

"A Chinese person told me that the British embassy is offering political asylum to student activists. What do you think about that?"

"I don't know," I said. "It's possible, but not likely. Who told you that?"

"I think it may be a trap."

"I just don't know."

"Can you ask about that for me?"

I told her I didn't know anyone at the British embassy but I said that maybe one of my "good friends" at the BBC did. Then I added my own advice. "Be careful about dealing with foreign embassies. If you go to a big embassy, it could be used against you politically. Maybe the embassy of a small, neutral country is better."

If she went to the US embassy I was afraid she would become a political pawn in US-China relations. I didn't think that the British embassy would be any better. Worse yet, what if it was a trap? What if the asylum offer had been made by an undercover agent, a trap set by Chinese police to discredit the nationalism of the students?

"Jin, I must go now," she said. "See you again!"

"Yes, it was good talking to you. *Xiao xin!*" I added, urging her to take care as she fell into a huddle with her comrades. "Be careful!"

I wanted to see her again. She impressed me as being sincere and passionate, but she was also deeply worried. Something about her embassy escape plans troubled me. Getting mixed up with foreign intelligence agencies was a slippery slope if there ever was one. Just the thought of it depressed me.

What was my proper role in all of this? I had started out as a demonstrator, then started freelancing for foreign media. Where ought one to draw the line of involvement? If I did nothing, I would be forsaking my belief in the universality of the human condition, but if I went too far I could be accused of interfering in another nation's domestic dispute.

Ever since I started to do freelance work with television news crews in 1986 I had been dogged with the accusation, sometimes uttered to my face but most often behind my back, that I must be some kind of spy. When I worked for NBC, the rumor got back to me that I was working for Chinese intelligence. Laughable perhaps, but speaking more than one Asian language made me a veritable poster boy for the CIA. Even taxi drivers had asked me if I was a spy.

Such misperceptions are an especially thorny problem for conscientious journalists, for whom trust and ethical concerns are paramount. Under the direction of President Jimmy Carter, the U.S. intelligence agencies pledged not to use journalistic cover for espionage, but Britain, for example, has no such restrictions, and one would hear jokes about the presence of MI6 even among BBC staffers. The journalist and spy shared a similar thirst for information, any and all information, but were guided by entirely different sets of ethics and priorities.

It wasn't just Bright bugging me about the BBC. I had my own doubts about wearing the occupational tag of journalist precisely because it overlapped—in the popular imagination if not in reality—with espionage. How do you prove you are not?

To go around denying it would be to "protest too loudly." To ignore it was one tactic, but that did not stop the whispers. It did not stop the suspicious gaze of real spies, which the Chinese bureaucracy, with few apparent moral qualms, routinely dispatched under the cover of interpreters, office assistants, drivers, strangers in the street, and of course journalists.

So what was I? Not a tourist, not a translator, not a journalist, not even a currently registered graduate student, but simply an observer. Recalling what Bright's father had said, I fortified my resolve. As nothing more or less than a witness to history, I had a right to be on Tiananmen Square.

I found Brian with the crew on the other side of the monument taking pictures of red flags, banners, and other things that were, well, colorful, but superficial. They hadn't missed me much; in fact, I had been made redundant the moment the BBC had finally found the broadcaster's holy grail, an English speaker willing to provide a string of sound bites for the evening news. They had set up the camera to record the performance of a likeable eccentric who was guaranteed to get a few chuckles back in England. Speaking before a curious impromptu gathering, a fellow Yankee, an orator told anyone who would listen—and the BBC was all ears—that he was here at Tiananmen Square representing the "People's Republic of Santa Monica." The wacky, self-appointed ambassador said that his people's republic supported the student movement and that "democracy is very important."

By now it was obvious there was a not-so-subtle linguistic imperialism in the BBC's news work, and the American networks weren't notably different. Better to have an irrelevant quote in English than a pertinent quote in Chinese. In this respect, Japanese television news had the right idea. They almost always interviewed people in their native languages and translated it with voiceovers or Japanese subtitles.

That an easygoing English-speaking tourist had a better chance of making it on the evening news than the imperiled leader of the world's biggest student demonstration illustrated the tendency to ascribe to one's native tongue a reality that foreign languages were somehow imputed to lack. It also showed how easily the medium of television could confuse news with entertainment.

Last Will and Testament

A petite sun-bronzed woman wearing a stained white tennis shirt and dusty beige trousers sits next to me in the back of the taxi, grimacing as if in pain, weeping quietly to herself. Named to the police blacklist, she says she fears imminent arrest. Up front, the driver sullenly surveys the streets, scanning the road for Public Security vehicles.

As the car glides down a leafy thoroughfare in the diplomatic district, Wang Li, who had been chatting quietly with the driver, turns around to make an announcement.

"The driver supports the students," he says. "He will help us."

"How do you know?" I ask.

"I know. Where you go?" he asks, switching into English.

"Tell him, let's see . . . I don't know, I just don't know."

Chai Ling, the so-called commander in chief of Tiananmen Square, had come to me this morning saying she wanted to "talk," but for the moment I couldn't get a word out of her. I had brought a small tape recorder and camera along as part of my hasty response to the startling and unsolicited request for an interview, but we had yet to find a safe place to talk.

A graduate student from Shandong studying psychology at Shida, she rose to sudden prominence during the world's biggest hunger strike. This morning she had approached me in the hallway of the Beijing Hotel as I was on my way to breakfast. It was so weird seeing her there, a fugitive from the police hiding in plain sight in a government hotel lobby. I naively invited her to join Bright, Wang Li, and myself for breakfast in the Western Restaurant in the old wing of the hotel. But this wasn't a Long Island kind of problem that could be worked out in a diner over a cup of coffee, bacon, eggs, and toast.

Face drawn with tension, almost morbidly silent, the famous hunger striker, who barely gave her food a second glance, explained in a low whisper that she wanted to record some kind of final statement, a sort of last will and testament. I looked at Bright, who declined to offer an opinion, though her eyes implored me not to get involved.

I got involved, mostly out of curiosity. It didn't make for a leisurely breakfast, and it left Bright, who had just come to see me, in the lurch, for in no time I was trying to secure a taxi at the front door of the hotel. Chai Ling had so far escaped the notice of the police, but not a group of hawkeyed journalists from Hong Kong, one of whom recognized her as the Tiananmen commander and begged to join us. There wasn't enough room in the taxi, so Bright, who was already less than enthused about radical student politics, offered her seat to Patricia, the Hong Kong journalist, and then we were off.

Now we were on the road. Where to, nobody knew.

"Let's go northeast," I suggest. "Take the road by Worker's Stadium, then go to the Great Wall Hotel, you know, around there. Do a big circle around the whole embassy district, okay, we just want to drive around for a while, okay?"

What should we do now? If the fugitive pressing against me in the backseat is truly in danger of arrest, maybe we should go further out of town. In any case, we can stay on the road for a while. The taxi is not cheap, but if no place is safe, is it not better to keep moving?

"If policeman follow," Wang Li says, turning around to peer at us, "I tell you, okay?"

He is speaking English again. What is it with his sudden switch? Who is he trying to impress?

"Where is camera?" he asks a moment later, and then I understand. He, a mere student at some kind of culinary school in the provinces, is trying to impress Chai Ling, the radical diva from Shida, who has already bagged a degree from Beida.

No sooner had I handed him my pocket-sized Olympus than he started snapping away with dramatic flair, as if he were a hotshot photojournalist.

While the driver patiently snaked up and down the leafy boulevards of Sanlitun, I suggested to the conspicuously silent woman warrior sitting next to me that we talk now, in the car, but she recoiled from the idea. True, some taxis were bugged, but the odds of that were slim. True, the car was probably too noisy to make a decent recording, but what was all this about, anyway? Even if the driver was later quizzed about suspicious passengers and duly filed a report on us, we would be somewhere else, sight unseen.

Despite Wang Li's eagle-eyed examination of cars going our way, he didn't think we were being followed. For the last few weeks, Beijing's secret police had been slacking off on the job, at least, it seemed that way. It was enough to make one believe in rumors; either politburo member Qiao Shi and his Public Security Bureau were sympathetic to the students or the pullback of policing was a deliberate trap.

Chai Ling, lost in a silence so deep that she seemed almost voiceless, quietly vetoed the idea of doing an interview in the car. Instead of talking, she penned a stark message on a piece of scrap paper:

"This may be my last chance to talk, I entrust (Jin Peili) Philip Cunningham to tell my story to the Chinese people of the world.

—Chai Ling, MAY 28, 1989 10:25 AM"

Her extended silence gave me time to contemplate the import of the note. I was both moved and disturbed that someone in fear of her life wanted me to speak "to the Chinese people of the world" on her behalf.

Holding in my sweaty palm what was essentially a last will and testament made me realize how quickly the tables had turned. Was this the same defiant young rebel who had risen to prominence during the hunger strike, supported by enthusiastic crowds of a million or more? Was this leader of the square, the strident voice of the public address system, the Joan of Arc of the movement who refused to talk to journalists?

Little of that was evident now. The intense young woman sidled up next to me in the back of the taxi was in a deep funk, vulnerable, isolated in her own heavy thoughts; the only ambition she betrayed was her quiet persistence in trying to arrange an interview.

"So, where are you going?" the taxi driver asks, shooting me an impatient look in the mirror. For all of Wang Li's shenanigans, he has failed to impress even the driver. It is also safe to assume that the driver expects me to do the paying, in FEC of course. But if he were greedy, he wouldn't have minded the last half an hour of going in circles. What he minds is the lack of clarity about our destination.

"I'm thinking," I answer. "Just go north for a while."

All I knew was that we had to get away from the omnipresent gaze of the state security apparatus. I gave the driver some seemingly firm coordinates, north, east, north, east, as I needed to keep him busy until I could come up with a safe destination. It was against the rules of martial law for journalists to interview student leaders, and I wasn't even on a work visa. I'd been arrested before for activities inappropriate for a foreigner and didn't relish being taken into custody again. Where could we do such an interview? I leaned forward, face in my hands, unsure of what to do next.

The temporary BBC office in the Great Wall Hotel came to mind, but it was a day too late, because yesterday was my last day working for them. And the BBC's London-centric producers were not exactly sensitive to things I cared about. For one, they struck me as nonchalant if not naïve about the degree of government surveillance that they themselves were under and the possible impact it might have on any Chinese who visited their well-watched offices. I knew better than to bring apolitical friends into such a fishbowl environment, let alone a student rebel on the police blacklist.

The American TV news outfits had similar security problems. Although I knew Eric Baculino, a former student radical from the Philippines, would be interested, NBC's office was no place to bring a fugitive from the police; they were located in the belly of the beast, renting facilities inside the state-run CCTV television center. CBS News had chosen to set up camp way out in the west Beijing boondocks, ensconced in the comfortable but remote Shangri-La Hotel, while CNN and ABC at least had the advantage of being on this side of town. But taking Chai Ling to a news bureau full of official snoopers and electronic surveillance was risky if not stupid. We had to go somewhere unofficial, somewhere off the map. The kind of place I'd take a friend, the kind of place I'd be comfortable taking a date.

"That's it! I know a place!" I announce, giving the driver directions to an expatriate apartment complex out on Airport Road. If we got past the front gate and then past the doorman in my friend's apartment block, we'd be okay.

The car picked up speed. After half an hour of random turns and amateur plotting on the part of the unusual collection of passengers, the driver was relieved to get some concrete instructions so he could be rid of us.

Finding an unmonitored residential location where foreigners and Chinese could mix without being carded and closely observed by guards at the door was a habitual problem in Beijing, especially vexing for stubborn believers in free cultural exchange like myself. Things were basically set up so that foreigners could socialize with other foreigners, tourists with tourists, and Chinese with Chinese. Maybe we could make that work for us.

On this day our group defied easy categorization, composed as it was of two Chinese citizens, one a fugitive listed on a police most-wanted list, the other a young rebel not nearly as well known as he wanted to be, and two non-Chinese, an aggressive Hong Kong reporter and an American freelancer less than enthusiastic about playing journalist with police on our tail.

In a way I was the most obvious problem. Being the only laowai made me a lightning rod for attention. Caucasians in China, whether newly arrived or resident for decades, did not have the option of disappearing like a fish in the sea of the people. We were rather more akin to lighthouses, forever emitting signals that revealed our presence.

So, the best way to become less glaringly obvious was to find an enclave where there were lots of other equally distracting people, such as a suburban hotel designated for foreigners or an expatriate residential compound.

I chose the latter. Living in gritty Beijing had given me some practical experience in seeking out comfort zones. Wanting to avoid the watchful gaze of the police rarely had anything to do with politics. It was more a question of pride, an effort to establish a sense of human dignity and to lead a half-normal social life. While I was aware that even native Chinese couples had problems of their own finding privacy, at least they could meet with relative anonymity in an apartment block or even in a gated park, whereas a mixed couple was an easy target for neighborhood snoops and zealous watchmen.

One place where I had found a semblance of normalcy on previous occasions was the Lido Hotel and its associated apartment complex, located on the northeast edge of town. Though the Lido was technically restricted to foreign passport holders, it had a large ethnic Chinese population from overseas and it was easy enough to bring Chinese friends inside to use the pool and eat in the restaurants there. Bright and Jenny both liked it; they found it less intimidating than the grander hotels. But it was still a hotel.

As the driver approached the Lido, I advised him not to enter by the hotel gate but instead to go around to the back in order to directly enter the apartment complex. The driver paused at the rear gate while the sleepy guard gave us a brief visual inspection. Waved through without incident, we all breathed a bit easier once inside the compound. I had the driver follow the meandering course of a private drive that led us past a pair of empty tennis courts adjacent to a low-rise apartment block.

Wang Li and I briefly discussed the merits of keeping the car, since taxis were a rarity except at the big hotels and a new one might be hard to find. But the driver had no interest in waiting, so I paid him and he sped off. If he were to be questioned, he could always plead ignorance.

I lead the way, taking a deliberately roundabout course to make sure we weren't being followed and detouring past some well-stocked shops, including a pharmacy and a grocery carrying pricey imported goods from Europe, Hong Kong, and America. As we walked past window displays and shelves stocked with consumer items that most Chinese could only dream about, Wang Li paused to clean his smudged glasses for a better look. I could tell he liked the place already.

Adjacent to the shopping wing of the Lido was a quiet path leading to the low-rise tower where Lotus and Albert lived. Wang Li sidled up to me as he surveyed the premises with interest. "Almost no Chinese around," he exclaimed, nodding his head in approval. Chai Ling and the Hong Kong journalist, both about the same height with hair about the same length, followed silently a few steps behind, like traditional women.

I shepherd our group past the front desk of the "foreigners-only" apartment building, hoping it won't be necessary to answer any questions, but if it is, it will fall on me to do all the talking.

As luck has it, the doorman is not at his station, so we easily slip into the dark lobby and hurry into a waiting elevator. I hear the guard returning to his post just as the elevator door closes. So far, so good. By force of habit, I check the ceiling of the elevator for the familiar protruding lens of the surveillance camera, usually wedged in the corner, but there is no sign of that.

We get out on the top floor and I run ahead to the door of Lotus and Albert's apartment, knocking excitedly. The door opens a crack.

"Who's there?" asks Lotus, clearly not expecting company.

"It's me, the homeless traveler," I say, joking so as not to raise alarm. The chain is undone and the door opens wide.

Lotus smiles warmly. "Philip! Good to see you!" she exclaims buoyantly. "I see you brought some friends. Come in. Welcome everyone. Come in!"

She greets me with her customary bear hug. "You just missed Al. He went out to play basketball with Justin."

"Lotus," I start, "I gotta talk to you. We have an unusual situation here."

"That can wait, Philip, first things first."

Lotus was possessed with the angelic patience of motherhood, the nonstop experience in dealing with unusual situations. She gave my disheveled friends an approving look and greeted each of them warmly in Chinese. She knew the face of someone in trouble when she saw it, and put her arm around the gaunt, almost catatonic Chai Ling as if to comfort her before I even had a chance to make introductions.

"Come on, come on inside!" she said. "Don't be so polite! You all look so hot and tired. Let me fix you something to drink."

"Lotus, this is Chai Ling, a student leader from Tiananmen . . . "

To Lotus the name or fame of a person mattered not a bit. But the fact that I brought along a protester from Tiananmen Square did. Lotus, still a sixties activist at heart and a true believer in people power, the power of ordinary, everyday people, that is, had been an enthusiastic observer of the demonstrations since the students started marching.

She had us sit down in the American-style dining room while she scurried about the kitchen, putting the kettle on and preparing some snacks. Wang Li scrutinized the apartment intently. Was he judging it for security features or just trying to sate his unquenchable curiosity about the world of luxury and privilege behind high walls, a world from which ordinary Chinese were normally barred? Unable to remain still for long, he leapt up and joined Lotus in the kitchen to get a closer look at some of the modern, imported appliances.

When Lotus tried to make some small talk in Chinese, she used a motherly tone of voice that reminded me of the way she spoke to her daughter in front of guests.

"Philip has many Chinese friends. Even though he is a foreigner, a white foreigner, he likes to be with Chinese people." She went on and on, sometimes switching to Mandarin, her accent even more heavily Cantonese-inflected than that of the junior journalist from Hong Kong.

"Lotus, come on already!" I was impatient, not only because I'd heard this description a dozen times before, but because we had more important things to worry about.

"This girl, I mean this woman, is on the run," I explained, imploring Lotus to give me her full attention. "She wants to talk about something, something serious."

Lotus looked at me with a quizzical smile, not fully comprehending.

"Sorry, I don't know if it was a good idea to bring her here, but we are really in a bind. I hope this doesn't get you into trouble, at least I don't think we were followed."

My friend in need read between the lines expertly. "Are you asking me if this place is bugged? The apartment I don't know, probably not. But the telephone? Yes."

"I don't want to get you and Al in trouble. I mean, he works for a big company, you've got your family here. This could be a bit risky."

Lotus and Al, like many of their peers from the top of the baby-boomer generation, enjoyed a solid income from the corporate world but still had a lingering fondness for radical causes. And they were sincere about it.

"Look, what are friends for? I want you to relax with your friends for a minute. I will talk to Al when he gets back."

"Where can we talk?"

"Just make yourselves at home," she answered.

"Boy, it's noisy here. What's that outside? Construction or something?" As I pulled the small handheld tape recorder out of my bag I realized with some disappointment that we had traveled a long way only to find a noisy location. "I want to do a taped interview."

"Nia's room is quiet," Lotus volunteered. Nia, whose name was inspired by the word *Tanzania* in recognition of early Chinese Communist efforts at diplomatic outreach to Africa, was just getting into her teenage years.

Lotus knocked tentatively on the door of her daughter's room. "Nia? Can you come out for a minute? I'd like you to say hello to Uncle Philip and his friends."

Nia reluctantly emerged, mumbled a shy hello, and ran back into her room, closing the door.

"Uncle Philip and his friends would like to talk in your room," Lotus added, trying to coax her pretty teenager out of her private fortress. "Is that okay, honey?"

The door popped open a crack and Nia peeked out, as if in partial acquiescence to her mother's request, but the look on her face indicated it was anything but okay. She was probably wondering why Uncle Philip and the visitors couldn't just talk in the living room like regular grown-ups did.

"Nia, please come into the kitchen. I want to talk with you about something," Lotus insisted. As soon as the teenager was pried from her room, we got the green light. "Okay, guys, go ahead. Sit down inside, sit down! Nia said you can borrow her room. Right, Nia?"

We awkwardly filed into the small bedroom, acutely aware we were invading the private realm of a teenage princess. There were dolls and teddy bears, a McDonald's poster, an unmade bed of pastel sheets, and an armchair.

"Everything okay?" Lotus inquires.

"I guess so, um-huh."

"Just a minute!" Lotus disappears, seeking to placate Nia, who is understandably confused.

After getting Nia settled in the living room to watch TV, Lotus busies herself in the kitchen. "That's a good girl," I hear her say to her daughter before she comes back to us with a tray of sliced oranges. "Sorry I don't have anything better than this."

"Oh, thanks," I say, taking the tray and putting it down.

"Philip?" Lotus says with a touch of admonishment. "Why don't you serve these to your friends?"

"Thanks, of course," I pass the orange slices around, then ask Lotus if I can borrow her video camera.

"You want the Handycam? You're lucky. I just charged the batteries. They will last for two hours. Is that long enough?"

"I certainly hope so," I answer with a laugh. I figure this thing, whatever it is, will be over in five, ten minutes, max. While Lotus goes to get the camera, I examine the room.

With the window closed and the air conditioner off, the room is quiet enough for an interview, but with four of us in there it is already starting to get quite stuffy. I decide to open the Venetian blinds for light, inviting in the dry heat of the sun. Wang Li peers out the window to survey the surrounding courtyards before settling next to Patricia on the floor at the foot of the bed.

Lotus comes back in and snuggles into the armchair, fidgeting with the dials and buttons of her camera. I move some stuffed animals out of the way so that Chai Ling and I can sit down next to each other on bed facing Lotus and the camera. I confer quietly with Chai Ling in Chinese, instructing her to introduce herself and tell us about the student movement.

"Do you have enough light, Lotus?" I ask, switching to English. "How's the sound?"

For some reason, Chai Ling takes my comments to Lotus as a cue to begin talking.

"The police are looking for me," Chai Ling starts, breaking her long silence. "My name is on a blacklist. If I am caught, I will get fifteen years in prison."

I get the tape recorder rolling, but Lotus is still fiddling with the camera. Meanwhile the cramped, poorly ventilated room is starting to feel like a sauna.

"I'm sorry, just a minute please," I say, trying to cue Chai Ling to the camera. "Lotus, are you ready?"

Our hostess has finally found a reasonably comfortable way to film without a tripod by scrunching up in the armchair, balancing the camera on her knees. "Okay, Chai Ling," I say, signaling the start of the interview. "Why don't you tell us who you are and how you got involved in the student movement?"

My interview subject is slow to react, as if weighted down by her own thoughts. She looks away from the camera, staring blankly at the wall.

"No, I think it's better if you look this way," I say, pointing to the blinking red light of the camera. "Here, hold the tape recorder yourself."

The student leader takes the compact cassette recorder and holds it in front of her mouth, as if she is addressing her followers with a megaphone. I motion for her to keep it down away from her face, to put it in her lap.

"Okay, let's start. What do you want to say?"

"I think these might be my last words. The situation is getting grim," she says, words emerging slow and methodically at first.

"My name is Chai Ling. I am twenty-three years old. Isn't it strange, my birthday was on April fifteenth, the same day that Hu Yaobang died?"

Her birthday marked the beginning of the student movement. She explains that she is from Shandong Province, a graduate of Beijing University, and is now studying child psychology at Beijing Normal University. Although her verbal delivery is fast and furious, her voice never gets louder than a desperate whisper. I urge her to speak up.

"Ever since April eighteenth I became active in the movement. It was very tense, everyone was hungry from waiting so long for Li Peng to come out and receive us. We wanted to pay our respects at the memorial service for Hu Yaobang."

Her words start to pick up speed, like a long pent-up torrent.

"But the government just put us off, so we were very angry. Some students wanted to break into the Great Hall of the People. But that would have ended up in bloodshed."

Bloodshed. So far there had been none—one of the most remarkable things about the student movement to date. But she was right to raise the specter of it, for, from the start, there had never been a moment when violence was not in the back of people's minds. A crackdown, sooner or later, had always been anticipated, and if I correctly surmised the rash and worried mood of this clandestine tryst, the idyllic peaceful days were over. Conflict was imminent.

MAY 28

◐

Clandestine Interview

Was it the eye of the camera working its magic? How to account for the transformation? Chai Ling, who had been brooding in utter silence to the point of despondency, was suddenly grandiloquent. Words flowed unceasingly from her lips, even as she sobbed and heaved and fought back tears.

"I went up in front of the Great Hall by the police line, and cried out on the megaphone until my voice was hoarse and I was in tears asking to voice student requests and grievances, but nobody paid attention. One of the PLA soldiers here said to me, 'Don't bother yelling anymore, save your voice.' Several of them offered me some water to drink. That was my first taste of water in over twenty hours."

She paused to look at me, as if expecting a question, and then continued without any prompting. I hadn't prepared any questions, but had simply asked her to tell us what she had been doing and what was going on.

"The mood was agitated. I asked my Beijing University classmates to join hands and leave Tiananmen Square together in order to avoid bloodshed. From that day I became a member of Beida's Student Preparation Committee. The same day my husband Feng Congde bit his finger and tried to write a message with his blood. He traced the characters for People's Premier, *ren min zong li*. But he could not finish. 'Why is there not enough blood?' he asked."

Chai Ling's deep narrow eyes are what the Chinese call *dan yan pi*, or single-fold. Almond-shaped and deep by the bridge of the nose, tears well up in the corners of her eyes. Then she sniffles and her cheeks are streaked with

204

tears. She purses her lips, as if she's on the verge of losing it, struggling to regain control. Before I can ask her if we should stop filming, she plunges back into her narrative.

"Our students kneeled on the steps for hours, arms upraised, holding a petition to the premier above their heads. They crouched respectfully but the government ignored them. Many of the students started to cry . . . On May fourth we staged another big demonstration and proclaimed the beginning of the New Democracy Movement."

She is walking us through the journey she had taken with her peers, a step-by-step guide to the movement. It is intense, fascinating, and coherent. Her delivery is soft-spoken but otherwise so fluent and forceful that I am reluctant to break it up with questions.

"But then the movement at Beida reached a low point. More and more students were returning to class. We wasted so much energy debating whether we should go back to class or not."

She says it was Beida student Wang Dan who told her about the hunger strike, and she joined in enthusiastically. That put her into conflict with other self-appointed student leaders who were against such a strike.

"On the night of May twelfth, the list of those who signed up for the hunger strike was posted at Sanjiaodi. There were only about forty names, but I was still moved. At the free speech forum I told my friends that the purpose of this hunger strike is to see the true face of the government, the true face of the people. Will they crack down or just ignore us? Does China have a conscience, does it still have hope?"

What's that noise, that rustling sound? I turn around to see Wang Li, the never satisfied, always hungry Wang Li, rummaging through the contents of a paper bag! Doesn't he know anything about recording? Why can't he sit still?

"We wrote a declaration of the hunger strike. The next day many teachers came to treat us to lunch and say good-bye. I felt terrible that day and couldn't eat, even though Bai Meng, a writing teacher, had made a special trip to a faraway shop to get us wonton dumplings.

"I heard one of my male classmates say, 'I used to feel I was Chairman Mao, now I feel so small. I love my parents, but I love the motherland more, so I join the hunger strike.'"

She relates that there was a big gathering at Shida around noon on May 13 that launched the great hunger strike. She adds that the number of students jumped to two hundred and then up to four hundred, initially all from Beida, Shida, and the Teachers Training Institute.

"Before we started the hunger strike march, I said to my friends, 'We are prepared to face death for the sake of true life. Only by facing death can we expect to leave a resounding, everlasting echo in Tiananmen. The oath we write with our lives will cleanse the skies above the Republic.'"

The morbid side of the hunger strike had troubled me—it brought to mind the tragic ordeal of Irish republican martyr Bobby Sands—so it's a tribute to her charisma that she makes it all sound so magnificent. She gives wing to words with her oratory, belying the fact that we are trapped in a stuffy little bedroom.

As someone still studying Chinese, with a long way to go before any sense of mastery, I envied native speakers like her; people who seemed to speak in poetry as effortlessly as an American could speak in prose. I wondered if the tendency towards aphorism and flowery rhetoric came from years of memorizing characters and classical poems, or was it more the influence of Communist slogans and artful propaganda?

I asked her if China had a tradition of hunger strikes, like in India with Mahatma Gandhi, but she said it was just something they thought up themselves. No sooner did I speak than I felt not only that my Chinese was inadequate to the task, but that I had somehow broken the flow of her narrative.

"The idea was brewing for a long time," she explained. "But it arose spontaneously."

She went on to say that the hunger strike immediately brought out differences among the leading activists. Wuerkaixi, she suggested, had fallen under the spell of government representative Yan Mingfu because he agreed with the idea that student strikers should move over, while remaining on the square, to make room for the official Gorbachev welcome ceremony. She was against this, and opposed anyone who supported such compromise, citing the weakness of the hunger strikers.

"Weren't you for dialogue?"

"Yes, but once we started the hunger strike, we were not going to budge until we had complete success. We would have had to carry some of the strikers on stretchers."

All at once, she starts choking up, suppressing a sob.

"Can you understand why it pained me so? It would have confused our supporters—first we're striking, then we're breaking it up."

Thereafter, almost entirely unprompted, except for my undivided attention and an occasional nod of the head, she goes on to talk about how the hunger strike evolved, from less than a thousand strikers to eventually three thousand.

I wonder about the nice round number, but without warning, the tone promptly gets darker. She cites a conversation with an apparent ally named

Li Lu, who said that if the government did nothing while students started to drop, they should consider more radical measures, such as self-immolation.

"'If the government is callous enough to watch its children starve to death, then I want to be the first to die.' I said this over the broadcast system. I said I was willing to be the commander in chief—I don't remember my exact words—I said the only criterion for a person to join the hunger-strike leadership was a willingness to be the first to die, so that other students could live on."

The intense young woman in the white sports shirt sitting next to me on my friend's daughter's bed had risen to the top of Tiananmen by being among the most bold, by using her own life as a bargaining chip. But did she really mean it, or was this more of a rhetorical strategy to seize power?

"At first the hunger strike was so united, so pure, even as large numbers of students fell to the ground and sirens wailed." Chai Ling pauses for a moment, dazed, or perhaps battling the contradictory emotions she is summoning up. Then she looks at the floor and starts sobbing uncontrollably. I fear she is having a breakdown on camera.

But nothing, not even her own heaving sobs, can stop her narrative once she is rolling. She presses on, talking about some incident of vandalism around the Great Hall, concluding that the hunger strikers, already too weak to walk, are ready to defend the sanctity of the Great Hall to the death. Anyone breaching the threshold is welcome to do so—over their emaciated bodies.

So much talk of daring, so much talk of death. I start to wonder if she might not be a bit suicidal. Lotus, Wang Li, Patricia, and I all sit in stunned and uncomfortable silence as the fragile-looking leader pours it out, sobs, then gathers her wits and resumes pouring it out. There seems to be no end to the thoughts she wants to share, some morose, others inspired, a heady mix of strident polemics cut with petty insights, beautiful phrasing mixed with bombastic drivel.

She even ventures into politburo politics, talking about how Zhao Ziyang and his people, though relatively open to reform and relatively responsive to democratic demands, had lost power, one province at a time, to hard-liner Li Peng, until now twenty-seven provinces and municipalities along with the six major military regions are solidly lined up behind Li Peng. The Zhao faction has been wiped out.

I ask her if she's had any news of Zhao Ziyang, because I keep hearing that he's somehow supporting the students, but she doesn't betray any particular knowledge of his whereabouts, other than to say that he has been knocked out of action, along with more than four hundred of his supporters. She talks about a student meeting of the day before, at which it was decided to carry out an orderly withdrawal from the square by May 30. She denounces this, saying it will have a negative effect, calling it harmful, saying the square is the only stronghold. She talks about the high points and low points of the movement so far when I ask her what comes next.

"Students keep asking, what is our next step, what can we achieve? I am saddened, there's no way I can tell them. What we are looking for is, it's bloodshed. In the end, the government will use the butcher's knife against the people. Only when Tiananmen Square is washed in a river of blood will the whole country wake up. But how can I say this to my fellow students?"

Hearing talk of blood and butchers gives me goose bumps. Does she know something too terrible to say? Is there an inevitability of bloodshed? Is the river of blood what she wants or is that why she's running away?

Her expression is too grandiose to take measure of, except when she is being petty and talks of power plays. She is hypercritical of the moderates who are urging protesters to leave the square before the government reaches its breaking point, singling out Liu Xiaobo and Wuerkaixi by name.

Personal animus aside, her point seems to be a tactical one. A government pushed to extremes will alienate moderates and extremists alike, driving more and more people into the camp of the discontents. But if the government somehow co-opts and compels moderate protesters to come back to the fold, it is the radicals, the most outspoken of the discontents, who are most likely to suffer from reprisals. Those familiar with government policing of past disturbances have few illusions that the top activists will be let off the hook. Whether it is the 1976 Tiananmen Incident or the Democracy Wall protests, long jail terms are to be expected.

"If they kill a large number of us now, if they crush us now, how many more years will pass before our people dare to stand up again? I feel really sad. I can't tell the students that we want bloodshed, to use young blood and lives to wake up the masses. They are definitely willing to sacrifice, but they are just kids . . . "

Bloodshed? Waking up the masses? Just kids? Chai Ling is only twenty-three, but she talks about her peers as if she exists on another plane altogether.

And now she's having another crying fit. Forcefully wiping away her tears, she expresses her disappointment with those who want to withdraw from the square. She says she left yesterday's controversial meeting with prominent intellectuals in tears, because it made her realize how much she loves the "tens of thousands" of student masses.

"Some people are struggling for power. I've never wanted power, but my conscience won't allow me to give in to the schemers and defeatists who attack us."

Alternately acidulous and serene, she vacillates between selfishness and selflessness. Like the Communist authorities she so roundly condemns, she shows little tolerance for those with whom she disagrees, such as those who have left the square. Not without some justification, though, she frets about the fact that some of the people at Tiananmen are just hanging around to see what happens in the end.

"I say to the people of China and to the Chinese people of the world, we are a tragic race, we must stop killing ourselves! We don't have many more chances."

She's so obsessed with her Chinese identity—she specifically asked me to convey her message to the Chinese people of the world—yet hypercritical of her race at the same time.

"I know Chinese shouldn't criticize other Chinese. But the truth is, I don't know if it's worth working so hard, if it's worth giving my life for the Chinese people. But then I remember all the good students, those with integrity and conscience, the workers, the citizens, and intellectuals."

She's sniffs softly, ignoring her tears.

"Yesterday I said to my husband, I don't want to stay in China anymore. I want to go abroad . . . perhaps it is impossible for us to obtain real democracy in the short period of one generation. If I live, I want to devote my life to helping the Chinese people. But I don't know if I'll have a chance to do that.

"When I joined this student movement on the twenty-fifth of April . . . it seemed that plainclothes agents had already infiltrated the movement.

"We were having a chat and I asked how many years does a political prisoner get? Someone said it used to be three, then five, then seven, and now it's seventeen years. That really upsets me. I'll be forty by the time I get out! I'm not ready for that."

The telephone in the other room rings loudly, giving me a jolt. Her intensely dark visions, the talk about secret police, have gotten me on edge. Al, who can be heard consoling his daughter outside the door, takes the call.

It isn't the police or Lido security, just one of his friends calling. We all breathe a sigh of relief and look to Chai Ling to see if she has anything else to say. It seems like a good time to wrap up the interview, so I ask what democracy means to her.

"I don't have any theoretical knowledge of democracy. But democracy is a natural need and desire, so everyone can be free and have the protection of human rights, to lead our lives freely, to express our political views freely."

Surely democracy is more than a mantra to her, but her understanding of it does not go much beyond platitudes. I follow up with a question about dialogue, one of the key student demands.

"Since the founding of the country, the government has never had a serious contender to speak on behalf of the people. The people should be able to engage in just dialogue, to monitor the government. To get involved in decisions, investigate illegal activities, not succumb to black controls in the name of national unity."

Ever since this morning, she has been hinting that she is at her wit's end and wants to quit. If the "people" blame her for it, so be it. She's gotten enough grief already. She hopes others would be able to fill her place. But what has it all been for? What is the real goal? She claims the government is afraid of dialogue. She feels that the Chinese people are still passive after two thousand years of feudalism followed by decades of Communist rule. As an example of this pervasive passivity, she cites the example of provincial students who came to her, deferentially, asking what they should do. She says she reprimanded them.

"Look at you! You have two hands, you have eyes, you can speak, you can use your ears. You can knit your own clothes and grow your own rice. You can do things on your own, make your own decisions. Of course, the good side of their eagerness was their respect for the leader's authority, but in fact some of them just evade responsibility."

I ask her whether or not Mao Zedong is an influence.

"Personally speaking, I don't have any respect for the man. If we were living in the time of Mao, there would be all kinds of horrible crackdowns and suppression. I just don't get much out of him."

Yet are there not similarities between this movement and the Cultural Revolution? Does not Deng Xiaoping, a victim of that period, have good reason to be nervous?

"As I told my fellow students, our hunger strike represented a leap into a new era, nobody expected all this to happen. But students and government alike make the mistake of viewing this movement with old prejudices."

Well, I am guilty of that, always on the lookout for precedents and patterns. I am also guilty of not arguing point by point where I disagree with her, but it isn't so much an interview as a full-bore confessional. Furthermore, I am drowning in a sea of words I neither fully understand nor fully grasp the nuances of. I just decide to let the tape roll. Lotus probably understands even less than I do, while Wang Li just takes it all in, uncharacteristically silent. Patricia rises to the task of asking some questions, but fails to achieve much rapport.

"On the first of May, my father, who always looked after me, came to Beijing . . . bringing a lot of things to eat. He said, 'I am going back, I can't be of much help to you here. How can I keep in touch with you?' I told him I would send a telegram every three days. Suddenly he asks, 'What if the telegram does not arrive?' I told him if that happens, don't come to Beijing, it will be of no use. I started to cry. My father said, 'Don't cry now, I must go. Good-bye, good-bye.'"

She breaks down, heaving heavily. I feel sorry for her father. I look to Lotus for help, wondering if we should stop, but again our resilient guest insists on resuming her narrative odyssey.

"My father went to medical school and became a doctor. He worked for the military, but he got where he is today by himself alone, by his own hard work. Now society is such a mess. Everybody wants to get rich. He asked about what happened to idealism? Did it disappear overnight? I feel sorry for my father. He still has a fond feeling for the Communist Party. He said that a person of peasant background like me could be where I am today because of the nurture of the Communist Party. I told him his generation should have gotten more out of life. I told him the Communist Party was the problem. He said he respected my right to my point of view. My father's an open-minded man."

She talks about her younger brother, sister, and her mother, touching on some family problems. Then I ask her what she thinks the government's response should be.

"The government is definitely going to take revenge on us. Chinese people have a vengeful streak, I don't have any illusions about that."

She was disillusioned and afraid, self-absorbed but not without profound convictions, and her outpouring moved me. More than that, it overwhelmed me. I had crossed some invisible divide, and had inadvertently gotten drawn more deeply into the vortex of China's complex troubles than I had thought possible or desirable. For the foreigner who was always looking to bridge the unbridgeable, East and West had just met head-on, and I was reeling from it.

MAY 28

◐

Going Underground

"Tiananmen," whispers Chai Ling.

"What?" I ask, comprehending without comprehension.

"I'd like to see Tiananmen, one last time."

We skip the turn to the train station—she and Wang Li had been talking about catching the first train out of Beijing—and instead continue east on Chang'an. As the car approaches the familiar student-controlled zone around Tiananmen Square, I try to make sense of what we are doing. I had just delivered to the international media a candid interview with a wanted student leader who said she is going to run away while speaking forthrightly about imminent bloodshed and the desire to overthrow the government. If she was at risk before the interview, she's at even more risk now. What is the right thing to do?

It wasn't just a question of abstract journalistic ethics; I suffered from the vague sense that I was the one being taken for a ride. I had no objections to being a partisan in principle, but the behavior of those I was trying to help was confusing me. Regardless of whether or not it was good form for a journalist to be aiding and abetting an interviewee's escape, I was willing to do so for humanitarian reasons.

And I admired the progressive, San Francisco–style chivalry of the sort I had just seen in Albert and Lotus when they offered Chai Ling and Wang Li a wad of cash, clothes, backpacks, and even footwear to abet their escape. I thought my part of the deal was to get them to the train station on time.

So what was I to make of Chai Ling's desire for a little detour to the student command center in the center of the most contested real estate in China? Was that not at odds with trying to help her escape to safety?

"It is not safe by the square," Wang Li announced crisply, as if aware of my doubts. His watchful gaze from the front of the car went momentarily out of focus while he removed his thick, black-framed glasses to wipe an oily smudge. "Too many plainclothes police."

I suspected he was right, but with plainclothesmen, and human surveillance in general, it was always hard to separate paranoia from precaution.

The car putters slowly in deference to the thin but irregular flow of pedestrian traffic as we cut across the largely empty north face of the square.

Chai Ling peers out the rear window, studying the scene of her rise to fame in silence. The precipitous drop in the number of protesting bodies is offset somewhat by the profusion of new tents. The bright tarps and canvas from Hong Kong make the student command zone at the monument look busy with color, if not people.

It seems crazy, taking this confused fugitive, alternately frightened, alternately fearless, to the place most likely to get her in trouble. Then again, Tiananmen is still more or less under the control of her people. Have I lost my faith in people power? Reluctantly, I tell the driver to swing to the south when we get to the Great Hall.

Traffic is light and what protesters there are are widely dispersed. The thinning ranks of student volunteers serving as traffic police do not demand to know our business today.

Waved on by a weary student sentry standing on the northwest corner of the square, we head south, halting when we reach the nearest point to the monument. All at once, Chai Ling seems to have second doubts, expressing a reluctance to get out of the car. She asks me to run over to the monument to see if I could find her husband.

"Tell Feng Congde I need to see him right away," she says in a grave whisper, leaning on me lightly.

"Where is he?"

"I'm not sure." She hands me another one of her little cryptic notes. "Please give this to him, my husband. He will know where to reach me."

"But how am I supposed to find him?"

"I think he is still on the square," she says.

"Where?"

"Probably by the broadcast tent," she clarifies.

"I'll go with you," Patricia volunteers, switching to English. "You and me, we can get out here and walk. They are in danger. They need the car, don't they?"

Wang Li is pleased to hear he will be left in charge of the car.

"When you find Feng Congde, tell him I must see him," Chai Ling adds. "Before I go. Thanks."

"So, wait. If I find him, where should I tell him to meet you? At the train station?"

"No, it's too far," she says, knitting her brow. The car is crawling at a turtle's pace, gently negotiating the random foot traffic near the busiest part of the square.

"Well, where then?"

If we are going to make a quick entry to student headquarters, this is as close as we can get on wheels. Patricia and I get out and do some reconnaissance. We scan the broad plaza, looking past the pup tents, army tents, umbrellas, and university banners. There are clusters of hurried activity and clumps of napping bodies on the ground, draped with the usual coats and blankets to block the midday sun. The student command center, wedged up against the southeast corner of the Martyrs' Monument, is about 150 yards to the east.

South of where we stand, just to the west of the intersection marked by Qianmen Gate, is the white and red signage of an American fast-food joint. I hurry back to the car and make a suggestion to the waiting fugitives.

"Why don't you wait for us at Kentucky Fried Chicken? It's walking distance for us, the driver can park there, and I think it will be safe."

"Kentucky?" They consider the idea. "Okay, Kentucky."

I pay the driver the meter fare plus some extra in case they need to make a quick escape.

"Be careful, you two," I say in parting. "Keep the car as long as you need to, it might be hard to find another one."

"Thank you, Jin," says Chai Ling, biting her lip, at once coquettish and shy about all the trouble.

"See you in Kentucky!"

Patricia and I ford a path through the thick but listless mass of daytrippers on the perimeter of the square, who give way to diehards, student wardens, and hard-core operatives as we get closer to the student HQ. Unwittingly imitating the government they speak of overthrowing, the student elite have become super-paranoid about security. Undercover police are undoubtedly a problem, I have noticed men taking my photograph ever since

May 4 and many of the photographers are older than the students, but so am I. Does that make me a spy in their eyes?

Latecomers to the cause from the provinces, for whom a mere claim of student status was initially sufficient to get access, were initially banished to the east periphery, but now are starting to squeeze closer to the center, vying for prestige by seizing central ground.

Access to the Martyrs' Monument is still tightly restricted, however, with security at the southeast corner being unusually tight, roped-off and zealously guarded for the exclusive use of the current pick of student leaders only. The center is bustling as before, but the surrounding crowd is a skeleton of its former self. The array of tents encircling the student command and control center stand open to passersby. Once tightly guarded university camps are violated by passing foot traffic. Worse yet, for one who still carries the afterimage of a million souls gathered peacefully and purposefully, large swaths of the square are empty.

As we wend our way through the depressing litter and mess, Patricia and I are stopped and questioned by student wardens and vigilante types, though the security is less comprehensive today. The burden of suspicion falls more often on Patricia, who flashes her Hong Kong press ID to get through. As for me, I have no press pass but an unusual and familiar profile—the Chinese-speaking laowai in the indigo shirt—and that generally suffices to let me move about freely.

As we neared the student-controlled inner perimeter, I turned around to check on the taxi, but it was gone. Once inside the inner zone, the security tightened, and we had to laboriously pass two more security rings before getting to the broadcast tent, where influential students still congregated. Patricia was immediately turned away, flatly told that the inside of the tent was off-limits to journalists. To get across the frontier of this final inner sanctum I had to produce the personalized all-points security pass signed by Commander in Chief Chai Ling.

The signature of "the leader" scribbled on a piece of cardboard did the trick and we were free to step inside. Gone was the tidy, homey atmosphere I remembered from earlier in the week. The inside of the tent was a mess, awash with litter and upended equipment, the mood chaotic if not frantic. Nobody seemed to be in charge.

There was no hospitality corner. There were no smiles, no offers to have a drink or take a seat. No one was willing to help us find Feng Congde, and no one seemed to care that I carried an urgent message from Chai Ling. It suddenly occurred to me I might be dropping the wrong names at the wrong time. What if there had been a student coup? Perhaps she and her husband had fallen from grace with factional infighting flaring up. Maybe that was why she came to see me in such a hurry; maybe that was why she was on the lam.

Sensing political fortunes had changed, I played it coy, the Wang Li way, asking if anyone had seen student commander in chief Chai Ling. The response was underwhelming. Although a few people paused long enough to show familiarity with the name, nobody seemed to know what was going on. There was an undisciplined, free-for-all, anything-goes atmosphere.

When I finally find a student willing to spare a few seconds to humor the foreigner, he states that I must go "upstairs" to the second level of the marble platform, just above the tent. When we try to go that way, we are stopped at a rope barrier. Adjacent to the checkpoint is a wooden table shaded by a canvas tent.

"This is the student information center," I am told. Although the tent is open to the elements on one side and flimsy in appearance, it has the dank bureaucratic air of a Chinese government office. Students who need to consult the leadership solemnly queue in line, impatient and irritable, hoping for "official" assistance.

Among those who wait in the sun like desperate travelers trying to snag seats on a sold-out train, there erupt shoving matches and shouts. Some of them are looking for lost friends, much as we are, passing back and forth notes scribbled on little scraps of paper, hoping to win the attention of a "responsible person" inside the student information bureau. This bureau is not only inefficient, but redolent of a bureaucratic arrogance. It is the holding pen one gets sent to when student guards are unimpressed with one's credentials. Trying to get an audience with the student leadership is an act in frustration, like petitioning Li Peng on the steps of the Great Hall a month before.

Impatient like everyone else on line, I resort to shouting out my request, hoping to get some immediate assistance. Whether it is my blond hair or amusing foreign accent that manages to catch the "responsible authority's" attention, I don't know, but at least I get an answer.

"We are not clear about that."

"But where is he?"

"His location is unknown."

"But . . . "

"Not clear about that either."

In such a chaotic environment, callous and dismissive attitudes rule. It is a miracle that anyone can get reliable information about anything.

While wasting my time with the student bureaucrats, I have lost Patricia. I climb up on the wall of the second level of the marble pedestal to better survey the flux of people. The area to the south of the monument looks like a campground: its colorful patches of red, yellow, and blue tarps and canvas bespeak tropical Hong Kong, not subdued, pastel-hued Beijing. The Hong Kong contingent, and those they support, have secured a patch of ground in between the massive revolutionary bas-reliefs leading to the entrance of Mao's tomb. The encampments north of the monument are relatively unchanged, a low-slung skyline of heavy-duty army tents and camouflaged gear that evoke the no-nonsense military style of north China.

Inasmuch as the square has a unique look each day, today it reminds me of a beach at low tide, littered with refuse and slime. As the number of feet pounding the square dwindles, the overall unsightliness increases, if only because the soiled ground is in plain view and garbage isn't being picked up anymore. Even in the open, the sharp counterpoint of odors on the square has become more pungent than the smoky incense-scented toilet stalls in the Beijing Hotel.

The flat basin of flagstones is punctuated with semi-permanent structures of wood, metal, and bamboo, topped with tattered banners and tired slogans. Not unlike the beady eyes in Mao's portrait, which seem to gaze upon every inch of Tiananmen at once, government monitoring of the square is ubiquitous but passive. Remote-controlled security cameras atop high lampposts silently pan the "rioters" while government infiltrators quietly go about their research.

"I found him!" Patricia calls out, pointing the way to Feng Congde. It turns out he has been inside a tent on the second tier of the monument only a few steps from where I had been asking for him. And naturally, nobody knew where he was.

I find him sitting like a colonial official in the shade under a broad canvas awning. He is lanky, long-haired, he has a pleasant, unpretentious air. He's a bit older-looking than the average student, and when he talks, despite the constant flow of aides pestering him, he is almost jovial in his expression. A natural complement to his wife; he's as laid-back and nonchalant as she is high-strung and self-aware.

As we exchange greetings, Feng holds a thick wad of cash in his hands. There are many similar piles of cash scattered on the table before him. A partially opened suitcase, a makeshift bank vault of sorts, is stuffed with thousands of renminbi notes, bringing to mind the loot of bank robber.

Thick packs of indigo-colored ten-yuan notes, the highest denomination commonly in use in China, are scattered on a table in the process of being counted. Looking at stack after stack of hard cash being shuffled and sorted by this taciturn man in the Western jacket makes me realize I have chanced upon the "Bank of Tiananmen" and he is the acting finance minister. The makeshift bank enjoys a prestigious location adjacent to the students' power center, much as the Bank of China enjoys a prestigious branch next to the Great Hall of the People, but the security is uncomfortably lax. The student bank has no vault, other than vigilant eyes, though it is protectively ensconced within the marble folds of the monument's pedestal, much like the command center a level below.

Feng Congde, eyes peering intently downwards through his glasses, intersperses pleasantries with business. He had paused long enough for cordial introductions; suddenly he is preoccupied again, issuing orders and counting money.

Patricia explains to me that he is in charge of student finances and that much of the cash we are looking at was raised in Hong Kong at events such as the Happy Valley concert where Hou Dejian sang along with Hong Kong stars in a fundraiser.

She and I hover uneasily at the bank entrance until a minor "official" offers us a seat on the cot, unceremoniously displacing two sleepy-eyed students who rub their eyes and exit without complaint. We sit it out while several thousand more yuan are counted out. One of Feng's assistants, apparently from the public relations section of the "bank," explains to us that the man we came to see is trusted and widely respected, so it falls to him to keep records of the money. Patricia had already told me that the Hong Kong press was accusing the Beijing students of mishandling funds, which, it now turns out, was one of the reasons why she and the other Hong Kong reporters had been on Chai Ling's tail this morning at the Beijing Hotel.

Ordinary people in Hong Kong had generously donated money to show their support for the Beijing students. A nice gesture, until the logistics were taken into consideration. Hong Kong dollars had to be physically carried into China and changed into local currency. This was not the kind of official transaction that could be wired and documented with a paper trail. Who was to say what constituted a legitimate expense along the way? If you wanted to give money to a democracy movement, whom did you give it to?

Just the sight of so much hard cash in a community of impoverished students was bound to raise a few eyebrows. Individual temptation and greed could not be discounted, nor was there any foolproof protection against theft or loss. The money may very well have been doing more harm than good. It took extra effort and discipline to guard it safely, determine how it was to be spent, and account for such expenditures. This multiplied exponentially the number of tasks the over-extended student leaders were pressed to handle.

At a time when Beijing students were getting weary and ready to go back to campus, there were two new jet streams of pressure. There was the Johnny-come-lately enthusiasm from the provincial students like Li Lu, from Nanjing, and Wang Li, from Xian. The hard-core ambition they showed in playing catch-up ball had the effect of raising the stakes for those more in a mood to compromise. Secondly, there were the overenthused, overly sentimental Hong Kong supporters, who in their own ersatz way were acting like humble provincials desperate to pay tribute to the new "leaders" in Beijing.

But the mountains of money from Hong Kong posed a stark challenge. Either the beleaguered Beijing activists must become efficient bookkeepers or they would be seen as corrupt politicos.

Accepting cash donations from well-wishers was not new. Only the magnitude had changed. From the earliest marches, Beijing students, a notoriously thin-walleted class of people, had taken in penny and dime contributions and donations of goods from local supporters. The free popsicles I enjoyed while marching in the hot sun on May 4 were part of the same phenomenon, as were free bread and soda pop. The crumpled and dog-eared yuan notes that trickled in from Beijing citizens in the early weeks of protest were sufficient to purchase new speakers for the student broadcast booths and megaphones for crowd control.

But the sheer volume of the new cash inputs raised tough questions about accountability. Was it first come, first serve? Who wouldn't be tempted to pocket a few bills when sitting right before one's eyes lay more cash than one's parents had earned in a lifetime?

Did some students have more right to the money than others? How much should go to the provincial students in need of food and shelter in Beijing? How about the leaders? And if student leaders felt the need to flee, was it fair game to pocket cash donations to expedite a mad dash to the border?

With power comes corruption.

The crowd facilitators who emerged from the anonymous masses to propel the movement forward were largely tolerated, though by no means elected or otherwise anointed by the crowd. Instead they assumed for themselves provisional leadership, taking control with security, secrecy, mood manipulation, and fiscal largesse. They had awesome portfolios: they were expected to maintain public safety, sanitation, traffic flow, and communications and ensure an equitable distribution of limited resources to thousands of followers toughing it out, living life in the open.

Incidents of crime were remarkably low by all accounts, but with what seemed to be an almost provocative retreat of state security, law and order was increasingly left to the students themselves. The Beijing student–led "citizen's arrest" of the provincial "vandals" who defaced the Mao portrait at Tiananmen, reportedly using eggs filled with ink, was a troubling example of vigilante policing. A violent melee or accidental death at Tiananmen would put student leaders under attack for negligence and recklessness. In early May, students rallied against government corruption and favoritism Now that they had a fledgling government of their own on the square, could they denounce corruption and favoritism without being hypocritical?

The student activist clique currently occupying the broadcast tent could be considered, for the moment, the "responsible cadre" in charge, but on what basis were they justified, let alone qualified, to lord over others on the square? The commander in chief was married to the finance minister. Their friends filled key posts. They weren't elected; they didn't have the time or inclination to consult those in whose name they acted. Through strikes, marches, and sit-ins they had created chaos, then assumed power by filling the vacuum. Power was up for grabs. It was a giant game of king of the hill. Some got to the top by speaking louder or more stridently. Others jostled for position by controlling real estate, controlling security, even stepping on toes. Were they not the spitting image of the establishment cadre they claimed to be rebelling against?

There were already signs of rampant hypocrisy. Subtly, sadly, but inexorably, student leaders started seeing themselves as special; like the rulers they opposed, they acted in the name of the people, but they were a little more equal than others. The core students, like their elders in the politburo, found it increasingly necessary to scheme and devote time to thwarting rivals, time that might have been better spent helping and inspiring others. To hold the high strategic ground, one had to be constantly on the lookout for usurpers, infiltrators, and potential rivals from within.

One way to rise to the top was through bold self-promotion (as in "I am Wuerkaixi!") and brazen clowning, such as Wuerkaixi's dramatic upbraiding of Li Peng at a televised event. Behind-the-scenes strategizing and building links among idealist contenders was more characteristic of the mild-mannered Wang Dan's rise to prominence. Chai Ling had caught public attention with passionate speeches and dare-to-die rhetoric.

I had to wonder if the way she had sought me out this morning, presumably as a conduit to the media, was a conscious strategy, a stab at international notoriety in order to thwart domestic rivals. If so, was I not an unwitting pawn in a game whose outlines I only dimly perceived?

The students denounced governmental information control and rallied for free press, yet they were secretive to the extreme. With the latest cash infusion from Hong Kong, the question of dubious outside influences could not be suppressed. Chai Ling had spoken to me more than once about secretive contacts with Western embassies. Was she beginning to assume, in addition to an impossibly heavy load of responsibilities ranging from law and order to propaganda, a foreign-policy portfolio as well?

It is weird and getting weirder. Chai Ling is running away, supposedly in fear of her life, and here I am daydreaming, whiling away the time in the middle of the command center at Tiananmen Square, waiting for the attention of her similarly blacklisted husband as he methodically counts out wads of cash!

At last, the finance minister is fully free to talk to us. "Sorry, I'm so busy. All this money from Hong Kong," he explains with a sigh, almost apologetically. "See? You see? We keep records."

The informal minister of finance delegated the daunting accounting work to some subordinates, freeing himself up for a chat on the cot. Even so, he seemed to be one of those people who couldn't do fewer than three things at once, for the whole while he talked to us he was jotting down notes and giving instructions to subordinates and helpers.

So fully absorbed was he with various tasks at hand, Feng certainly did not look like someone who was about to throw in the towel. Then again, maybe he was playing it cool, so when he left, abruptly and without warning, it would be a complete surprise to those who watched his every move. I decided not breach the subject within earshot of others. The constant interruptions and frequent distractions made coherent conversation difficult. I slipped Chai Ling's note to him, but no sooner had he inspected it than he turned his attention back to other matters.

Dare I tell him in front of the others that his wife is hightailing it to the train station? Does he know about the embassy deal she whispered to me about?

I ask if we can talk somewhere else. He reluctantly stands up and leads me to an empty roped-off zone on the northern tier of the marble pedestal. We stand high on the steps, surveying thousands of bobbing heads in the foreground, backed by the reassuring architectural lines of Tiananmen Gate at a distance.

In a few words, I relayed that his wife had done an interview for television, which I had delivered to ABC News, and she was now waiting for him nearby, at a fast-food joint. He listened intently but without the slightest tension. He came off as so unruffled and unperturbed, I got the impression he was merely humoring me. Nothing I said seemed to fully register. Chai Ling had told me he'd been to a consulate, and he had a good chance to study abroad. She said it was his plan to study law, sociology, and math, and then come back to China to write a new constitution. Did he already have a ticket out of here? Why the laconic confidence?

It was hard to believe Feng and his associates were actually fugitives on a police blacklist. They didn't seem to be in hiding, or if they were it was a brazen kind of hiding in plain sight, like here, in the middle of the square, or in the long corridors of Beijing Hotel. What happened to the legendary efficiency of China's secret police?

At my urging, Feng took another look at the note from his wife while I tried to fill him in on more details.

"*Xie-xie!*" He is cordial but dismissive. "My wife worries too much. It's not as bad as she thinks."

"Well, I just think you should know she is traveling, er, south. She says you know how to find her . . . "

"Yes, I know."

"She is very upset. She was crying."

"Where did you say she was?"

"Kentucky Fried Chicken."

"I've got one more thing to do here and then I'll go see her."

He shook my hand heartily, saying, "Thanks, Jin Peili. See you in a little while." Then he went back to his comrades in the accounting department.

Patricia and I exited the students' secure zone and hoofed it to "Kentucky" at a normal walking pace, weaving through light people traffic all the way to Zhengyanglou, the monumental gate on the south of the square. From there, we crossed Qianmen Avenue, walked past the tidy row of poplars that partially hid the unsightly billboard advertising Kentucky Fried Chicken, and entered the parking lot. The taxi was nowhere to be seen, so we stepped in, figuring our fugitive friends were inside, and I fully expected to see Wang Li alertly casing the joint while munching away on chicken wings. I checked both floors, but there was no sign of them.

"Maybe they're already on their way," I suggested. "You know, the train station."

"But why didn't they tell us?" Patricia, who started out the day not liking Chai Ling very much, had sort of been won over. Now she sounded hurt.

"Maybe they got worried about the timing."

"But they promised . . . "

"Well, anyway, it's more important that they get off safely than stick around and risk getting caught."

"I don't think they made it to the train," said Patricia, airing her concern. "We must find the car!"

"Do you think we should we should look for them at the train station?"

"What about Feng Congde?"

Patricia and I agreed that searching for the student leader at the train station might bring unwanted attention, but why were we doing all the worrying? Feng's laidback attitude and Chai Ling's impulsiveness were incongruous. And what was Wang Li's role in all of this?

We checked every last taxi in the vicinity of the rendezvous point and then waited. The wife was gone; the husband hadn't bothered to show. Finally, we gave up and walked back to the square. Where else was one to go?

"What happened?" I asked Feng, who was back on the job when we finally located him.

"I went there but I couldn't find her," he explained. "Sorry, I am very busy now." His sangfroid made me more confused. Did he know something that she didn't know? Did he have some guarantee of support?

"Don't worry about it. She'll be all right," he said.

Midnight Rendezvous

For the second time in a day, I'm on the run with Chai Ling. For the second time in a month, I find myself in a beat-up jalopy racing towards the Beida student center at Sanjiaodi. Again I am huddled together with members of the vanguard, only this time it's not musicians wanting to know what the students are up to but the student leadership itself.

The interior of a moving van is a reasonably private place, assuming the driver is trustworthy and the vehicle is not bugged. Chai Ling sits behind me in the third row, curled up like a kitten, snuggled next to her puppy-dog husband Feng Congde. They look like feuding lovers who have just made up. I am seated in the middle of the second row with a bodyguard named Yang on one side, a professor on the other. Way in the back, and up front, yet more students are squeezed in, keeping pretty much to themselves.

The driver turns north, then eventually works his way west. Chai Ling is reviewing the familiar scenery with the intense appreciation of someone ready to take an extended trip abroad. Both she and her husband had been talking about studying abroad; maybe they had one foot out the door already. Start a revolution, then fly away in time for the start of a new school year.

"There's that restaurant!" she exclaims. A few minutes later, she gets nostalgic about another landmark known to her and her husband. "Remember the time we went there?"

The mop-headed driver, who could have passed for the fifth Beatle, zooms at high speed along the ring road, only shifting gears to slow the van down when we get to the busy streets of Haidian District.

"Do you think we could visit Beida one more time?" Chai Ling asks. She does not seem to be addressing the question to anyone in particular.

"That's possible," the bodyguard next to me says after a pause. "But let's wait till it gets dark."

"Beida, Beida, I want to go to campus! I want to go home one last time!" she pleads with a girlish flair.

Talk turns to politics again. I choose to not intrude and cannot fully grasp what is going on, but I don't want to bring undue attention to myself by asking too many questions. From what I can gather, Chai Ling is still on the verge of running away, but due to the intervention of her husband and some friends, she dumped Wang Li and is now going to postpone "going underground" until a more necessary and appropriate time. More importantly, she seems to be enjoying some kind of high-level support for her political line, and even the protection of bodyguards. If so, who is the ultimate protector?

Are the students working in tandem with protégés of the fallen Zhao, or perhaps a military protector? There have been rumors of old generals being supporters of the cause, but students also like to say they are free agents, not aligned to any faction. That's what the May 27 meeting was about.

Who can possibly be lending support to the students at this late stage, enough tacit support to make them utterly unafraid of arrest in the Beijing Hotel? Is it Public Security? A rogue intelligence group? Or just plucky citizen volunteers?

And how does the interview we did this morning fit into all this? At that time, she expressed disappointment with fellow students, but she also talked of overthrowing the government! ABC News has already indicated they are going to use the tape, and it is nothing if not highly incriminating. If Chai Ling is still in town when the interview is aired, her likeness and passionately expressed antigovernment ideas will be all that much better known.

Finally, I decide to interrupt their backseat musings. "Chai Ling?"

"Hi, Jin Peili," she smiles as I turn around to face her.

"You know, that interview, the interview today, you said a lot of things that could, like, get you in trouble. Are you sure you want it to be broadcast?"

"Yes."

"It's not too late to call ABC and ask them not to air it, or at least delay it," I advise. "If your life is in danger."

"I want it to be broadcast," she answers pointblank, without batting an eyelash.

"But you said some things . . . like about the government, you know, wanting to overthrow it."

"When will it go on the air?" asks Feng, with a sudden perk in interest.

"Sometime tomorrow."

"Don't worry, we will be gone by then."

"You're sure?"

"Yes. After we visit Beida, one last time," he says.

I am beginning to feel the immense responsibility that goes with putting something provocative on the air, especially something political. Millions will see it, but more to the point, it will be closely monitored by Chinese security.

Feng grins at me to dispel my doubts "Don't worry, you've done a good job. We all appreciate your help."

"Since satellite transmission has been cut," I explain, "ABC has to take the tape out of China by hand. It will be carried to Hong Kong or Japan, and then relayed by satellite to New York. The earliest it could be on the air is the evening news, American time, which means early tomorrow morning here."

"It's fine, no problem," he says. Feng is disarmingly self-assured.

"It's not too late to call, if you need more time."

"Jin, don't worry. We will be gone by then."

So they still plan to run away, and this little jaunt, this little joyride they have invited me to partake in, is for what? For fun? Or a mix of business and pleasure, saying good-bye while just taking care of some last-minute logistics?

I have trouble putting together the young woman who confessed and cried her heart out earlier today, face contorted and full of pain, with the breezy young woman in the van.

What's going on? Why is Feng Congde so confident that nothing will happen to them? Is he reckless or does he know something that his wife did not when she made her mad dash for the train station? What happened at the train station, anyway? There are so many things I want to ask, but given the gentle cooing sounds behind me, it doesn't seem like the right time.

Chai Ling was no stranger to the Beijing Hotel; she had been there twice today. A few days before, I had seen her meeting there at midnight in a darkened coffee shop with Wang Dan and Wuerkaixi. Yet on the square, one had to pass through all kinds of security ropes just to get in her vicinity.

The student leaders seemed unnecessarily stringent in their security, but an illegal movement of that size required vigilance. So why was it that, in the most heavily monitored hotel in town, the student rebels seemed so at home, if not outright welcome? I knew from talking to the floor attendants that many ordinary workers supported the students, but ordinary workers also knew not to get in the way of police.

Beijing Hotel workers had marched under banners indicating their work affiliation and a gigantic ten-story banner proclaiming solidarity with the striking students had been draped from the top of the hotel during the height of the protest. The multistory banner, partially draped in front of my room, each character the size of a person, read:

WHO IS TO SAY WHAT IS THE FATE OF SO VAST A LAND? DEMOCRACY AND FREEDOM ARE THE SHARED IDEALS OF ALL HUMANITY!

With a banner like that suspended from the seventeenth floor running all the way down to the seventh floor, right past my window as it turned out, one could imagine why the students might be attracted to that particular building, but why was the banner permitted in the first place? Was there some kind of connection between the security staff of the Beijing Hotel and the student movement?

If there was support, it was hidden and erratic. Even now, the van took precautions in ferrying us across town. Not only had the driver made some unnecessary turns on the way, but he took to circling Haidian District like an airplane awaiting official permission to land.

When I ask about this, the bodyguard explains that the driver is killing time, waiting for the cover of darkness before slipping onto campus. But Beida is a gated community. Would the guards let this vehicle, the student command on wheels, pass through the gated checkpoint? It was no secret Beida harbored activists. Wouldn't the secret police be looking for student radicals on campus, or were they such Keystone Cops that it never occurred to them to look in obvious places?

As Yang shrewdly observes, the driver will not attempt to enter Beida until darkness falls. When he at last pulls up to the front gate on the south side of campus and greets the guards, I worry how they might react to my presence—did the presence of a foreigner make the entourage look less innocent, or more? One guard presses his face up to the window, mentally registering my presence with eye contact, but it ends with that. We are then waved in. Once inside the huge walled campus, the driver again adopts a defensive posture, crawling in long slow circle around the lake and tree-dotted grounds while Chai Ling and her friends heatedly discuss if they should get out of the van, and, if so, where.

The tentativeness of the travelers upon arriving at Beida reminds me of my midnight visit to Beida with Cui Jian on the eve of May 4. Sitting inside a vehicle creates a certain perception, perhaps illusory, of security. One feels safer inside than outside. For me, sitting in the back of a car reminds me of the security of childhood, when everything important was decided by your parents sitting up front. For an American like me, being in a car has deep associations going back to childhood. But what comfort does the hum of a vehicle give Chai Ling and Feng Congde, for whom riding in a car is still a novelty?

The tree-shrouded campus is quiet and dark. We make a clockwise sweep, tooling past Shao Yuan, the foreign dorm; then the library; and then back down a dirt road leading to the Chinese student dorm adjacent to the hot spot of Sanjiaodi.

The van draws up to the stairwell of the dorm and the driver tells everyone to get out. As soon as we have all clambered out, he hits the pedal and speeds away. We are whisked into the unlit hallway by waiting escorts. We mount a dark, dank stairwell, then turn down an empty corridor. A door is opened, revealing a plain room lit by a bare bulb, a room packed full of people.

Once we are inside, the door is closed and Chai Ling is greeted with hugs and pats on the back by her comrades, like a war hero just in from the battlefield. A few of her supporters eye me curiously, with stares neither friendly nor unfriendly, because I arrived with her group, but the attention is clearly focused on her.

We are led up another flight of stairs and into another room. Again the door is closed quietly but firmly behind us. Chai Ling is no stranger to the makeshift student headquarters, and quickly assumes the role of host rather than guest. Sensing my bewilderment if not discomfort, she leads me by the arm into an adjacent dorm room, where the furniture has been rearranged to serve as an office. She is a known entity on her home turf. Just being seen with her makes my presence more acceptable, just as being with me made it easier for her to navigate the Lido Hotel earlier in the day.

We squeeze into a dorm room that has been converted into a primitive communications office. There are three bunk beds and a desk in the middle of the floor. From the ceiling dangles the usual no-frills lightbulb. In the corner there is a rack of metallic washing basins, hot-water mugs, toothbrushes, and thermos bottles. What makes this room different from nearly every other dorm room in China is the addition of a communications device both rare and highly useful: a telephone.

Seeing the phone made me think of my friends. Was Bright still waiting for me back in my room? What about Lotus? And where did Wang Li run off to after Chai Ling changed her mind about taking the train south?

"Can I make a phone call?" I ask.

"You may," one of the students answers, "but be careful about what you say, the phone is bugged."

As often is the case in China, convenient communication comes at a price.

"I want to call the Beijing Hotel."

"Go ahead."

I dial my room number, wondering what cryptic words I should use for a phone call bugged on both ends, but no such luck for the eavesdroppers tonight. No answer.

Chai Ling is preoccupied, instantly immersed in student dealings, though she manages to flash a friendly little smile my way every once in a while. For the second time today we sit on the same bed, she on one end, me on the other. At one point she breaks from her group to come over and offer me a drink of water, perhaps trying to return the hospitality of the morning. But basically she is too busy to chat, let alone field my questions.

I lean back against the wall, sipping hot water, trying to take it all in. One by one her friends and followers pop in to talk with her, sometimes waiting on line to do so. It's like a campus version of the broadcast tent.

Some of the talk is semiconfidential, judging from excited whispers, cupped hands, and hushed tones. I overhear talk about going somewhere by airplane. I hear talk about the military. Just at a moment where the conversation takes an interesting turn, with military overtones, my appointed companion Yang, the young bodyguard, takes a seat next to me and, almost deliberately it seems, begins to distract me with a different sort of conversation.

"What sports do you like?"

"What are your hobbies?"

"Do you like music?"

When I tell him that I like to play guitar, he gets up and retrieves a cheap folk guitar that had been abandoned on the other bed. He presses me to play something, anything. I refuse several times but can't bring myself to say I'd rather be eavesdropping than singing, so at last I yield to his request.

I strum a few chords, tune the strings a bit, and strum some more. The reverberations of the guitar comfort me and without even a glimmer of conscious thought, my hand starts to finger chords to "Tiananmen Moon." I strum lightly and sing quietly to myself, in a whisper really, because I don't like to perform. The song sounds so innocent, so anachronistic now.

> "Midnight moon of Tiananmen,
> When will I see you again?
> Looking for you everywhere,
> Going in circles around the square."

My almost inaudible, understated performance earns a few polite smiles, but it lacks the pizzazz to stop the intense conversations going on around the room. Bodyguard Yang is all smiles, giving me a thumbs-up of approval. He then confides that he, too, plays guitar and he sings a song for me. We take turns singing and strumming for half an hour or so, our amateurish folk guitar rhythms providing accompaniment to the more strident political negotiations in progress.

A group of four or five unsmiling young men come barging into the room, shooting a few less-than-friendly glances in my direction. They claim urgent information about arrangements for getting on an airplane, catching a flight, something about getting to a military base. Out of the blue, or perhaps in response to a cue undetected by me, Yang puts down the guitar and makes an incongruent offer.

"Ice cream?"

"What?"

"Ice cream," he repeats. "Let us, you and I, go out to get some ice cream."

"Oh, no thanks, I'm not hungry."

"No, I insist, the treat's on me."

I obviously am not meant to be party to whatever clandestine discussions are going on, so I take up the offer of ice cream. Assuming that we will return to the room right away, I leave my Air China bag holding my camera and notebook on the bed next to Chai Ling. I try to get her attention before I leave the room, but it is hard to get eye contact as she is huddled with her comrades, deep in conversation, musing on some new development.

"We're going out for some ice cream," I announce softly. She shoots me a quizzical look at the mention of ice cream before turning back to more weighty matters.

Yang and I descend a dark staircase, emerging on a lively courtyard. Around the corner is Sanjiaodi, which boasts an air of normalcy, as bustling as a night market.

"Buy a jianbing!"

"Popsicles for sale!"

"Ice cream over here!"

Street vendors, who were rendered all but invisible by the influx of poster-perusing social superiors during the height of the movement, are still at it, hawking their wares, a reassuring assertion of normalcy. The vendors are poor but pragmatic survivors, long accustomed to living on the margin, long since liberated from the quasi-toxic dreams of youth.

Staccato voices emit from a slapdash speaker system mounted on the dorm building where Chai Ling confers with other self-appointed leaders. Unseen announcers implore students not to give up hope, to continue the peaceful struggle. Fresh big character posters about martial law and the newest twists in student strategy are plastered over hopelessly dated messages, such as MARCH ON MAY FOURTH! and THE PHYSICS DEPARTMENT SUPPORTS THE STRIKE.

My bodyguard/butler bought me a *zhuo bie lin*—vanilla and chocolate ice cream on a stick—and when he saw that I liked it he bought me another, perhaps slyly buying time for his busy comrades upstairs. It was called a "Chaplin" because the shape and color vaguely resembled the Hollywood tramp's mustachioed face topped with a chocolate hat.

After downing two Chaplins, Yang made it clear he wanted to sit outside for a while, so I returned the favor by buying a couple of orange sodas and fresh-grilled savory pancakes to share with my assigned friend. I could not help but feel I was being tested and watched, but for what reason I could not fathom. Yang was more relaxed away from the others. He told me stories of his childhood and how he loved the martial arts, recounting a memorable visit to Shaolin Temple as a boy.

"Where are you from?"

"Henan Province."

"Been here long?"

"No, I only came to Beijing recently."

"Are you really a bodyguard?"

"I was trained by Public Security. I was an agent but I didn't like it so I quit."

"What about now?"

"I support the students. It is my job to protect them."

It occurred to me that Yang might be working for some powerful political figure who was lending clandestine support to the student movement. Despite the stoked-up tensions and harsh rhetoric associated with martial law, it would be wrong to assume a Manichean divide, government against the students. The students were young Communists, would-be Communists, cream of the progeny of the Communist elite, and ultimately the future of the party. They were a force to be co-opted, if not a leading force; they were part and parcel of the body politic.

That the students had erred was party line. Deng Xiaoping made it so with his strident and inflammatory editorial. On the other hand, they were the sons and daughters of the Communist elite and were thus, by and large, eligible for forgiveness. The self-identification of students with top leaders and top leaders with students allowed for a degree of mutual sympathy and care that might otherwise be lacking, as in the case of a militant minority group like the Tibetans, who had been so harshly cracked down upon, or hapless uneducated laborers, who could be exploited because they had no connections, no voice.

So the students undoubtedly enjoyed some sympathy from old men in high places, if only as a reminder of their own youthful infatuation with grandiose ideas and the spirit of rebellion. On the other hand, the party was paranoid about challengers and would out of habit, in addition to or in spite of any genuine empathy, infiltrate the movement to guide its course.

Offers of access to airplanes and logistics involving military bases of the sort I had just overheard seemed incredible but not impossible. Like the offer of help from foreign embassies, they reeked of sympathy mixed with Machiavellian opportunism and could not be taken at face value. The Communist Party was no monolith, nor were its actions and impulses entirely coordinated. It was entirely possible that one arm sought to embrace the students—who were themselves divided into different groups—while the other batted them away.

In that sense it didn't matter if Yang was a government infiltrator or a freelance supporter. Either way, his protective policing reinforced the idea that students were part of the cherished elite.

In a society where taxi drivers and cleaning ladies take it upon themselves, or are instructed to, spy and report on "questionable" individuals in their midst, should it be any surprise that bodyguards might have mixed loyalties?

Yang had effectively steered me outside, away from a hush-hush discussion. Had he done so by instinct or at someone's request? Was he just a bit of amateur muscle who had found a role for himself in an unfolding drama, or did he have a brief to steer events in a certain direction? Who did he answer to?

To be fair, I was probably as opaque, if not more mysterious, to him as he was to me. And maybe that's why he shepherded me the way he did. I liked his understated style; he would have been a good helper to a freelance reporter or a foreign film crew. His self-presentation to me, much like mine to him, was not necessarily untrue but woefully incomplete.

Sometimes no explanation was more satisfactory than an incomplete one. The more you learned, the more questions you had. The more one tried to deter suspicion, the more suspicious one might seem. All this was everyday psychology heightened by trying to function in a society notorious for surveillance. Living in China had bred in me the habit of assuming that what one saw in public self-presentation was only the tip of the iceberg. And yet even armed with such an attitude, I had undoubtedly been duped into suspecting innocents and seeing innocence where there was none.

Never knowing for sure who is who, who can really be trusted, is one of the chilling legacies of Soviet-trained Kang Sheng and Mao's security henchmen who imported divisive KGB techniques to Communist China. But it is not fair to blame it on the Communists alone. Chinese leaders have always pitted people against people to maintain the social order. Chinese communities far outside the control of the Communists, even outright anti-Communists, are full of secrets, secret societies, gangs, and triads. Was the violence-enforced order of old, be it enforced by emperors or triad chiefs, really that different from the barrel-of-the-gun politics of Mao and the PLA?

We talk and linger in the cool night air of Sanjiaodi for about half an hour before making our way back to the room. When we get back upstairs, I am a bit taken aback by the news that Chai Ling and Feng Congde are already gone.

Even a laconic bodyguard might be expected to lose his cool if he just lost the very VIP charge he was supposed to protect, but the martial arts expert from Henan is unfazed. Maybe he hasn't lost her; he has found me. Or maybe he is just another Wang Li, dispensable, if not completely forgotten, in the context of more pressing personalities.

Or was Yang just running interference, in which case everything is just as it should be?

The student command room is still busy with self-important types, but I'm not in a social mood. I quickly gather that Chai Ling and the others have just left, spirited away to some kind of secret meeting.

"Where?" I ask impulsively. Not asking enough questions has gotten me in a bit of a fix.

"Tiananmen."

I can't believe it! Tiananmen? Again?

Yang takes the news in stride and calmly announces that we will have to hitch a ride with some other student delegates. It turns out there are several beat-up cars of Beida students going to the same secret meeting inside the Museum of the Chinese Revolution. Yang thoughtfully secures a seat for me in one of them.

As we cruise back to the downtown plaza, tugged by the immense gravity of Beijing's beating heart, my fellow passengers talk in hushed, assured tones. None of them pays me much notice. All of them are strangers to me. They are in an upbeat mood and express high hopes about tonight's meeting. My mind races ahead even as my body is slumped in the backseat with exhaustion. It's midnight. First the running away, then the train station, then Tiananmen, then a sentimental farewell to Beida, now it is back to square one?

And how are we going to get into the government-run history museum at night? I feel a total loss of personal autonomy as I move down the deserted streets of Beijing with a car full of plotting students.

As we draw close to the museum, my silent, sleepy presence is taken note of. There is a whispered debate as to whether or not I should be allowed to attend. "If you looked more Chinese," explains one of the young commissars, "you could join us." The verdict is that I am too visible as a foreigner. His words are meant to be soft and comforting, but I have heard them before and it grates me.

It brings to mind the time I was rejected, invitation tickets in hand, at the door of a gala Communist celebration at the Great Hall of the People. "We could let you in if you looked more Chinese," said the guard.

Now, on the exact opposite side of the square with a group of rebels who purport to be in opposition to the Communist Party, I am turned away for the exact same reason.

The hurt on my non-Chinese face must be visible, even in the dim light of a car parked in front of the museum. Yang consoles me, saying it has nothing to do with race. Rather it is fear of attracting unwanted attention from the plainclothes police who prowl the square at night.

I am left sitting in the car with Yang and the driver. Dark as it is, with streetlights providing the sole illumination, I decide to jot down some notes. When I grope for my notebook, I realize that I left my bag with Chai Ling. Does she have it with her? Yang finds a messenger to go inside the museum to look for her while I wait in the car. The messenger comes back to say that Chai Ling had indeed picked up my bag on her way out but had then deposited it in another dorm room at Beida. I wait in the car for a few minutes more while the "laowai" problem is discussed and reviewed within earshot. Then Yang goes inside. When he comes back, I am fighting drowsiness in the back of the cramped car.

"Chai Ling said she won't be going back," he explains, "so you better go to Beida and get your bag now."

"How can I get it now?"

"We've arranged a car," adds Yang. "Come with me."

Although the streets are totally deserted, the driver plods along at a steady, measured pace. He brings the car to a complete halt for every last stop sign and traffic light, more cautious than a driver on a police-lined street in broad daylight. It takes us almost an hour to get back to the northwest quadrant of town and by the time we tool into the courtyard adjacent to the student HQ at Sanjiaodi, everything has quieted down. Yang runs into the dorm, retrieving my shoulder bag, and asks me to check its contents. It's just as I left it, camera and notebook inside.

Soon we are back on the slow road to Tiananmen. Once again, the monotonous ride in an underperforming vibrating vehicle takes forever. This time I lose the fight to stay awake. At last, Chai Ling's kindly bodyguard gently rouses me, instructing the driver to drop me off at the Beijing Hotel. I thank him for his help. He waves me off and disappears into the shadows under the columns of the Museum of the Chinese Revolution.

PART IV

NO MOON

◑

Troops Are Coming

"Hello, *ni hao*! Where are you army men from?" I put my question to a band of soldiers in white T-shirts and khaki pants who had just broken through a series of civilian barricades to make it all the way to Wangfujing Intersection. They were under such discipline that only a few even reacted to the sound of my voice, looking my way with clay eyes. Lined up in a row, still as statues, faces etched in the stark shadows of the nighttime street, I thought of *bing-mayong*, the terra-cotta warriors.

"Ah, *ni hao*!" I said, sensing an opening when I had finally gotten a glint of eye contact.

The soldier in question looked around me but not at me, making me feel as invisible as a cloud in the night sky. He pulled out a cigarette and lit it with feigned nonchalance as if he were back in the barracks. The other men looked agitated, a bit frightened even, and shifted uncomfortably. The smoker, in contrast, struck an almost theatrical condescending air. He blew a puff of smoke in the air but looked the other way, which reminded me of the studiously cold reaction I once got from an old Caucasian gentleman in the Beijing Hotel just before the filming of *The Last Emperor* got underway. I made the earnest mistake of asking the tall, foreign man at the table next to me if he needed any help ordering food, pitying the way he was reduced to using his hands to communicate with the noodle shop waiter, who spoke little English.

The laowai with cold blue eyes stared right through me until he found something interesting to look at on the ceiling. It hurt to be ignored. When

I rode my bike back to Shida, I made a point of responding attentively to every random greeting on the street. The next day, back at the hotel for coffee, I was offered an interpreting job on the film by a cast member who had witnessed the noodle shop encounter. He explained that the man I tried to help was Peter O'Toole, and he had only been toying with me.

But the solider wasn't play acting, he was dead serious.

At last I heard one soldier speak, and then only a word.

"Where are you all from?" a young man in thick black-framed glasses had asked, addressing the group of soldiers who were ignoring me.

"Hebei," answered a military man with a fresh crew cut. The student and soldier were about the same age, but occupied very different rungs of China's hierarchical social ladder.

"What are our friends from the country doing here in the capital?" the student asked, with more than a hint of social condescension, as if Beijing were the center of the world. The friendly soldier was at a loss for words.

"Don't bother talking to them!" another soldier warned.

I pulled out my little camera to snap a picture of the frustrated dialogue. The moment my flash went off, the soldier who had been only furtively eyeing me up to that point jumped up and lunged angrily, fists waving in the air. I probably would have been hit and my camera confiscated had not the student intervened.

"Don't fight, don't fight!" the bespectacled student screamed, putting himself between me and my assailant.

"We are sorry! He's a foreigner, he doesn't understand, we will tell him," my self-appointed translator breathlessly promised.

I backed away, thanking the student who, however conceited, had gamely intervened on my behalf. Voice now shaking, confidence shot, the student retreated; the polarity of student-soldier social status had suddenly reversed.

I saw similar conflicts reenacted, with civilians verbally hectoring soldiers unwilling to talk. Then I saw the feisty Kate Adie, running to and fro in the BBC's best style, her blonde hair a pale flash in the dark. She approached me explaining, almost out of breath, that she had lost her government interpreter, which I could readily believe given the uneasy, erratic movements of the troops and agitated civilians.

Kate Adie, the lone woman among the BBC correspondents in Beijing, was the most energetic of the lot, perhaps working harder to make it in a man's world.

"What's this man trying to say?" she demanded. "Can you tell me what he's saying?" The pressure was on, and before I could react, another question. "And what about this one, what's he saying?"

"The troops are from, ah, Tongxian," I said, straining to make out the words of the man who was mumbling beside her.

"Well, just what does that mean?" she asked, impatiently, hand on hip.

"Tongxian? Well, that's the next county over. You see, *xian* means county," I said. "It is kind of, well, it's to the east of here."

"So what?"

"He is saying . . . something about how they jogged in, about eighteen kilometers, and with, with more troops coming. He says it is dangerous."

And then Kate Adie was gone, as fast as she had first appeared, chasing the story in her own inimitable way, or perhaps she had just spotted her guide, or maybe she decided to run all the way to Tongxian. Meanwhile, the white T-shirt offensive was petering out. As things quieted down and the soldiers withdrew from plain sight, my adrenaline level dropped and my legs shook and I suddenly realized how exhausted I was. The protective blanket of the crowd was unreliable and wearing thin.

Even after returning to my room, if I slept an hour it was a fitful one. Every time men in khaki were spotted or there were sudden shouts or a collective roar went up or some motorcycles zoomed by, Wang Li would wake me, announcing the crackdown had finally come. Then we'd work the phone, sharing reports with others. With the lights out and all attention on the street below, it was some time before I noticed that Wang Li had coagulated blood on the top of his forehead, partially obscured by his hairline. He said he had been hit, not by a soldier but by a person he described as a plainclothes agent. The agent stole his tape recorder, which is to say my tape recorder, which is to say the one I borrowed from someone else. Incredibly enough, he had also "lost" the backup copy of my first interview with Chai Ling. And there was the matter of the pink panties drying on the towel rack.

"A girl from Tianjin," was all he had to say about that.

I was tempted to crawl back into bed and refuse all calls when I heard someone at the door.

It was Bright. Radiant and rosy-cheeked as ever, despite the doom and gloom outside, she had come to room 1413 with eggs, bread, and sausages wrapped in napkins. Wang Li joined us and we ate quietly on the porch, watching with unspoken fears as the city uncannily assumed a practiced normalcy, as if June 3, 1989, were just another day. Would that it were. Why couldn't the army just pack up and leave everyone alone?

I told Bright about my nightmarish encounter with angry troops on my way back to the hotel last night, telling her how the mood on the street had suddenly turned humorless, how the inability to negotiate with the latest military contingents did not bode well for the students.

"I missed you," she said. "And I will miss you," she added, subtly shifting tenses.

That's when I realized Bright didn't have the time or interest to talk about troop movements and speculate about crackdowns. She had just told me, with a shift of tense, that the crackdown was imminent, and I hadn't been paying attention. I felt like an idiot trying to impress her with BBC news crew bravado and the latest political gossip.

The arrival of fresh troops in downtown Beijing was a critical development, even if it had not resulted in the final, apocalyptic battle of Wang Li's feverish imagination. There was so much I wanted to talk about, if only we could arrange some quiet time together. It had not yet fully hit me that Bright had come to say good-bye.

"You don't understand," she said, looking down with great solemnity. She shifted uncomfortably and swallowed several times, but did not go further.

"Understand what?" I asked, heart starting to beat anxiously.

"Nothing. I must go now." There was a steely determination in her voice I had not heard before.

"Well, let's meet tomorrow," I offered.

"No, not tomorrow," she said, "and not the day after that either."

"Why not?"

I looked at Wang Li, who was more of a third wheel than ever, hoping he would take the hint to give us some time together, but he seemed intrigued by the encounter.

It wasn't as if Bright had given me no warning. I had known from day one that working for the BBC subjected her to unwanted scrutiny and the web of state surveillance designed to snare foreign journalists might inadvertently get her in trouble. We had already agreed not to meet in this hotel anymore, which is why I was so surprised to see her at my door this morning. At first I thought she had come by to announce that she needed to keep a strategic distance until the storm blew over.

Wang Li, who continued munching on the remains of the boxed breakfast as if nothing was out of the ordinary, at long last got up from his chair.

"Be careful, little brother!" she said to him.

"I will," Wang Li replied. "You be careful too!"

"And you," she started. "You . . . "

She winked at me, batting her eyes with a forced playfulness as she picked up her bag and made a motion to leave. "Be a good boy!"

She came back to kiss me lightly on the cheek, then turned shyly away.

"Good luck, Jin Peili, in whatever you do!"

"But wait!" I pleaded.

"Ah, I really must go," Bright said, stepping out into the hallway.

I ran after her.

"I'll go down by myself," she whispered. We both knew the elevator was bugged and had a video camera in the ceiling. "Please go back to your room now."

"Little Conservative!" I called out.

"This is China . . . " she answered, using the opaque rationale I dreaded more than any other.

"And I'm a foreigner, right?" I said, giving voice to the unspoken part of her message.

"No, please don't tease. It is hard for me."

"It's hard for me, too."

"I'll call you later. Be careful!"

She pressed the elevator button and we waited in silence, well aware that we were not alone. She stepped into the elevator, giving me a girlish little wave good-bye before the door closed.

Back in my room, I didn't have the time to ponder what it all meant or the privacy to mope. Wang Li, who used the phone far more than I did, wanted to talk about the latest troop sightings, distracting me from the import of what had just happened. Soon he was on the phone again, calling Hong Kong on my dime to give newsy updates to journalists he somehow had numbers for. Despite his noisy communiqués, I tried to nap, but in vain. There was a knock on the door, but not the knock I was listening for. This time it was Jenny Clayton. Even in the worst of times, she had the British flair for a kind of forced cheerfulness.

"Good morning, Phi-lip. How are you today?" As for Wang Li, now reclined on the bed, she pretended he wasn't there.

"Okay, I guess."

"Here, I've got your assignment!"

"You didn't hear about last night?" I asked, wondering how she could be in such a chipper mood.

"We heard all about it in the office," she said crisply, handing me a sheet of paper, a copy of a BBC fax marked with the letterhead of the Palace Hotel. "Can you take the crew out and get these shots for me today?"

I looked at the shot list with amused disbelief.

BUSY MARKET SCENES, LUXURY CARS, PEOPLE SHOPPING, NEWSPAPER BULLETIN BOARDS, HIGH-RISE HOTELS, BARS, COFFEE SHOPS, BICYCLE PARKING LOT

There might have been a revolution erupting on the streets below, there might have been a volcano erupting on Tiananmen Square, but from the comfortable cocoon of the BBC's Beijing bureau, but a shot list stamped and approved in distant London had more immediacy and import.

Jenny Clayton, whose company I had enjoyed so much when we recorded the joyful sights and sounds of the high tide of the movement, suddenly sounded inexplicably foreign to me.

"The markets and the bicycle parking lot are most important," she said. "You absolutely must get those!"

If I was disappointed with the absurdly narrow scope of the assignment, I myself was partly to blame. Many of the items on the list were ideas I had submitted over a week ago—which seemed like an eternity given recent events—coming back to us on the rebound a few days late after getting paper approval from London. Rather than argue, I said I'd see what I could do, figuring we could get some of the generic shots for the script while covering the larger story of Beijing on the brink of disaster.

As soon as I got outside with the crew, I pocketed the shot list and instead asked the cameraman to shoot some newly hung banners, put up not by the students but the government. Bad news was not only dominating the airwaves, it was being draped down the facade of the hotel. The long banner about democracy and freedom was gone, replaced by equally long vertical banners that read like excerpts from Li Peng's martial law speech.

FIRMLY SUPPORT THE FOUR CARDINAL PRINCIPLES!

RESOLUTELY SUPPORT THE COMMUNIST PARTY!

It was almost impossible to find a taxi, another sign of the controls being imposed. Normally I would have chosen to go to the square by foot, but the camera gear was heavy and the crew wanted a car. In desperation I chatted up a scruffy-looking entrepreneur and agreed to rent his car sight unseen. The fact that it was an illegal gypsy cab was not an issue; being captive to a state employee driving a state-owned vehicle at a time like this would involve a certain kind of risk as well. Ingo and Mark had just told me about a journalist who had just been kicked out of China because of conversations secretly taped by a driver cooperating with the authorities.

The gypsy cab, however liberating in principle, turned out to be a bomb on wheels, stinking of exhaust and much smaller than anything we had used before. The rusty shell of a vehicle was just big enough for the lot of us if we boarded in just the right order and held our breath. The most troubling feature of our ride was the broken back door, of the sort that could only be opened from the outside. It wasn't that I didn't trust the driver, he seemed dependable enough in a slightly unsavory sort of way, but being locked inside could be dangerous in an emergency.

When I complained about the faulty door, the spunky driver demonstrated with great verve how quickly he could hop out of the car, run all the way around back, and pop open the door within seconds. We decided a bad car was better than no car and maybe even better than a good one. As the driver negotiated a path through a thicket of bicycles and an obstacle course of people on foot, the advantages of the junky car became obvious. The beat-up wreck on wheels was so unlike the fancy government-owned vehicles usually assigned to journalists that it permitted us to venture down back alleys or even into tense situations without attracting undue attention.

After two hours of random explorations and fitful filming, getting snippets for the shot list as well as trying to record in some demonstrable fashion the precipitous decline in public spirit, as exemplified by our being chased away by guards, police, and indignant townspeople, we found ourselves relying on the driver to keep us both safe while hovering as close to trouble as possible. We had been physically prevented from filming in front of the Qianmen Kentucky Fried Chicken, of all places—it had been my idea to show the contrast of newly posted martial law edicts with fast-food slogans. Unlike assigned drivers, often gossips and tattletales, our driver refused to answer police questions or identify us; he even went as far as urging we make a quick run for it when cornered by some snarly cops. He was a real trouper and had the makings of a natural journalist.

Although the extreme tensions of the previous night had largely dissipated with daylight, the square was getting dicey, difficult to approach on wheels.

What a difference a day could make. Only yesterday morning I had been back at the tent again, almost feeling like a regular, hanging out with Chai Ling in her tent headquarters, chatting and observing as she played the role of queen bee, running the business of the square. I had never seen her more breezy and confident. She was wearing a bright green and white striped shirt and short khaki shorts and seemed to enjoy basking in her newfound media limelight. Dozens of reporters and photographers watched her, and I found it no trouble at all to interview her again, though her answers this time seemed rote and scripted, in accordance with an unduly optimistic party line. About the only negative note she introduced was to say that it would take at least seventy years to introduce democracy to China. While chatting with her I was introduced to Hong Kong TV personality Johnny Shum and a gaggle of other Hong Kong supporters, who knew about the May 28 interview from rough transcriptions and written reports Patricia and I had offered the Hong Kong press. Impresaro Johnny Shum and company had just flown into Beijing bearing financial gifts reaped from the Happy Valley fundraising concert.

Hou Dejian had played at that Hong Kong concert, a personal turning point that had led him to getting involved upon his return home to Beijing. I wondered about him now. He was at the monument, on a hunger strike of his own, along with Liu Xiaobo, Zhou Duo, and Gao Xin. I could readily identify with all of them, not just because I had met them all at one time or another. We were all in our early thirties, caught at that tempestuous age when the caution and circumspection that comes with maturity can still be overridden by the lingering enthusiasm of youth.

Suddenly we hit a chaotic intersection with a jolt. Our way forward was blocked by pedestrians milling about angrily on West Chang'an Boulevard by Liubukou, not far from the guarded entrance to the leadership compound at Zhongnanhai.

The wide street was free of traffic but choked up with the carcasses of three smashed buses and shards of broken brick and glass. We stepped out of the car cautiously, not sure the bricks had stopped flying. The tension in the air was almost visible, like heat hovering over a hot road. The buses reminded me of beetles, attacked and stripped of meat by an army of ants. The interiors had been picked clean by the mob; upholstered seats ripped apart, metal bars bent out of shape. This was no ordinary case of looting, but an expression of hatred to the fingertips, hatred to the bone. Why the anger, the sacking of a bus? I asked around and was told the story of the Trojan horse. The bus had been full of lethal weapons, ammunition, and other military supplies.

"Guns!" one of the vigilantes explained. "Military issue! There were also hand grenades on the bus."

But why were the seats pulled apart, the windows smashed?

"The army tried to trick the people," another man cried out.

"They tried to make it look like we had the weapons! It was a trap. They are looking for an excuse. It is they who are criminals, not us!"

A student brought me over to see the evidence. Rifles, machine guns, tear gas cylinders, daggers, and grenades were piled on top of the bus for all to see, but wisely placed out of reach. There was a twin danger: a distraught demonstrator might be tempted to grab a weapon and turn it on his tormentors or the conscientious men guarding the weapons might be accused of collecting them with violent intent; either way creating an excuse for crackdown in a country where gun laws were so strict that mere possession of the same could bring on a violent military response.

It had all been so sporting up until now, a battle of wits, a battle of wills. A battle of empty hands, empty stomachs, incantatory voices, and tired feet. The introduction of military hardware changed the game entirely. It made a mockery of a month of nonviolent struggle. Who was funneling in the weapons? Were they a pretext for a pretext to crack down?

"The bus and the weapons are part of a conspiracy to smuggle in troops and weapons to attack Tiananmen," explained a young man in a white shirt.

"But what happened to the soldiers on the bus?"

"Those cowards, they ran into the gate of Zhongnanhai. They ran away, they are afraid of the will of the people," he said, choking up with anger. "They are afraid . . . "

Although I did not disagree with his words, the strident and unforgiving tone of his voice unnerved me.

"If they didn't run away," added another self-appointed spokesman, "they would face the justice of the masses."

"Justice of the masses," echoed another man approvingly.

Mass justice, vigilante justice, just what did that consist of? By now I was worried that our BBC crew might become embroiled in a misdirected mass action for some perceived slight, so I erred on the side of caution, quietly asking permission to take some pictures on the bus. Permission granted. While Ingo and Mark recorded the scene, I studied the tense, shiftless ring of bodies lining the intersection between the broad boulevard and the side road that led to the music hall. There were angry scowls, twitching limbs, and nervous facial tics, and palpable worry in people's eyes. It was spooky and made me want to leave.

While the film crew did their job, I jotted down some of the antigovernment slogans and graffiti on the roadside walls.

DON'T BETRAY THE PEOPLE!

NEVER TRUST THE MOTHERFUCKING GOVERNMENT!

IS THE PEOPLE'S ARMY AFRAID OF THE PEOPLE?

Thousands of people stood around shiftily, but their faces lacked the reassuring neutrality of the idle loafers one normally encounters in China. There wasn't much to do, but there was much to think about. Things were way past the point where people wanted to practice English or know where we were from. A number of the young men near the bus leered at us, dumb with rage and fear perhaps, nerves frayed by caustic thoughts. Conversation, even when on the same side of the barricade, was difficult. Loquacious small talk, the lubricant of Beijing street life, had all but dried up. What was happening to the marchers, once so resilient, so peaceful, so optimistic for so many weeks? Were these the same people? If so, were they not fast approaching a psychological breaking point? It pained me to look at them; there was venom in their eyes.

Chai Ling had given a clue as to the true nature of the movement in its current decayed state; it was about blood, but with a twist. Both sides taunted and provoked, intimidated and humiliated, hoping the other side would attack first. Once the blood started to flow, all sorts of unreasonable actions could be justified. Once the blood started to flow, an upsurge in sympathy would accrue to those most effectively portrayed as victims of the violence.

That's what made the hunger strike so effective. If one side could claim victimhood, the other side started to look like a cruel victimizer. Maybe that was why the government was recklessly sending in probes, discarding weapons in plain sight: setting up a pretext. If the people attacked the soldiers, if the generally beloved and legendarily heroic PLA themselves became victims, the polarity of sympathy could be flipped, with the students and their ilk seen in a novel way, not as lambs being led to slaughter, but as wolves in sheep's clothing.

The mounting war of nerves, with each side trying to make the other side look like the predator, brought to mind the haunting lyrics of Chyi Chin: "the northern wolf, cold fangs bared, dust and wind blowing, ready to strike."

The weather was an irritant in its own right. It was hot and muggy, and yet dark for midday. What sun there was, was filtered through a thick haze. The air was stiflingly still. We took our establishing shots, asked a few more questions, and beat a quick exit, and not a second too soon. It occurred to me that in a moment of mass panic, our gear could be mistaken for weaponry. Once we broke ranks with the raw, barely contained crowd, a number of unfriendly comments were hurled in our direction, as if we were abandoning them or somehow colluding with the government.

Even with our heads bent low, we might inadvertently become targets for the pent-up anger around us. The driver sensed this, and got in the habit of patiently and deferentially fielding questions from those around us, even those who banged on the car demanding to know who was inside. The driver knew what to say and when to say it. He had uttered not a word the time we were cornered by the police, but was quick to mediate when we got caught up in civilian disputes, such as happened in a backstreet hutong near Qianmen when a posse of indignant residents prevented us from filming.

The atmosphere was so edgy, I started to fear the undisciplined crowd more than the highly-restrained soldiers. There were more than a few people looking to vent their anger on anyone, anything. Mercifully, the driver's gift of gab helped keep things on an even keel and served to deflect those who might otherwise see us as a convenient target.

The rusty jalopy, loaded down with our oversized Western bodies and heavy gear, lurched and sputtered along the agitated, littered streets in the direction of the Great Hall of the People. Before we had a chance to establish where we were going, the driver pulled over to the curb and opened the door for us.

"Take pictures here," he instructed matter-of-factly, as if he had suddenly become our producer, and in a way he had. "I will wait for you in the car."

We went along with the driver's suggestion, taking some of the gear with us, but we didn't even bother to set things up. Nothing of importance seemed to be happening; maybe that was the point, a chance to rest in the shade. The Great Hall of the People towered to the east over the tiled rooftops of low-rise brick dwellings.

Back alley residents moped around listlessly. There were the usual drifters and loafers, but the habitual stares were glazed over a bit. A brick wall blocked our view of the nearest intersection, but we weren't looking for escape routes. It was calm, perhaps a bit too calm given the bulging eyes and absence of earthy voices, but calm enough for our attention to revert back to things BBC, talking about our recent trip to the countryside, to look for nonexistent signs of unrest there, and other excursions I had been on since getting rehired by the Beeb on May 29. I distributed popsicles to the thirsty crew as we shuffled slowly in the direction of the Great Hall.

We were sufficiently inattentive to the oddly muffled crowd dynamics to get us on the topic of what to do for lunch. But when we turned the corner, all conversation ceased mid-sentence.

Before us a thousand soldiers in full battle dress occupied the street. They had staked out a bit of strategic high ground, lined up in formation on the street behind the Great Hall, arranged in long rows, some sitting, some standing. Whoa! Where did they come from? How did they get past all those people on Tiananmen? Had the square been breached? Then I recalled the Beijing whispers, long predating this crisis. There were said to be secret underground tunnels all around Tiananmen leading to and from the Great Hall, Zhongnanhai, and other government power centers.

It was as if they just popped in out of nowhere. The uniformed military men, well over a thousand strong, were in crisp formation, unlike the ragtag army units we had seen the night before. Though surrounded by civilians pleading for peace, the men looked beyond persuasion, quietly fired up, ready to kill. If the soldiers in white T-shirts and green pants who jogged into town last night could be characterized as slightly unfriendly, then the fully equipped soldiers today were outright hostile. The only saving grace was their utter immobility, like an army unearthed from a century's sleep.

To see a battalion of People's Liberation Army soldiers facing down a mass of unarmed protesters on the back steps of the Great Hall of the People was incongruous and unsettling. The tough men were organized in units, some helmeted, some carrying backpacks, others carrying field radios with thick black antennae sticking up into the air. Their self-restraint and inaction encouraged us to move around for a closer look. I helped the crew get set up on the wide marble steps of the back door to the Great Hall. The dignified solidity of the building somehow stiffened our resolve; after getting our establishing shot we approached the ring of soldiers for close-ups. We inched in on the soldiers, careful to look for an escape path in case something untoward happened.

In front of us a tense negotiation was in progress as members of the neighborhood and student negotiators pleaded with the men in green. The discussion appeared to bear no fruit; argument seemed futile, but at least it was still possible to talk. The soldiers, however, were clearly under some kind of discipline that made them impervious to the naïve charm of fellow citizens begging for peace.

The situation could get out of hand all too quickly. I scanned the ceremonial cityscape for possible escape routes and hiding places. Would it be safer to go back to the steps of the Great Hall or dive into some courtyard? Would the thick walls of the public bathroom over there provide cover? Would the soldiers use tear gas or clubs? What about guns?

The troops deployed today were the real deal. This was the sort of iron-fisted response to political protest that I feared most when I joined Bright and Jenny as they stepped through the gates of the university out onto the streets of Beijing on May 4. We broke the law against demonstrations and nothing happened. Students took to the streets day after day and nothing happened. Students took over the square and nothing happened. Soon the numbers swelled to a million, student leaders talked of overthrowing the government, and nothing happened.

No crackdown, no nothing. The blossoming of the Tiananmen movement was as much the result of inaction as action. It was widely believed that the government, at least part of it, supported the students. China was going through some sort of paradigm upheaval, bigger than any of the parties involved, and yet to date it had been a mercifully peaceful transformation. The natural outcome might well be political reform that allowed for more personal freedom and open discussion. Or so it seemed.

The army units now entering Beijing by stealth were game changers. In a matter of days, the government's alleged patience took on a more sinister air. The unwillingness to crack down the day martial law was declared did not mean there was tacit support for the students, nor did it reveal a compassionate desire for reconciliation; it was just a logistical logjam. It had taken two weeks to move the army into place, and now that the troops were finally face-to-face with the protesters, things were a lot less ambiguous than before.

I went back to our pre-arranged meeting spot and looked for the driver to discuss a plan of action in case all hell broke loose, but the driver and the old jalopy were gone. What a time to abandon us! I paced up and down the street where he had told us to wait for him, furious at his betrayal.

"Are you all right?" asked a man who had been watching me. My consternation was visible.

"What?"

"Are you lost?"

"No, I'm looking for someone."

"The driver? Perhaps he has gone."

I had trusted him. Was I really such a poor judge of character?

"It is not safe here, but you will be okay if you walk in that direction," the man said, pointing south.

"But I have to find the car, our stuff is in it!"

"What can I do to help?"

The stranger surely meant well. Then again, how could one know for sure? Judging the trustworthiness of strangers was in the best of times an inexact science, but at a time like this it could be the difference between escape and entrapment.

I thanked the man for his advice and retreated to the wall near the intersection to commiserate with the crew. Being penned between mazelike *hutong* and the back of the Great Hall with thousands of soldiers blocking traffic made for claustrophobic feelings. Some of the gear was gone but we were unharmed and the soldiers, for the moment at least, seemed content to leave us alone. Perhaps we could hoof it back to the hotel, if we could only squeeze by the south flank of the Great Hall, cut across the square, skirt past the Public Security compound and work our way north to Wangfujing.

The crew wanted to bail, but just as soon as we commenced our roundabout retreat, there was a surprise.

Our driver was back! He ran up to us, waving to get our attention, huffing and puffing out of breath. "Sorry, friends, I was busy."

"Where'd you go? We were looking all over . . . "

"I took an injured man to the hospital," he said, wiping his sweaty forehead with his sleeve.

"What? The hospital?" I was almost going to shout "but you're working for the BBC!" when I realized that I could hardly fault him for an impulsive act of compassion. "What do you mean, hospital? What happened?"

"A man was beaten by a soldier, he was bleeding all over. The hospital is far, all the way over by Chongwenmen," he said breathlessly. "Sorry. It took so long."

"No, forget it. I guess what you did is more important."

"Thank you for understanding," he said, shaking my hand, nodding to the others. "You are true friends of the people."

Touched by his concern for others, but not in a comparably altruistic mood ourselves, we decided to return to the hotel with our gear while we could. On the way, the driver suggested we stop by the hospital to take a look. He suggested we try to film some of the people who had been wounded and we quickly agreed. The broken-doored jalopy offered scant comfort but it did give us a low profile as we meandered through streets that were increasingly falling under martial law control. Getting out of car quickly was no longer the issue. The streets were menacing. The driver veered south, edging his way around the square, patiently snaked around clusters of people left and right, and finally made it to Chongwenmen Intersection via a series of back alleys.

The driver pulled up to the emergency room entrance of the hospital. A middle-aged woman with bobbed hair wearing a white smock shook her head no, dismayed at the sight of a car full of foreigners with cameras, emphatically shooing us away. Wang Li and I got out with the help of the driver and approached the prim-looking lady.

"*Ni hao! Women shi yingguo dianshitai laide.* We're from BBC television, we'd like to talk to some of the patients who were injured today . . . "

"You are here in violation of martial law!" she railed loudly. She then parroted word by word a few lines from the martial law regulations. Unmoved by her reasoning, we repeated our request.

"We won't take any pictures, we just want to find out what happened and talk to anyone injured in the fighting."

"As I said," she rejoined, raising her metallic voice an octave, "You are in violation of martial law!"

Wang Li asked me to slip him my little camera; his plan was to slip into the hospital unnoticed while I distracted the woman. She was sounding more and more like a Communist Party tape loop, especially when she repeated her martial law statement for the third time.

"Would you like to say that to the camera?"

By now Ingo had the camera rolling and he was coming our way.

"Get that camera out of here!" she screamed.

The officious lady ran after Ingo and Mark, allowing me to slip inside. Wang Li waved me into a sickroom. One man, heavily bandaged, said he was struck by the military police outside Zhongnanhai. There were several other patients recently wounded. I ran out to see if we could somehow get Ingo in with the camera. This time the woman in charge planted her body between me and the entrance.

"As I said, you are in violation," she sputtered. "If you don't leave immediately I will, I will . . . "

I tried to win the support of a small circle of onlookers hoping to swing things in our favor, a technique that had worked well when we were of one mind with the masses.

"Just admit it," I said to her, keeping an eye on the noncommital eyes around us, "You're only saying that because you have to, right? In your heart you side with the people, don't you?"

"Get out of here!" she screamed, raising her arm as if to hit me.

What could we do? She may have been a broken record, but this was her workplace. My bid to win lateral support failed badly. No one budged an inch. I backed away from the enforcer and told the crew to pack it up.

A familiar-looking young man with a wispy beard came forward. He was wearing a loose-fitting mint-green cotton top that looked like hospital garb, and I would have taken him for a patient wandering the halls were it not for the stenciled words "1989 Democratic Tide" and telltale autographs scribbled across his shirt.

He was a student and he had been watching us in silence. Just at the moment when we gave in and started to pack up, he came over to me to talk.

"That woman is unreasonable. She should have let you in."

"Thanks for the encouragement," I said. It was a relief to find someone willing to take my side when I had been arguing, rather rudely, with another Chinese.

"Sometimes I wonder if I should even bother."

"I heard you," the young man added. "You have the right to say what you said."

Even though you're a foreigner, he might have added.

The young man's sun-scorched, high-cheeked face reminded me of someone. Where had I seen him before? Apparently he had a similar sense of déjà vu.

"Aren't you with ABC?" he asked me.

"No, BBC, England, though I am from America."

It struck me as uncanny that he should ask about ABC. The police had closed down ABC and inspected the office after a copy of the May 28 tape was intercepted at the airport. I had to assume they were looking for me since they were somehow tipped off about the interview I did with Chai Ling.

"My name is Meng, I am a student from the Central Academy of Drama," he said. "You look familiar."

"Why did you ask if I was from ABC?"

"Oh, because during the water strike I was interviewed by ABC News."

The water strike. It finally dawned on me where I had seen him before, and he me.

"Phil, let's get out of here!" yelled Ingo.

The crew was packed up and waiting impatiently.

I wanted to talk more to this winsome kindred spirit, but the crew couldn't wait.

"Hey, do you need a ride anywhere? Why don't you come with us?"

"Okay, just a minute . . ." He stepped aside to speak quietly with some student friends who were holding vigil at the entrance of the hospital.

Meng, though a large-boned man, was skeleton-thin after the hunger strike. Even so, he could barely fit into the van. I sat in the back so I could talk to him, giving up the navigator's seat to the grateful Ingo, who had the build of rugby player.

"You were in the water strike, right?" I said to Meng, who was squeezed between me and Wang Li. "Remember the day I was there, when the student guards let me in but not the correspondent? He's still mad about it!"

It was immediately obvious that my roommate was not happy about the latest addition to our crew, as if two activists in tight quarters was one two many. Wang Li, after striking out with Chai Ling and the radical crowd, had focused on BBC, trying to perfect his role as media intermediary. He emphasized his links to the British crew by refusing to speak Chinese with his fellow citizens, using his shaky English instead to make a point. The urbane Meng, for his part, indicated no interest in chatting with the rough-hewn provincial either.

Instead he talked quietly to me about how students were monitoring news by posting teams at the entrance to major hospitals, fully expecting the government to lie and cover up in the event of casualties.

On the way back to the hotel Wang Li did something that crystallized my growing doubts about him. While practicing English with Mark, he alone in the thirsty crew sipped on a can of Coke that he had taken from the minibar in my room. After sucking it down to the last drop, he nonchalantly flipped the can out of the car window as we buzzed along Dongdan Road. The red can bounced a few times in the middle of the road, nearly hitting a cyclist.

"What did you do that for?" I asked in disbelief.

"Someone will pick it up," he said callously.

Wang Li. That's what he called himself anyway. A name as common as John Smith or John Doe. Was the other name he once whispered in my ear his real name or another nickname? Who was the real Wang Li? A student activist? Was he a student at all? An entrepreneur? An opportunist? Who, if anyone, did he work for?

The dusty jalopy jerked to a halt in front of the posh Palace Hotel, where uniformed doormen tried in vain to open the rusty back door, but only the driver knew the trick to that. I thanked the conscientious driver for his extraordinary help and paid him twice what he asked for. Meng took one look at the fancy lobby of the PLA-owned luxury hotel and told me he didn't want to go in. I wanted to talk more to the idealistic activist, if I could only get Wang Li off my back for a few hours.

"Hey! You guys having dinner now?" I called out to the crew.

"Haven't had a thing to eat all day . . . " Ingo answered.

"Could you spot Wang Li a meal?"

"Sure. Hey, matey, you coming with us?"

"Not yet. See you later," I said.

Meng and I walked towards Wangfujing, comparing notes on the day. Tear gas had been used at Liubukou. Police were swinging clubs. One of the first victims was a girl who had her leg broken.

When we moved on to other topics, Meng had a few choice things to say about Wang Li, whom he suspected of being with the secret police. A con artist I could believe, but not a cop. Such things were possible, but I wasn't willing to believe it.

Still, the contrast between the two of them was evident enough. Meng's unvarnished political idealism reminded me of my mood when I marched in early May. Wang Li's desire to master the media, to take in stride the punishments and rewards that went with it, echoed my more recent activities as a stringer for the BBC and ABC.

Wang Li, not unlike myself, found comfort in fancy hotels, whereas Meng wouldn't even step inside the Palace Hotel, and I had a hard time getting him inside the Beijing Hotel for a quick meal. He insisted on ordering nothing, then settled for the cheapest thing on what to him was a sorely overpriced menu. He seemed like he couldn't wait to get back outside.

After a bowl of noodles in the hotel dining hall, where we ran into Eric and Fred relaxing on a well-earned but ill-timed night off, and then Louise, who was talking with Harrison Salisbury at another table, Meng and I went back outside for a stroll along Chang'an Boulevard, taking measure of the dissipated crowd, trying to see for ourselves if soldiers were anywhere close to the square.

A column of soldiers burst out of the shadows near the construction site at the western extremity of the hotel and started running along the sidewalk. They ran in formation, maintaining a disciplined single file until their path was blocked by a gang of indignant civilians. Some of the onlookers booed or jeered, others even shoved and harassed the unarmed soldiers. Activists wearing headbands, most probably students, could be seen pleading with both the civilians and the soldiers for patience and conciliation.

We ran closer to get a better look. The soldiers had been stopped in their tracks by a handful of protesters, which suggested not so much the indomitable strength of people power but rather a reluctance to clash with civilians. Were the soldiers divided in their sympathies? Afraid? Or were they under instructions not to clash, not for now? What was their plan and where were they headed? Were they slyly inviting trouble, hoping to create an incident, a pretext for further action?

People argued among themselves at emotional high pitch. There was a marked division of voices; some spewed abuse at the soldiers, others pleaded for nonviolence and negotiation. A single file of older men in uniform cautiously edged their way along the metal fence that surrounded the western perimeter of the hotel. They were eventually cornered and pressed up against the fence, jostled by the unfriendly bystanders until they dispersed.

The soldiers gathered closest to us looked physically fit and wore trim crew cuts, but some of them had gray hair and appeared close to middle age. Were they officers? Unlike the relaxed, unafraid gait I associated with men of power in uniform in China, these men looked stiff, unsure of themselves, and tense. I snapped a few photos and we tried to talk to some of the soldiers, but they blankly refused to respond to any of our questions. They avoided eye contact, as if looking into the faces of the people they were being ordered to put down would weaken their will. Were they waiting in the wings, poised to smash the protest and retake the square?

Despite the stern countenances, the soldiers we ran into around the hotel were gentlemanly almost to a fault. The same curious reticence had been noted in the case of the troops we had seen by the Great Hall and the troops that jogged in from Tongxian the night before. As far as I could observe, the PLA had not yet been willing to breach, let alone smash and ride over, the patently flimsy barricades scattered around the downtown area. The only serious barrier keeping the troops from the sacral ground of Tiananmen Square was human flesh; the fear of confronting fellow citizens.

For the unwanted but otherwise unobjectionable military men, the only way to get downtown without mowing down barriers was the same way as everyone else, on foot. Given the fact that the soldiers were unarmed and apparently ambivalent about doing their job as soldiers, they did not enjoy a clear advantage over the adrenaline-spiked protesters. One might even say the soldiers were at risk, depending on how effectively the crowd controlled itself. While Meng and I mused over such things, the column of army men that had slithered through the protest crowd just moments ago had broken rank and melted away into the shadows, exiting the boulevard along a side street running north.

In addition to the new troop arrivals that we had just encountered, the troop concentrations we knew about included the many hundreds packed on the street behind the Great Hall of the People. If rumors Meng had heard were to be believed, there were troops hiding in secret near the Great Hall in subterranean tunnels and perhaps on the other side of the Zhongnanhai wall where he had fasted.

We knew that strategic areas adjoining Tiananmen Square, such as the Museum of the Chinese Revolution, the Forbidden City, Worker's Park and Sun Yatsen Park, had been declared off-limits according to martial law declarations. Was that a crowd control measure or were troops being stealthily amassed in those normally public places? Why had the troops posted behind the Great Hall not yet made a move on the square? Was there still serious division in the politburo on how to proceed? How many troops armed with clubs and tear gas would it take to disperse a protest that was collapsing in on itself out of sheer exhaustion?

We found it increasingly hard to move about and monitor political developments on the street over the heads of overly excited civilians in an increasingly short-tempered crowd. The power of the PLA as an institution and the instinctive fear of authority in this authoritarian state was so strong that the mere appearance of men partially in uniform, even unarmed, and as well-behaved as the most recent dispatch of soldiers appeared to have been, was inciting and incendiary.

Then the soldiers disappeared into the night, abetted by the lack of electric street illumination, which was limited to the big boulevards. There was no glowing backlight to the overcast skies. The only thing worse than seeing so many soldiers so close to the square was suddenly not seeing them at all, but knowing they lurked nearby.

JUNE 3

◑

Of Tanks and Men

Disquieted by the disappearance of the soldiers, Meng and I briefly went up to study the street from a more comprehensive vantage point before setting out for the University of Democracy on the square. Lotus, who was on the phone when we entered, was flustered, saying her husband wanted her back home immediately. No sooner did she leave than there was a loud knock at the door. It was the BBC *Panorama* crew and they wanted my help with something. I led them to the porch to take a good look at the commotion below, fully expecting to be hit with a renewed request to cover the disco assignment.

"We got your message, Phil," Jenny Clayton started, while John Simpson remained in the background, uncharacteristically unobtrusive. "It's a shame we can't go to the disco, because this is our last Saturday night here." She paused for a moment, gazing at the agitated blur of motion in the street below. "But you are right, this is more important."

She was straightforward and curt about it and that was the end of that. There was no reprimand; rather, they were asking for my help, which in turn made it hard for me to tell them I had lost interest in freelancing for them. At least we were of one mind about wanting to go to the square.

Jenny Clayton, gracious as she had been to me, could not entirely let go of her desire to get the "cultural" shots she needed for her documentary. She got in an unpleasant argument with John Simpson that started in front of the hotel and lasted for the duration of the long walk to the square, which given cumbersome night gear including lights and the distractions of a skittish, un-cooperative public took longer than usual.

There was tension in the air, something atmospheric, like the irritability and depression associated with the falling barometer before a storm. Something had to give, and give soon.

I put my ear to the wind, hoping to pick up what wisdom the crowd might possess. I was starting to think of the trembling mass as one large amorphous jellyfish or one throbbing, contiguous body that would seize up the moment any part of its perimeter was breached or sustained attack. The eyes and ears and nose and instincts of the crowd extended far beyond our individual senses. It was a collective extension of ourselves, almost a vital, living thing. If something should happen on the far side of the square or further down Chang'an Boulevard, word-of-mouth warning transmitted by hundreds of contiguous voices might be the only warning available to us.

What was that rumbling sound? Thunder? It was overcast, not a star in the sky, but it didn't exactly look like rain either. Again we heard a faint, grinding, metallic sound, distorted and swallowed by distracting voices near us, and a crescendo of muffled shouts in the distance. Something appeared to be happening to the west, but we couldn't make it out.

The battle of wills between reporter and producer led to a halfhearted search for a place to do a standup while also on the lookout for newsworthy developments. This resulted in a zigzag path that took us first towards and then away from the ghostly beauty of the hopelessly dim Goddess of Democracy and finally over towards the hackneyed but clearly illuminated Mao portrait.

In doing so, we followed the general flow of foot traffic along a boulevard almost entirely empty of cars and only lightly peopled. We moved in silent communion with hundreds of others, assuming the habitual counterclockwise movement that led one straight across the top of the square and then down in front of the Great Hall of the People.

"There's supposed to be a ceremony at the so-called University of Democracy tonight," I said as the crew paused to consider a stand up. But I was rather consumed with curiosity about what Chai Ling, Feng Congde, and the diminished ranks of student protesters were up to. "Can we go over there first?"

"No," Jenny countered, looking not at me but at her colleague. My question had the effect of reigniting her argument with John and the stand up was scrapped.

Mark and Ingo exchanged knowing glances while I took Meng by the arm and suggested we lead the way and let the crew follow. I needed to tune out the distracting voices of argument in my native language to better make sense of the jittery Chinese voices around us.

We worked our way through thickets of protesters while the crew followed us in tandem. As we got deeper into the crowd and closer to the beating heart of Tiananmen, I checked my watch more frequently. It was nearing midnight.

The producer and correspondent ambled together in an uneasy silence, broken by bursts of audible antipathy. Ingo lumbered down the crowded street, pausing now and then to adjust a bolt of black cloth that he draped over his camera. Mark followed close behind and Wang Li just a step behind him, tripod in tow.

As always, racially observant comments greeted the crew.

"Look! Laowai!"

"Are they going to the square?"

"Look! Foreigners! Journalists?"

"Don't the laowai know about martial law?"

Not all of the comments about us are in Chinese. An unexpected taunt on the part of a passing foreigner proves harder for the crew to ignore.

"Ha, ha! Look at that man!" cries an American-accented voice. "He's carrying a big camera. Look, he's got it hiding under a black sheet."

"They can laugh all they want," Ingo mutters. "If things get bad I can use this to hide the camera. It could be a matter of life and death."

The cloth-draped camera did look odd, resembling a magician's prop, but it was no joke to a news professional like Ingo, who had been shot at before.

"Sniper fire is often aimed at people with cameras," Ingo explains to no one in particular. The producers are locking horns again while the two student activists studiously ignore one another. Who isn't feeling irritable, afraid, and confused on this evening? Some kind of confrontation is imminent. The sweet scent of anticipated success has given way to the acrid odor of fear and failure.

At certain junctures, the flow of the crowd seemed to reverse itself, provoking heated exchanges between those entering and those exiting the square.

"Why are you going that way?"

"Cowards! What are you afraid of?"

"Going home already?"

"Someone said the fighting has started to the west!"

"Got to get out of here before one!"

It was getting scary. Who wasn't frustrated, if not afraid, as the transformative dream of the collective crumbled and the crowd spiraled out of control? Self-preservation, not self-sacrifice, was the ascendant trend. The "pulse" of the crowd grew irregular, erratic. Every shiver a shudder, every paroxysm packed with apocalyptic portent. The ability of the mass to transmit sympathetic vibrations had not been fundamentally altered, but the content of the message had been, as contagious enthusiasm was replaced by malevolent desperation.

You didn't have to be a fortune-teller to know Tiananmen was the target, but what were they going to hit it with and when? The long-anticipated crackdown had been postponed so long that getting it over with might bring a certain amount of relief, if not resolution.

To think I could have gone to a nightclub "to see what young people were thinking" on the other side of town with the *Panorama* crew this evening, an absurd assignment, but at least a safe one. Bright probably would have approved.

But for reasons I couldn't explain to myself, let alone her, I had to be on the square. It was like there was a Tiananmen virus and I had been infected by it.

Still, Bright's cryptic phone message echoed in my ears. The way she practically ordered me not to go out was so out of character. I thought of how she easily she had acquiesced when Chai Ling "hijacked" our day off, or when I said yes to a new job at the BBC, only days after quitting, to work on a BBC documentary.

"Don't go out tonight," she had pleaded over the phone, reaching me in my room just after dinner. I told her I was going out with or without the crew.

"Well, if you must go out, make sure you go home by midnight. If not midnight, definitely go back by one!" she said in a whisper.

"Why?"

"Please, I can't tell you any more. I can't say . . . but please, stay in your room!"

What was I to make of her plea? Was it just the latest missive in her campaign to get me to quit working for the BBC or was it code for something else?

It suddenly dawned on me that I might be endangering the crew by my stubborn, irrational insistence on going to the square. How could I convey to them that I believed this was the night, based in part on instinct, in part on a college girl's solicitous warning? Would they listen or laugh?

I duly told the crew that things might get dangerous after midnight.

"I'm responsible for the safety of the crew," Simpson responded, deftly appropriating the information while subtly asserting rank.

Wang Li was rising to the occasion. He had initially attached himself to me, then briefly to John Simpson, and after managing to annoy both of us respectively had found in Ingo yet another BBC "boss" to cling to, but I didn't begrudge him this. Ingo, who had been the first of us to voice safety concerns, was appreciative and generous.

The cameraman needed an alert pair of eyes to watch his back when he had his face pressed to the viewfinder and Wang Li was observant. In no time at all, Wang Li learned to move with the crew in almost perfect concert, as if he had been working with them for years.

Despite some gnawing doubts about Wang Li's actual identity and motivation, I thought he was plucky, a natural journalist, and an excellent addition to the BBC crew. Even if he wasn't really a student, an operator like Wang Li might well be an asset if the going got rough.

In contrast, the idealistic Meng, my direct line to the hunger strikers, was something of a liability, as much as I liked him. The cachet of wearing a red headband and student-issued shirt emblazoned with the "1989 Democratic Tide" was plummeting by the minute.

Simpson and Clayton finally resolved to do a camera setup near the portrait of Mao. Wang Li opened the tripod and tested the lights, Ingo set up the camera, and Mark tested the sound.

Meng and I decided to do a little reconnoiter within a short radius to better gauge what was going on. The "University of Democracy" was only about two hundred yards away to the southwest, but we hesitated to leave the crew alone for the uncertain duration of time it might take to get there and back.

"Leave the square for safety of life and limb!" a disembodied taped voice blared out over a public-address system. The sound was not coming from the broadcast tent but rather from government-controlled loudspeakers mounted high upon lightposts around the square. Li Peng's grim propagandists were back in action.

The student loudspeakers rigged up in the center of the square were still audible, but just barely so. I thought I heard Chai Ling's high-pitched voice, but it might have been my imagination since she had very much been on my mind. Would the hyperbolic rivers of blood she spoke of truly come to flow across the square?

Scratchy amplified voices issued by portable speakers not far away from where we stood also begged for attention. It was a group of workers, their spokesmen shouting something along the lines of "Vow to defend the students to the end." Meng explained that the workers were led by Han Dongfang, pointing out a thick cluster, mostly men, gathered in the northwest quadrant of the square.

We were being hit by the static of three strident outbursts at once, each distorting the other, making for a noisy, nightmarish war of words.

Again I heard, or thought I heard, a low rumbling sound like that of distant thunder. Turning back north to hurriedly rejoin the crew, I found my route blocked by an undulating human wall. Without warning, the workers and students around me first stiffened, then surged en masse towards Mao's portrait, like rambunctious Red Guards turning to the red, red sun of their hearts. Sparked on by some cue that I had missed, thousands more young men and women snapped to attention and began a rush to join some unseen fray somewhere.

Being part of the teeming mass, I had little choice but move in tandem. It was well nigh impossible to stand still; to move against the flow would beg injury. Only when I reached the concrete and steel divider in the middle of Chang'an Boulevard, guided by those in front, pushed by those behind me, could I pause and wring myself free of the seething throng long enough to climb on top of a cement road barrier to get a better view of what was going on.

A military vehicle that looked like a tank came careening recklessly through the sea of people like an icebreaker cracking through thin ice. Tanks on Tiananmen Square! It was crazy, what was the PLA doing, what did they think this could achieve? The armored vehicle roared down thickly peopled Chang'an Boulevard as fast as its heavy treads would permit, not as a peacekeeper, but as a provocateur. Then there appeared another metallic monster, begging for a clash, beckoning blood.

The reckless charging of two heavy vehicles in the middle of a crowd of thousands shocked me; the rules of engagement had changed. The military's admirable discipline and restraint had been abandoned, giving way to reckless, violent acts. The tank was so unforgiving, so heavy, so hard, the bodies it bolted past so vulnerable and soft. So far, no one had been hit or run over, but it could happen any second now. It was a deadly game of "chicken," in which the winner is the last to flinch, but the game was unfair, pitting tank against man. I shuddered in dread of seeing people mowed over, but amazingly the men and women around me seemed emboldened rather than frightened.

It was as if the daredevils possessed a belief in mind over matter, like the martial arts warriors of the late Qing Boxer Rebellion who convinced themselves they were invulnerable to bullets. I'd seen plenty of people tempt fate crossing streets in busy traffic, but never did I dream it possible to slow a tank's advance by jumping in front of it!

Numb and immobilized, I watched daredevils dart back and forth in front of the armored vehicle, taunting the unseen driver. The armored tank continued to penetrate the crowd, slowing to turn around, speeding up on the straightaway, heading directly at the flag- and banner-waving provocateurs like a mad bull aiming for a matador. With each sweep, the crowd parted, some running for their lives, others holding their ground, tempting fate.

The passionate insanity of the moment was contagious. After a second silent signal, which caused the people immediately around me to snap into action, I stumbled, and then without really thinking about it, joined the fray.

The heavy concrete and steel road divider that I had been standing by jerked sharply and suddenly lurched into the air. I lost balance and fell hard. I tried to right myself, but was pressed down by others, like a surfer who had just wiped out, only to get caught in an undertow. When I got over the shock I was found myself at the mercy of those around me.

I was floundering below a turbulent crowd that was attempting to yank a heavy road divider from its moorings. A lengthy section of the concrete and iron barrier, once broken free, was lifted and positioned to block the boulevard, rotated from its original east-west mooring to follow a north south axis. The heavy beam, made featherlight by hundreds of hands, was dropped to the ground with a thud, right in the path of the tank-like intruders.

Once I regained my footing, thanks to the attentive assistance of the two young men closest to me, I joined the crowd of workers in its tug of war. We heaved-ho over and over until the divider was repositioned to better block the boulevard. We moved it in slow increments, like the jerking second hand on an old clock, moving, resting, moving, resting. Whose idea it had been was impossible to say, for nobody was really in charge. No one had told me what to do either, for that matter; rather, it was instinctive, a collective move to slow the arrival of hostile invaders. I doubted it would seriously deter the movement of army vehicles such as the ones we saw buzzing the crowd, but taking fate into one's hands and doing something felt better than doing nothing.

By the time we had the concrete barrier in place, the offending vehicle had moved on, disappearing from view somewhere to the east, and the people around me breathed a collective sigh of relief. Only after the intense and immediate sense of danger had subsided did those around me realize, or have the time to react to, the unusual fact that there was a foreigner on their team. Several sweaty men in T-shirts, massaging their aching arms after the sudden bout of intense weight-lifting, beamed at me offering congratulatory handshakes.

"*Huanying ni!*"

"*Pengyou!*"

One man welcomed me, the other called me friend. As stilted as the exchange might sound, their words moved me, almost to tears. The verbal embrace was at once nostalgia-inducing and reassuringly real. But I didn't have time to linger with my newfound comrades, to lose myself in the horde. I had to find the BBC crew.

When I found them, I was breathless with the news of my exciting encounter. "Did you see that tank? It was crazy. I can't believe the way that tank went speeding through the crowd!"

"That was not a tank, Phil," Simpson crisply corrected. "That was an APC, an armored personnel carrier."

"Well, whatever it was, it nearly killed a few people," I said, gesticulating wildly. "It was speeding through the crowd like crazy." Although Simpson had been only about a hundred yards away, he had seen it differently.

"Perhaps it was sent in to survey the crowd," he said, in keeping with his unruffled demeanor.

"I think we should have an emergency plan," I suggested. "Like if something happens. Let's go over by Mao's picture or some safe place like that."

"Phil, see if you can find some people to interview," Simpson suggested, trying to reestablish some control over the mutinous crew.

"No, John. We're going to do the standup from here," countered Clayton. "Ingo, Mark, are you ready?"

"I don't want to do that now!" Simpson snapped.

"This is not a news crew," she answered, "This is *Panorama*, and you, John, you are the presenter for this documentary."

I had to agree with Simpson. This was no time for a fuckin' standup.

As if still intoxicated by the red-blooded bonding and instant solidarity I had felt while moving in concert with the militant workers, I tuned the BBC out.

I craved to be with my Chinese friends, rooted in the land, in full possession of the moment. Even though there was a hint of terror in the chaos, there had been an almost preposterously joyous though highly irrational moment when time had stood still and I felt at one with a mass of unknown strangers, bonded by a primitive attempt to stop a tank.

Meng, who had been separated from me by the erratic movement of bodies when the APC came streaming through, had closely observed the roadblock incident from the other side of the divider.

"I saw that. They are taunting us," he muttered bitterly. "They are trying to break our will. They are trying to incite violence."

"So, what's next?" I asked, wanting to know, wanting him to have the answer.

"Nothing will happen, I think. The government is just trying to scare the people."

We backed away from the crew, scanning the swarming multitude for some indication of what might happen next. Suddenly Meng's face lit up in recognition of some familiar faces coming our way. Two women were walking their bicycles, weaving through the jumpy crowd in front of Tiananmen Gate. After negotiating the uppity throng gracefully, they parked their bikes next to the BBC's tripod as if it were a parking meter. Soon they were deep in a whispery conversation with Meng, pouring out words too fast for me to keep up with. I stood back, content to watch the beautiful, expressive faces of three people who knew each other well baring their souls in the subdued lamplight on the square.

"Jin Peili," Meng said, pulling me over, trying to include me, "these are my classmates. They study acting at the Central Drama Academy."

We all shook hands, exchanging smiles. Despite the unsettled and frighteningly murky outlook of the evening so far, time was becoming very malleable, and that languid moment was imbued with a poignant beauty. Ordinary life, as we had come to know it, was slipping away by the minute. Nothing would be the same; nothing could be taken for granted. Win or lose, the final showdown was at hand. Yet even with the despondent mood and the alert about violence breaking out to the west, the two drama students, vivacious and self-possessed, made me nostalgic for life in the peaceful hutong alleys around the drama academy, for the reassuring rhythms of daily ritual on a college campus, for the apolitical pleasures of life without fear.

How wonderful it would be if we could make all the bad stuff go away and just return to normal times and just hop on bikes and go off for a long ride into the night. Somewhere far from politics, somewhere far from Tiananmen.

"Blood has been spilled, the fighting has already started!" the one closest to me said. "We just came from Muxudi."

The other woman, still talking intently to Meng, was saying something about blood, about people being shot, adding ominously, "The army is coming this way now."

With the BBC crew now crowding around the actresses, I translated their whispery news updates from Muxudi, while conveying their request not to be interviewed on camera.

"We are leaving now," the one standing close to Meng said, smiling weakly.

"We must go tell the news to others," the one nearest me repeated for my benefit, looking at me with kindness, maybe even pity.

"Wait, where are you going now? It would be good if we could talk longer," I said, rambling on in Chinese, hoping to stretch the moment. I felt a flash of panic as they remounted their bikes, poised to put foot to the pedal. I ir-rationally feared their departure, as if with them went any chance of nor-malcy. It was as if the departure of Meng's muses would deal a body blow to the collapsing congregation, as if their withdrawal would diminish the very luck of those left.

Meng's two drama classmates, now perched on their bicycle seats, huddled in consultation about another urgent matter for another minute or two, the pale outlines of the Goddess of Democracy glowing behind the trio in the darkness. The night sky was absolutely black—no moon, no stars—limiting visibility. The Central Drama Academy classmates exchanged heartfelt farewells with a solemnity befitting an unknown outcome. It looked like Meng, the stoic hunger striker who had already courted death, was getting yet another send-off, only this time his journey was mine.

"Jin Peili!" the girl I had briefly commiserated with cried out in parting. "Be careful!" They pedaled slowly away, cycling east along the northern perimeter of the square. I stood shoulder to shoulder with Meng, watching their shadowy figures recede until they were swallowed up in the shadows between street lights.

I was suddenly overwhelmed with a sense of foreboding, the bitter pre-sentiment perhaps intensified by the pumped-up adrenaline coursing though me ever since joining the mob in erecting a tank-stopping barricade. Inex-plicably I was succumbing to a desperate longing for cycling in the moon-light, for the bright days of May, marching in the spring sunshine with friends and friendly strangers.

Nobody was sure what to do next, but the haunting words of a someone I had met during the rowdy drum performance celebrating the installation of the Goddess kept running through my mind: "To walk away is best."

"Where are you from?" she had asked, a surefire way to jump-start a friendly foreigner, interrupting my quiet conversation with Cui Jian, with whom I stood, watching with awe and wonder as the Goddess was unveiled. He had his fans and I had mine, and such interruptions were frequent, though mine were largely unearned.

"I'm from America, and you?"

"I'm Lina, from Beijing," the sociable middle-aged woman said. She had approached us on the southern side of the roped-off area where the structure, its name not yet formalized as the Goddess of Democracy, was wrapped in temporary tarps and scaffolding, getting its final touches. The neighborly plain-faced woman introduced me to her friends, mostly soft-spoken, self-effacing teachers in their late thirties and forties.

"My friends come from many different parts of China," she said. "We are intellectuals in support of the movement. After the death of Hu Yaobang we decided to support the students."

"Why?"

"Hu was a good man," she said. "And he did such a great job as the head of our school!"

"What school is that?" I asked.

"Why, the Communist Party Cadre School of course!" she said, "We are all from the cadre school."

"This is illegal, isn't it? I mean, you know, martial law?"

"We are not afraid," Lina said on behalf of her associates. "We are teachers and researchers. Being here is our responsibility."

The topic turned to the Cultural Revolution. Lina and her friends, unlike the current crop of student protesters, who were just toddlers at the time, were old enough to remember that topsy-turvy and tumultuous period clearly. Among themselves they commenced to speak animatedly about the tragic fate that befell many party members back then. Dunce caps, cowsheds, loyalty dances, banishment, and suicide. The violence was not so much committed by the state; rather, the state had first provoked things, then withdrawn precipitously, stoking populist passions and allowing persecution and humiliation to follow. The radicals riled up the masses and then let them fight it out. Lina abruptly asked me if I had ever heard of a man named Deng Tuo.

"He was a writer, persecuted in the early sixties, wasn't he?"

"Yes. Deng Tuo was my uncle. So you see, I must be here tonight. We must stand witness."

It touched me to see, hovering tentatively at the foot of the Goddess of Democracy, these party members, repentant Red Guards, making a modest show of support for the students. They knew better than anyone that political frictions could release ideals like a genie from a bottle, all but impossible to control. But as teachers of communism, they also knew that idealism was an integral part of communism.

Lina tightly clutched a book in her left hand. Twenty years ago it would have been the sayings of Chairman Mao. What was she reading?

"Oh this? It's the *Thirty-sixth Strategem.*"

"Something from *San Guo, The Three Kingdoms,* isn't it?"

"Yes, it's also a philosophical guide. Do you know what the thirty-sixth stratagem is?"

"Tell me."

"If you face overwhelming odds, it is best to walk away," she said, pausing for a moment. "You must remember that!" she said in a motherly tone.

"I get it."

"Here, please read it for yourself," she said, handing it to me.

"Are you sure? I mean, like, you haven't finished reading it."

"I want you to keep it. Someday you can tell me what you think about it; my name and address are written inside the cover."

I found myself thinking of Lina as the mechanical groan of a heavy treaded vehicle could once again be heard, coming in from a distance.

Zou wei shang ji, the so-called thirty-sixth stratagem, the wisdom of knowing when to walk.

Had the time come at last?

J U N E   3

Eve of Destruction

A dull grinding sound caused a collective shudder. The armored invaders were back, clawing across the thickly peopled pavement, heading our way. The ominous rumble and thunder brought an instant and unceremonious end to John Simpson's hasty on-camera introduction to Tiananmen Square. We scrambled to the side of the road for safety—sticks, camera, lights, and all. Due to the sudden escalation of tension, the "according-to-instructions-from-London" argument was abandoned.

An armored personnel carrier careened in from the east, hurtling down the Boulevard of Eternal Peace with the abandon of a drunk driver. The square's lampposts provided as much shadow as light, making accurate estimates of trajectory and distance difficult. Like its reckless predecessor, which had buzzed the crowd along the central concrete divider, this metallic vehicle tended to veer off to the side as if out of control, oblivious to or scornful of the many people in its path. Self-appointed vanguards snapped into action again, daring the vehicle to head towards them, dodging it when it did, and pounding the vehicle with bare hands as it rolled by, like cavemen taunting a giant armor-plated dinosaur.

Armed only with chunks of broken concrete and makeshift spears, iron poles extracted from the broken road divider, men and women in the path of the beast focused weeks of pent-up anger and frustration on the green monster that dared to violate the sovereignty of the people's square. For a while, the sheer pluck, reckless taunting, and almost superhuman willpower of the demonstrators seemed to have the desired effect. The rumbling sound faded and the hated armored vehicle disappeared from view.

This time I was not so much with the throng as a witness to it, and the relative objectivity that afforded me prompted me to join the crew in a cautious retreat to the sidewalk on the north rim of the square. The camera crew took a moment to catch their breath and scan the open plaza for danger, then swiftly mounted the camera on its tripod, facing the center of the square. The raised curb offered a slight degree of protection, if only psychological, in contrast to the open road. Within minutes, the camera was rolling.

As the throngs around us grew thicker, even the newest member of the crew became the object of unwanted attention. Wang Li, whose plan to impersonate a British citizen offered him no meaningful protection in this context, was being roughed up and elbowed, causing him to struggle with the gear and drift off target. The lights bobbed left and right, up and down, drawing even more attention.

Some of the background faces caught inadvertently in the light were macabre and frightening. We were floundering, blinded by our own lights, illuminating ourselves as a target. The peripheral location we had retreated to was thick with rabble of a different caliber from those close to dedicated demonstrators near Han Dongfang's worker outpost. Here on the edge, there was no sign of the brave workers manning barricades, or gentle students urging restraint, or clean-cut marchers singing "The Internationale," nor even the idly curious onlookers.

The May Fourth spirit was gone, replaced by something murky and malevolent. There was a new element I hadn't noticed much of before, young punks decidedly less than studentlike in appearance. In the place of headbands and signed shirts with university pins they wore cheap, ill-fitting polyester clothes and loose windbreakers. Under our lights, their eyes gleaming with mischief, they brazenly revealed hidden Molotov cocktails.

The unsung heroes who had kept the peace for over a month could retroactively be appreciated by their disconcerting absence; at best, student types were in scant evidence this night. Instead there were warriors with agendas unknown pressing in on us. No overt hostility was directed at the crew per se, but the anger and seething lust for violence was palpable. Our lights, in this dark and troubling hour, seemed to attract all species of insect.

"Turn off the lights!" I yelled at Wang Li. "This isn't working, turn off the lights! We better get out of here!"

Who were these punks in shorts and sandals carrying petrol bombs? Gasoline was tightly rationed; they could not have come up with these things spontaneously. Who taught them to make bottle bombs and for whom were the incendiary devices intended?

Lights still blazing, Ingo started shooting from the hip to capture some pictures of the provocateurs. The noose of spectators tightened.

Lights out, the shoving match subsided. But the troublemakers lingered, smiling inappropriately as they stared at us. Frustrated, I led the crew to the most obscure and least crowded spot I could find, the moat by the massive outer wall of the Forbidden City. Not surprisingly, we were jeered for making an apparent retreat.

"Look, foreigners! Ha, ha!"

"What are they doing there?"

"The foreigners are scared!"

"Hel-lo? Where are you going?"

"They don't care about China!"

"Cowards!"

"They are running away!"

Some of the comments sounded like veiled threats. I pretended not to understand in order not to have to react. We were not running away, but I didn't owe them an explanation. The technical requirements for a well-lit interview were hard to meet under such agitated conditions.

Could the mass yet turn on us? Were we dealing with rational individuals or an irrational collective? How could one possibly distinguish good from bad in such a vast gathering of people? We walked with our heads down in silence, a solemn file of five Caucasians and two Chinese. Finally we set up the tripod and camera next to some trees alongside the majestic vermilion wall lining Worker's Park on the northeast corner of the square. On the other side of the wall was a potential sanctuary, the entrance courtyard to the Forbidden City.

The relatively secluded location gave us about a minute to tape before things got out of control again. There were ogling onlookers as before, but the random mix of townspeople in our new location was less implicitly threatening than the Molotov cocktail gang. When things got tight, merely switching the lights off sufficed to relax the stranglehold of the instant gaggle that coalesced around us.

Looking at the indecision and fear on the strange faces watching us, I felt we were much alike in our unspoken desperation, looking to one another for cues on how to act, grasping at straws in the wind trying to figure out what was going on. Given the communal uncertainty, it was easy to understand how an incandescent circle of light on a dark plaza might be mistaken for a meaningful vortex of activity.

While Simpson brushed his hair, Clayton made notations on her producer's sheet, Ingo unwrapped his camera, Wang Li fumbled with the lights, and Mark readied the sound gear, I would try to explain to the usual knot of people closing in on us what we were doing in order not to excite too much attention.

"We are the BBC, English television, we're just doing a random interview, please step back, we appreciate your cooperation, thank you."

In no time at all, interviewer became interviewee.

"What do you think will happen?"

"What information do you have?"

"How many killed at Muxudi?"

While I was trying to cope with such questions, Simpson shouted that another APC was heading our way. Everyone dropped what they were doing, immobilized by fright, as the green monster bore down upon us. As before, the horde parted only reluctantly from the path of the careening vehicle, and as before not a second too soon, leaping away left and right, defiant till the last possible moment. The BBC crew swiftly backed onto the sidewalk, wisely regrouping behind some trees that offered a modicum of protection. The threatening vehicle then lurched to the left, veering away. Assuming a westerly direction on a boulevard still awash with demonstrators, the treaded APC, dull gray-green under the streetlights, headed straight for the highway divider that I had helped lift, rotate, and reposition in the middle of the road.

Encountering chunks of concrete and rubble on the ground, the vehicle, unsteady in its trajectory to begin with, slowed down. When it did, it was mercilessly bombarded with a volley of metal poles and rocky chunks from the broken railing. Everyone around me was reaching for the ground to pick up something, anything, in his or her hands. Time kicked into slow motion. When another APC careened down Chang'an Boulevard, I was possessed by the hot roar of the crowd to pick up a rock from the curb by the tree and leap out into the street in concert with a hundred others.

Before I knew what I was doing, a walnut-sized rock left my hand and joined the barrage of homely missiles hurled at the armored vehicle. In an instant too short for rational thought, I was transformed into a member of a tribe, a complete and utter partisan for the movement. The rock I had thrust hard into the black sky landed a few feet short of the target, hitting the APC weakly on a bounce. The rock-throwers around me smiled approvingly when they saw me cast the stone, but I was scared about what I was getting into. I stilled myself and shirked from further attack.

The collective power of hundreds of enraged men and women had surged right through me, causing me lose my autonomy. I needed to cool down, to collect my senses, in order not to act in such an autonomic way. So when the army of civilians leapt ahead, I checked my pace, moving forward with caution. When the horde shouted words of hatred, as if screaming for blood, I remained quiet.

Why did so many people choose to pursue the APC once it had safely passed? I watched the BBC crew move abreast of me, tenaciously following developments as the mob closed in on the errant vehicle. It made me proud to see the crew, Wang Li included, recording the chaos that was unfolding without flinching.

Then the hundreds of shoes hitting the pavement came to a sudden halt. A chorus of voices erupted in a primitive war cry. The monster had been stopped! People had stopped a tank with their bare hands!

That should have been enough, but the rabble, enraged and almost unstoppable now, raced like an arrow in flight, anxious to come down on target. The camouflaged vehicle was attacked on all sides. Angry fists and chunks of concrete had pounded against it without much effect, but one of the metal poles, strategically inserted, had gummed up the treads.

My pace quickened as I approached the stalled vehicle, infected by the toxic glee of the mob, but then I caught myself. Why was I rushing towards trouble? Because everyone else was? I slowed down to a trot in the wake of a thundering herd that was of one mind. Breaking with the pack, I paused to summon up the concentration necessary to free myself from the unspoken imperative to follow others forward.

Oddly, I was reminded of the fanatical actions of sport fans after a big college football game, in particular an emotional Michigan–Ohio State contest in a stadium holding one hundred thousand people. When the time clock finally ran out after a tense game with emotions running high, tens of thousands of spectators poured onto the field, following some deeply felt tribal instincts, trampling several people in the process. I too rushed onto the field, mainly because everyone else did. But there are always those aggressive enough to distinguish themselves, even in a huge collection of people. Daredevils mounted the goal posts while others tried to pull the posts down. The goalposts came crashing into the assembled fans and bodies went flying, but miraculously nobody was seriously hurt. And that was just a football game.

If the hyped-up fans of "Team Democracy" got out of hand here on the square, there would be no stopping them. Shocked at how susceptible I was to such unthinking tribal behavior, I snapped out of the mass trance and backed off, looking for Meng and the others.

Despite my pacifist inclinations, it gave me a secret thrill to see a gang of men pound on the tank with bare hands. The treads of the APC had somehow gotten enmeshed with mangled poles from the road barrier. The engine whined, putting out hot smoky exhaust, but without traction, the wheels of the APC spun uselessly. The crowd-crushing machine, so terrifying a moment ago, was now as helpless and immobile as a beetle on its back.

Adrenaline raced through my veins. We had done it! We had stopped the monster! Meng found me and held my arm, getting more and more skittish as we watched. Someone tossed a Molotov cocktail, setting the APC on fire. Flames spread quickly over the top of the vehicle and spilled onto the pavement. The throng roared victoriously and moved in closer, enraged faces illuminated in the orange glow.

But wait, I thought, there's somebody still inside of that, it's not just a machine! There must be people inside. This is not man against dinosaur, but man against man!

Meng protectively pulled me away to join a handful of headbanded students who sought to assert some control. Expending what little moral capital his hunger strike signature-saturated shirt still exerted, he spoke up for the soldier.

"Let the man out," he cried. "Help the soldier, help him get out!"

The agitated congregation was in no mood for mercy. Angry, bloodcurdling voices ricocheted around us. "Kill the motherfucker!" one said. Then another voice, even more chilling than the first, screamed, "He is not human, he is a thing."

"Kill it, kill it!" shouted bystanders, bloody enthusiasm now whipped up to a high pitch.

"Stop! Don't hurt him!" Meng pleaded, leaving me behind as he tried to reason with the vigilantes. "Stop, he is just a soldier!"

"He is not human, kill him, kill him!" said a voice.

"Get back, get back!" Meng started screaming at the top of his lungs. "Leave him alone, the soldiers are not our enemy, the government is the enemy!"

The former hunger striker howled until his lungs failed him, his voice weak, raspy, and hoarse.

Meng's headbanded comrades descended on the stricken vehicle but were unable to placate vigilantes keyed up for action.

"Make room for the ambulance," one of the students yelled. "Please cooperate, please step back!"

I watched from twenty to thirty feet away as the students tried to extract from the burning vehicle the driver who had nearly killed them. He had trouble walking. He appeared to be injured and in serious pain, but the quality of crowd mercy was uneven.

"He's not a person, he's a thing, kill him!" voices continued to shout out. Hotheads were deliberately instigating violence, putting them at odds with conscientious demonstrators who had no intention of hurting anyone.

The assembly surrounding the armored vehicle shared a paroxysm of joy in stopping it, but was of more than one mind about what to do next. At least one surrendering soldier was safely evacuated to a waiting ambulance, but then the ambulance itself was attacked, the back door almost ripped off by protesters determined to punish the man in uniform. Up until now, the volunteer ambulances were symbols of the movement's caring side, carting collapsed hunger strikers away from Tiananmen to hospitals for physical restoration. Until this night, city ambulances, plying slowly through the pack with that familiar, almost reassuring up-and-down wail, had been sacrosanct and untouchable.

A man with a metal pipe smashed the rear of the ambulance, breaking the taillight. Two or three other men pounded on the back door demanding that the limp body of the soldier be handed over. The driver desperately begged the vigilantes to leave the injured man alone, to let him be taken to the hospital. The back door of the ambulance swung open and the injured soldier was about to be extracted for a bout of "people's" justice when the vehicle lurched forward and raced off in the direction of the Beijing Hotel. Student traffic directors trying to impose a semblance of order did their best to hold back those seeking blood, just barely allowing the ambulance to escape.

So it had come to this. The dream was over, people were killing each other. The mutual restraint, one of the things I admired so much about all parties in this monumental conflict of wills, was breaking down.

The students had lost control, the crowd had started cracking, and the movement was breaking up into splintered mobs. There were calls for cooperation and shouts for vengeance. The blood thirst made me nauseous.

Meng was distraught. "Don't use violence!" he yelled, straining his voice to persuade anyone who would listen. "Don't fight!" he cried hoarsely, over and over. But whipped up into a state of true turmoil, few cared to listen.

The ambulance was gone; the APC was now a flaming hulk, billowing black smoke that masked the sky. The ghoulish glow of distant fires—one could only imagine what might be going on elsewhere—reinforced the gloom of this moonless night.

The BBC crew reassembled, shaken but unhurt. Before we could gather our wits, however, the sky was suddenly pierced with red shooting stars.

"What in the world?" I had never seen anything like it before.

"Tracer bullets," shouted Simpson. "We better get out of here!"

The red traces of speeding projectiles crisscrossed Chang'an Boulevard. The cracking sound of gunfire was steadily audible in the distance. The now seething mass was not easily intimidated, and became only further enraged. Empty-handed civilians cursed the government, venting violent epithets.

I looked at the anguish in Meng's face, tears welling in his eyes.

"This is no longer a student movement," he said. "This is . . . " He paused, fists clenched with rage, face pained with resignation. "This is a people's uprising."

As the fighting worsened, with gunfire close by, I had to physically drag Meng, so reluctant was he to leave the street, towards the Beijing Hotel for shelter. There he joined the BBC crew, along with Wang Li and myself, in room 1413 to sit out the lethal madness. Patricia, in fear of the police roaming the hotel, joined us shortly afterwards.

The Beijing Hotel was no longer a safe haven. "What are you doing here?" one of the guards had barked at Meng as we crossed the threshold. In our haste we had failed to notice that the gatekeepers were in place again, guard posts fully operational.

"He's with me!" I answered firmly. Not wanting to get stuck at the guarded elevators, I had to take Meng by the arm, treading away from the heavily monitored entrance into the long red-carpeted corridor ringed with dimly lit lobby lounges. The guards did not follow us, so we first lingered there, taking comfort in the incongruous fact that the deserted coffee lounge was still operational. We gathered up an armful of yogurts and soft drinks for the crew and went up to 1413 by a less guarded passage.

From my balcony high above Chang'an Boulevard, we surveyed the horizon. It looked like nothing less than war as I had imagined it as a child: fire and flares in every direction. Burning vehicles emitted an oily smoke that funneled upward, linking with its long black columns the murky sky and the ground. Screams and gunfire could be heard almost directly below. More distant cries and rumbles were intermittently carried by the breeze. Tracer bullets fired from somewhere across the street arched upwards along a parabolic path and fell behind the hotel. The frequency of gunfire intensified.

We watched in stunned silence as the tanks rolled in. We heard sporadic gunfire all night long. Someone said a few shots hit the room next door. Police started to patrol the hotel corridors, going door to door on inspection. We hid our videotapes in a ceiling vent and passed a fitful, fearful night together, taking turns watching from the porch, like one big dysfunctional family thrown together by crisis.

Patricia cried quietly, Jenny Clayton read a book, Wang Li lay sprawled out on the carpet, Meng kept to himself. Simpson and I spent most of the time on the porch with Ingo and Mark, who tried to get some footage in the low light, camera lens trained on the northern rim of Tiananmen Square. We could not determine what was happening there, and the base of the monument, where students were gathered, was blocked from view by the museum, but we saw smoke and heard gunfire throughout the night.

We couldn't see much; it was too dark, we were too high, too far away, and even through the telephoto lens not much detail could be worked out, not in the direction we wanted to see, Tiananmen Square. But the detritus of battle could be observed below, right in front of the hotel: smoldering clouds of tear gas, burning vehicles, repeated gunfire, bloodcurdling screams, fallen bodies, hasty civilian evacuation of those injured, some rushed away on carts. There was a body placed face down on a cart, shirt back oozing with blood. Why were people being shot in the back?

Lotus called me several times from her suburban outpost with shocking but unsubstantiated reports, mostly gleaned from her satellite dish–fed TV. It was tempting to think one could just turn on the TV and find out what was happening, but from what she was telling me, the newscasters didn't know what was going on. TV news relied on people like us, who had been on the streets with cameras, who remained near the scene, to fill in what happened. There was no satellite transmission going out and would be none. The BBC's tapes would have to be smuggled out of the country before anyone could see a bit of what we saw.

I called Bright. She was safe and sound, but choked up, not at all talkative. She said she'd heard that the fighting was fierce and the casualties were heavy outside the square, with "several hundred dead." She was glad to hear I was back in 1413 and all but commanded me to stay inside.

I dialed another friend whose father was a retired member of the politburo. The phone rang a long time before it was answered.

"No one's here now," answered a familiar voice. It was the family nanny from Anhui; she had a distinct regional accent. She immediately recognized my distinct "regional" accent as well. "How are you?"

"Is anyone home?"

"They were here before," she said, hesitating as if unsure how much to reveal. "They went to a meeting."

"Where?"

"I can't say."

"What's happening out there?"

"They said about three hundred people were killed, but don't worry, everything's under control."

"Three hundred?"

"That's all."

"What do you mean that's all? Where is everyone now?"

"I'm not clear about that."

"Take care."

I put down the phone and sat in quiet meditation. Three hundred dead, with tanks still rolling down the street and volleys of gunfire still rattling the night.

By the time dawn broke, the people's army had shot its way through the streets of Beijing and taken control of Tiananmen Square. How many people died to save that big empty piece of concrete and stone?

One of the wall posters I had seen on campus a month earlier turned out to be eerily prophetic. It was a florid poem, submitted anonymously on May 5 by someone who signed as "the wild one": "Drawing blood on Chang'an Jie until the dawn dawns red, smashing to bits the bona fide dream of the people."

With the first inkling of dawn comes a light rain, damping the metallic stench of the cordite-scented air, but insufficient to cool a city in flame.

"Even the sky is crying," Meng declares, staring vacantly in the distance.

"It's dangerous," I warn him, tugging on his sleeve. "Come on in."

"I don't care."

"Don't be crazy, I care, we care," I implore. "Please, come in!"

"Let them come and get me," Meng swears under his breath. "I'll fight to the end!"

I grab him by the arm, but he refuses to budge. Finally I have to drag him off the porch.

"Xiao Meng! Get inside, it's too risky out there."

"I want to die tonight. My friends are dying," he answers. "I want to die!" After dragging him inside, I close the porch door and the curtains.

"I don't care if the police come, they won't take me without a fight . . . "

The unsettled dawn of June 4 brought not hope but more despair as the vestiges of a night of horror became evident. Blood on the street, bodies being rushed to the hospital on flatbed bikes, civilians taunting soldiers, soldiers bullying civilians, buses burning, barricades smashed to bits under the weight of the mighty column of tanks that had passed in front of our hotel and now guarded the square.

The dream of changing China died on a night of no moon.

The sun rose and shone briefly.

And then it started to rain again.

JUNE 4

◑

The Sky Is Crying

At a time when I was busy hand-carrying videotapes from the Beijing Hotel to the BBC office on foot, tapes hidden under clothing to avoid getting questioned in the soldier-controlled streets, a memorable photograph and related video footage were taken from my room and several other south-facing rooms in the Beijing Hotel of a man standing in front of a tank. When I viewed the footage on a video deck a short time later, it did not strike me as being important or in any way extraordinary. By then the square had been emptied and the fighting had died down. The tanks, though terrifying to countenance, had not fired even once, and at that particular instant were in slow retreat from the square.

Countless acts of resistance abounded at the time and the man in front of the tank was just one of many. Later I could appreciate the power of the image, a singular man staring down an almost immobile tank, but it paled in comparison to the memory, still fresh but already seared in my mind, of a hundred men stopping a speeding tank with their bare hands.

Wang Li did furtive errands for the BBC a few days more, then took the money and ran all the way to Hong Kong. Before I said good-bye to Meng, who insisted on remaining in Beijing, we traded shirts. He gave me his autograph and sweat-stained "1989 Democratic Tide" shirt, his Central Academy of Drama pin, and his headband in exchange for a set of clothes less likely to make him a target.

By even the most conservative reckoning, hundreds of people died that night, mostly on the outskirts of the square. China television made no secret of the fact that in other big cities where there had been rioting and unrest, many were arrested, with a few poor souls executed as an example to scare others.

Chai Ling and Feng Congde went underground. I heard that Crazy Zhang was shot three times but survived. Thousands of youthful protesters were imprisoned in the "white terror" that followed, but particularly harsh accusations were directed at older teachers, writers, and activists such Dai Qing, Wang Juntao, Han Dongfang, Chen Zemin, Chen Xiaoping, and Liu Xiaobo. Hou Dejian, the idealistic musician who had written the unofficial anthem for a united China, was unceremoniously put on a boat to Taiwan. Wang Dan, who did not fancy life on the run, returned to Beijing from Wuhan and got locked up in the notorious Qincheng Prison. Deposed party chief Zhao Ziyang lost all power and lived out his life under house arrest, though he was permitted to travel sometimes, and even play golf. Less prominent Tiananmen demonstrators, including most of my friends from Shida, escaped reprisal by keeping a low profile, putting their ideals in their pockets, and going back to school.

Eventually the Chinese government would acknowledge a death toll in the hundreds, a still-disputed figure, while the estimate most routinely offered by the Western press gradually went from "thousands" to "hundreds," or, hedging it, New York Times fashion, "hundreds, maybe thousands." The minimum number of casualties documented by hospital visits, body counts, photographic evidence, and testimony gathered by relatives of the slain led by the remarkable Ding Zilin is at least several hundred dead, which accords with chilling early reports I got while the fighting was still going on. Given official neglect and twenty years of incrimination, whitewash, and denial, the full toll may well be higher, but it will never be precisely known.

But the essence of the crime remains the same: it was grievously wrong to turn weapons against people who had none. Different government factions had each been trying to wrong-foot the other, and a clampdown was expected, but the gratuitously violent crackdown was indefensible.

But there is also a sense in which it was not as much any individual as a dysfunctional system that was to blame, a system that time and again devoured its own, though never to the extent of turning its guns on civilians in the capital. To pin the blame on structural problems may not be as emotionally satisfying as sticking it on a recalcitrant Li Peng or crooked Beijing party chief Chen Xitong or old man Deng himself, but to be fair, they were products, and victims too, of a flawed political system that created the conditions for the state terror. They acted with hubris, haughtiness, and the force of habit in a country that was founded on barrel-of-the-gun politics and has been wracked with periodic social convulsions ever since.

The foreign media was at times ill-informed and unduly self-referential, making mistakes in the heat of the moment, seeing a reflection of its own obsessions wherever it looked, but it had no real competition, and will have none, so long as the Chinese media has its hands tied. Reporters are only human, honest error is to be expected, and playing to the home audience is part of the TV game, so the swashbuckling pretensions and London-centric thinking that so vexed me while working for the BBC seem less important now.

But because the Western media ran so fast and so far with its basic narrative, a narcissistic, Manichaean construct which might be crudely expressed as "there are good and bad people in China and the good ones want to be more like us, democracy and Statue of Liberty and all," it has been difficult to convey a sense that Communist Party members were victims too.

Then there is the pernicious influence of what might fairly be called an anti-China narrative, composed of outright false claims, inflated statistics, and irresponsible treating of rumor as fact simply because the Beijing government lacks the ability and credibility to make valid counterarguments.

But why make such unsubstantiated claims when the unvarnished truth was sufficiently devastating, the question of who fired upon whom was never in dispute, and the courage of participants and witnesses never in doubt? It's as if Tiananmen Square, having caught the public imagination in a way that framed the event as bigger than life, demanded bigger-than-life stories of unthinkable perfidy, ranging from rape and massacre to rivers of blood. Beijing's penchant for information control is certainly complicit in this; rumors abound when facts are hard to come by, but that is hardly a green light for journalists and rights activists to run with rumors.

If anything, it appears that the Beijing government, itself so prone to exaggerate the centrality of Tiananmen in order to assert its legitimacy, actually took care to avoid killing on the square, while showing no such compulsion at other locations. Whether Tiananmen was kept "clean" out of awe, by order, or as the result of on-the-spot discipline, it speaks to the almost sacred nature of the space. But the square was bloodied, figuratively in the public mind and more literally by the drops of real blood from real killings committed just steps away.

Ever since, Beijing authorities have been doggedly insistent on using the square to stage feel-good PR events of the highest order; the black sky over Tiananmen must be obscured, but not the square itself. Consider the gala celebration of the return of Hong Kong, the celebration of winning the Olympic bid, the memorializing of the heroes of the anti-Japan struggle and the incessant, obligatory photo ops for diplomatic summitry. It's almost as if the regime wants to imprint as many new memories on the space as possible to suppress the old ones, though the effort often backfires.

Covering the 1998 Clinton presidential visit to Beijing I saw this first-hand. Endless ink was spilled over the official welcoming ceremony, with a bizarre twist: it was the Americans who were claiming the controversial event didn't take place on the square while the Chinese insisted it did. The White House side tried to sidestep the controversy by saying the salute was not held at the square but in front of the Great Hall of the People, just the kind of hairsplitting obfuscation that Beijing has made an art of.

Tiananmen is continually being scrubbed and reinvented; not just spruced up and cleaned of litter but also scrubbed of people, especially the "un-washed" masses, during sensitive political junctures and anniversaries.

The damage inflicted by the June 4 crackdown on the square itself was mostly symbolic, with tanks knocking over the Goddess of Democracy and cracking the marble steps on the pedestal of the Monument to the People's Heroes. Given the incessant cleanups, renovations, and replacing of flag-stones that once bore the weight of a million protesters, it starts to look like the obsessive washing of hands, as if the keepers of the square were trying to remove the oddly indelible stains that linger there.

Too much blood spilled on the ground at numerous locations where sol-diers shot and killed civilians, such as Muxidi, Liubukou, Fuxingmen, Nanchizi, and Jianguomen. But these peripheral intersections, linked to the square by Chang'an Boulevard, don't have the instant recognition or media resonance of Tiananmen.

Indeed, there is something about Tiananmen that captures the mind's eye. Even as an eyewitness to the outbreak of bloodcurdling violence, first on Chang'an Boulevard and later in front of the Beijing Hotel, I found myself thinking not of what was happening in front of my eyes but of what might be happening on the square, without realizing that it was probably safer to be on the square than near it. The tense but orderly evacuation of hundreds of stu-dents from their emotional last stand on the monument to the open streets south of the square on June 4, 1989, an exodus bravely negotiated by Hou Dejian, stands as evidence of that.

During the first year after the crackdown, when the whereabouts and wel-fare of vanished students such as Chai Ling were unknown, I defended her consistently, both out of concern for her safety while she was still "under-ground" and out of a lingering solidarity from a shared day on the run.

I was relieved to see her and Feng Congde emerge from hiding alive and kicking, and I met them in Paris shortly afterwards, where they were guests of President Mitterrand and his wife. And I was even secretly pleased to learn that the rapscallion Wang Li had escaped to Hong Kong by selling a bootleg copy of the May 28 interview, even though he had lied to me about it, claiming it had been stolen. And by a serendipitous coincidence, I was a Nieman Fellow at Harvard at the same time that Tiananmen veterans Chai Ling, Wang Dan, Wang Juntao, Gao Xin, and Chen Xiaoping were in Cambridge, a year that saw both Jiang Zemin and Wei Jingsheng visit campus as guest speakers.

As the producer of the single most telling, and by some accounts the most incriminating, videotape interview of the entire student movement, I have contributed, if only indirectly, as much to the dismantling of the myth of the valorous students as to the construction of that myth in the first place.

Chai Ling broke from the student party line during the May 28 interview to say things that were alarming, insightful, and provocative. Her unusual candor comes off as self-incriminating in some instances, but her awkward honesty has been unfairly used to lay too much blame on the students to my liking. Heated things were said in those heated times, including irresponsible things, but that was all part of a real-life dialogue, whereas the opaque, impersonal style she readopted once she was back in the fold of the student command center, as evidenced in her June 2, 1989, follow-up interview with me, mirrors the soul-stifling style of party-line rhetoric and propagandistic platitudes.

The story of how Chai Ling braved on and escaped with the help of high-up Chinese patrons and clandestine foreign support is hers to tell. She is indeed a complex character—her own words tell us as much, and she has much to answer for—but her remarkable prominence in the movement has to be understood in context of how little real power any individual possessed, a sense of which I have attempted to provide with my account.

To put it more emphatically, the crackdown was not the fault of the protesters. Certain hard-line elements of the government precipitated a bloody crisis by trying to manipulate unrest and then seizing control during a crescendo of tensions that almost exploded into civil war. The handful of individuals most culpable for the violence—the sycophants who fed distorted information to the paramount leader who then ordered a crackdown which was in turn carried out in a gratuitously cruel way by certain underlings— have evaded justice because of the residual power of their political cliques. The result is an odious and self-serving official silence.

For the Chinese government to acknowledge wrongs committed is, ultimately, as important as it is for Japan, for example, to acknowledge the truth of its war of invasion and pillaging of Nanjing, or America its debacles in Vietnam and Iraq.

But it is also wrong to say the Chinese government, in its entirety, was wrong. Blanket condemnations and blanket apologies obscure the fact that many "good" Communists did care about keeping the peace and found themselves in sympathy with the student protesters and civilians who joined in. This was evident from the start; children of the elite, teachers, researchers, intellectuals, party members, and at least some close associates of party chief Zhao Ziyang engaged in the protests with a passion. Perhaps even more remarkable is how ordinary workers and vendors and backstreet aunties and uncles all pitched in at one time or another to show their support of the striking students by providing food, transportation, security, and words of support. It looked, sounded, and felt like social and cultural renewal, a time-honored process with lauded historical precedent, such as the student demonstrations of May 4, 1919. As the movement became more radical, it also began to resemble Communist youth movements and associated political self-cleansing campaigns, most notably the Cultural Revolution, and by the end it had the hallmarks of a people's uprising.

The telltale dynamics of such deeply indigenous social dynamics were on plain display at Tiananmen Square in 1989, including the May Fourth–inspired marching, the pithy four-character slogans, the belief in rapid self-transformation, the sly shifting of the party line, the utopian idealism, the outreach between social classes, the crude stigmatization of the enemy, the appropriation of symbolic space and revolutionary symbols, and the students' reliance on their own version of the orthodox "blue skies over Tiananmen" rhetoric.

Inasmuch as the startling success of the hunger strike intimated that a new mandate of heaven might be in the offing, the stakes were high. But the incoherence and severity of the crackdown suggests a skittish and divided regime, not a monolithic one. The secretary general of the Communist Party of China famously opposed the crackdown, and of course was immediately demoted. Zhao Ziyang's refusal to turn guns on the citizens of Beijing, at the risk of his political career, was a bold stance, supported by at least some commanders of the 38th Army, and a laudable act of civil disobedience. More than a few people high in the Communist Party showed a felicitous concern for the striking students at the time. Part of the tragedy of Tiananmen is that hard-line minority opinion was intolerant of, and eventually prevailed over, more moderate majority views on both sides of the divide.

In any case, it was not crowds running wild that threatened China, or even heated student rhetoric, but entrenched power holders who did their best to play the crowd, and failing that, used the crackdown to carry out a putsch.

The U.S. evacuated its citizens, and other nations followed suit, not because of unruly protesters with headbands and banners, but in response to signs of conflict within the military at the highest level.

It has been suggested, by writer-activist Dai Qing among others, that martial law itself was an attempt to contain the hard-liners and avoid violence rather than lay the ground for it. Likewise, one could look at the Goddess of Democracy as a double-edged sword—a substitute for protesters on the square, allowing students to go home without further incident, or the ultimate provocation, staring down Mao, challenging Communism to the core. That sincere moves by each side were thwarted, misconstrued, or ignored by the other is part of what makes Tiananmen 1989 a tragedy of Shakespearean complexity.

Coming to terms with such a vexing domestic trauma is not easy and, alas, appears to have been put on hold indefinitely. The real problem now, as memories fade and young people grow up oblivious to an event that has shaped and constrained their lives whether they know it or not, is how to remember it. It is too easily dismissed as *liu si* or June Four, a shorthand term with controversial connotations, a tag that can't even begin to do justice to the remarkably peaceful, transformative, and uplifting weeks that preceded the crackdown. The challenge remains how to teach a chapter of the past that current power holders continue to deny, how to appreciate the good and bad of it, and, if possible, to draw appropriate lessons.

How should the hundreds of individuals who died that night, soldiers included, be remembered? How should the extraordinary courage of students, townspeople, and party members who struggled to redefine China under such punishing conditions be commemorated?

Accountability and transparency, even late in the day, can serve to heal. China wounded itself badly, dangerously betraying the trust between the people's army and the people, and all but severing the bond of consent between the government and the governed. After a remarkable month of mutual restraint, it took only a single evening to trample the dream of a generation, and in doing so, to tread precariously close to losing the mandate of heaven.

With so much time gone by already, the taboo of silence needs to be challenged, not to lay blame on the perpetrators, many already passed from the scene, but to move towards truth and reconciliation for the sake of the living.

Afterword

In the many years that have gone by since the eventful nights and days described in *Tiananmen Moon*, Beijing's central square remains a bittersweet haunt. From my earliest days in Beijing I liked the openness of the space, albeit in a naive and apolitical way before 1989, and sometimes still try to see it that way now. But each time I set foot on the square, memories rush in and I find myself looking for people around my age and wondering if they, too, might have been *there*. If they, too, might be out taking a nostalgic stroll, recollecting a vivid chapter of the past. On any given day, how many—if any—of the others were pilgrims who had been witness to, or maybe even taken part in, that remarkable yet unspeakable peaceful uprising?

Over a million people in Beijing alone were drawn into the gyre of demonstrating, whether out of principle, caught up in the excitement, out of sympathy, or in solidarity.

Among those people were a few friends of mine.

Bright, Jenny, and Lily remained in Beijing, as did Cui Jian and Liu Yuan. I went to Hong Kong to produce documentaries and eventually found work doing China programming at Japan Broadcasting Corporation (NHK) in Japan. Although I continued to write and produce on China, I did not return to Beijing for five years.

By the time I returned, I had completely lost touch with Bright, though I often wondered about her. Almost eighteen years to the day that she and I exchanged our hurried good-byes, I found her. I was writing in the lakeside cafe of a popular Beijing park and stepped outside to take a walk in the cool evening air. As with most parks in China, even today, there is minimal night-time illumination, and the people one passes in the night—joggers, couples taking a stroll, kids playing—appear more as phantasmal apparitions than recognizable countenances. As I treaded the tranquil, shadowy path, I saw the silhouette of a tall, thin woman in a long billowy dress. I knew her instantly; it took her a moment longer to recognize me.

"Is it you?" I asked. She froze, and then we both laughed. After getting over our mutual astonishment, we took a walk around the park, exchanging the normal directory details: when did you get married, how old are your kids, what kind of work are you doing, and who are you still in touch with. Before long a cascade of memory brought us back to 1989 during the height of the protests.

I asked her how she regarded the Tiananmen protests now, looking back.

"People say it was pointless, but it changed everything, didn't it?" she answered. "I mean, what we have today is because of what we went through then."

I wasn't so sure. If the upheaval at Tiananmen truly had a positive legacy, if it accelerated reform, indirectly made good things happen, why does it remain so difficult to talk about openly?

"Social stability is the key now," she answered. "We are not ready for democracy yet."

I sensed that her otherwise sensible and sensitive views had been obscured and overlaid with a veneer of the standard answer to the standard question. In China, stability is truly important, perhaps more so than elsewhere, due to the way things are set up and the way crowds run wild. She and I knew that all too well; we had once been part of such a crowd.

The next time Bright and I met, Jenny joined us. We sat together and pored through my snapshots of May 1989, over a hundred photographs that had been "lost" for nearly two decades, all that time inadvertently stashed away in a Japanese newspaper office, then discovered and returned to me by a sharp-eyed editor.

As we reviewed dated pictures of one another and dated pictures of the crowd, the past came rushing back and we began to share excited recollections about the drama of the day, that faraway time in recent history when young people took to the streets animated by hopes for political reform, and in doing so discovered a collective joy that has rarely been evident since.

People lived closer to the street back then—most homes had few comforts to offer and bicycles were a necessity—and it was possible, if only fleetingly, for pedestrians to take back the streets, something hard to imagine in today's car-choked Beijing.

The skies over the Beijing Olympics were not as blue as the authorities would have wished, but the inclement weather turned out to be a good time for reunions. Lotus, Albert, and their children were also in town, as were Shida friends I hadn't seen in years. I took Lotus to Liu Yuan's jazz club, and also to CCTV, where I often appear as a guest commentator on the current affairs show *Dialogue*. I heard news about Lily, who is doing well, and Meng, who has enjoyed a measure of success in his profession. Cui Jian remains a favorite minstrel.

Talking with old friends, the topic often drifted back to the China we once knew, the world before private phones and private cars, the world before red light bars and the real estate boom.

The Shida campus remained pretty much its old sleepy, shabby self for the first ten years after the failed uprising. Then, in the late nineties, it was drawn into the demolition and construction cycles coursing through Beijing and much of China. Commercial buildings and chain eateries began to encroach on the school grounds. But the first thing to go, way back in 1989, was the old hot water shack.

After I told U.S. journalist Ted Koppel that the hot water spigots served as a village well of sorts, he subsequently did a television standup introducing *Tragedy at Tiananmen* in front of the hot water shack on campus, suggesting, with just a touch of journalistic flair, that this was "where it all started."

Twenty years is a long time, more than a decent interval. China has moved on, all the while subtly haunted by that which it pretends to forget.

In trading political freedom for stability, great things have been accomplished, even while glaring injustices continue to go unrecognized and historical truths are reduced to whispers. The state-imposed apartheid-like system of separate and unequal hotels, shops, and residential compounds along with FEC and an unwieldy two-tiered economic system has been dismantled, and the Big Brother–like system of assigned jobs, assigned housing, and strictly monitored social relations has largely crumbled. But the nation's nouveau riche, typically party members dabbling in business or businessmen greasing the wheels of party politics, are finding ways to create new walled enclaves for themselves. Especially odious in the eyes of the sometimes feisty and relatively unfettered Beijing press are cold-hearted coal mine owners who gobble up pricey real estate with blood money and ill-gotten gains.

While new horrors are uncovered daily by the Chinese press, Internet bloggers, and academic researchers every day, whether it be corruption, or the lack of a safety net, or the poisoning of the environment, much good has come from the industry and discipline of the Chinese people in recent years.

One night during the 2008 games, I entered the magically illuminated Olympic Village with tickets to attend a track-and-field meet with my family. The event was held at the monumental but architecturally intimate Bird's Nest stadium on August 15. Seated in a mostly hometown crowd of over one hundred thousand, I observed with satisfaction that the people most inconvenienced by the games, namely ordinary Beijing residents who had endured years of noisy, dusty round the clock construction, forced relocation, and drained public coffers, were there in abundance and enjoying themselves.

Indeed, I had not seen such a cohesive crowd in China since 1989, and while a sports stadium is a controlled environment and the spectacle is not political in any obvious way, it brought back a rush of memories. There's something wonderful about being surrounded by tens of thousands of cheerful, well-behaved people momentarily at peace with themselves and the world.

In 1989 the student-dominated crowd was composed mainly of what might be described as a nascent middle class, beneficiaries of the Communist regime, connected and confident enough to take to the streets in the first place. Likewise, there was a distinctly middle-class cast to those filling the rafters in the Bird's Nest, the toiling migrant workers and construction crews who sacrificed so much to make Beijing dazzle having mostly been sent out of town.

The plight of migrant workers in today's China is an uncomfortable reminder that the age-old Communist promise of a more equitable society, which briefly took wing during the height of the Tiananmen protests, only to be shot down, has been repeatedly frustrated since. Although leaders such as Hu Jintao and Wen Jiabao rightly seek social harmony, their best efforts have not been sufficient to stem increasingly harsh social disparities, especially in the countryside.

The Olympics were a resounding success, but in trying too hard to make them so, something was lost, too. It wasn't just migrant workers who were sent packing, or unsightly apartment facades that were whitewashed in order to make Beijing shine in August 2008. Nor was it just the color of the skies that was modulated, nudged from gray to blue with a little help from silver iodide cloud-seeding rockets, for the authorities were busy modulating information flow as well. China pulled the curtain on vital civil debate with a near-complete media clampdown on touchy issues such as Tiananmen and the more recent problems in Tibet.

China is, at best, at an uneasy peace with itself. Thousands of small disturbances and medium-sized demonstrations break out across the vast terrain of the People's Republic every month. Some target police stations or torch luxury cars, others result in violent pitched battles, growing out of frustration about pollution, stolen wages, police abuse, and land disputes.

As in 1989, many ordinary citizens are enraged by corruption, nepotism, rights denied, and freedoms curtailed, but for the moment, only pitchfork uprisings in remote areas are tolerated, and then only barely so. The party has clearly learned tactical lessons from its past mistakes, even if it doesn't admit to committing them. Protest is quickly nipped in the bud where possible, though it may be allowed to simmer or even play itself out in places where core party interests are not at stake.

It is possible to live in Beijing and feel very far from such things, given the physical and social gulf between the city and the countryside and the compartmentalized nature of a society which seems to put up a new wall every time it tears an old one down. Where the Chinese-foreign divide was once clumsily governed by FEC scrip and friendship hotels, now only a stoked-up Han chauvinism is required to put individual Chinese at odds with others, be it minorities, such as the Tibetans, or things French, if that be the flavor of the week, while Japan's historical crimes and American interventionism are two big perennial bugbears that can be trotted out on a moment's notice.

Given the ways nationalism has been manipulated, exploited, and occasionally let to run out of control in recent years, a case in point being the anti-Japanese demonstrations, it was necessary in 2008 for Beijing newspapers to run sports etiquette supplements just in case the zeal for team China got out of hand.

The crowd around me in the Bird's Nest did lose it briefly, albeit in a good-natured way, when a Chinese athlete snagged an unexpected gold medal, and flag decals and patriotic red shirts were much in evidence. The incessant emotional venting of the excited crowd that night, one hundred thousand hurrahs, reminded me of the muddied line between a crowd and a mob, between collective joy and communal terror.

As before, I admired the ability of Beijing citizens to be so composed in the midst of so much agitation and retain their individuality in the midst of so many others, even when standing up on cue to do "the wave." There were thousands of young volunteers drawn from Beijing universities to act as facilitators, directing the crowd, enforcing rules, trying to keep the peace, as if appropriating and reprising the role played by the headbanded student organizers in 1989. Despite the general effectiveness of such gentle social engineering, I found it possible to talk my way past guards from front-row field-side seats to the highest row of the upper grandstand, a reminder that the cachet of a foreigner speaking Chinese is not completely a thing of the past. Nowadays many more foreigners speak Chinese, and indeed are expected to.

Earlier in the summer, I had published an essay entitled "August Moon over Beijing," noting that the rising and falling cycles of the moon had corresponded with the changing mood of the crowd in 1989, and wondering whether the Beijing Olympic Committee's request to move the Olympic start date to August 8 might not boost morale, as it allowed for the full moon to reign over the height of the games.

Unfortunately for the Beijing Olympic Committee and Zhang Yimou, maestro of the lavish opening ceremony in the open-air stadium, a prolonged, uncharacteristically wet spell hit North China, enveloping the city in fog (almost invariably described as pollution by the journalists with an attitude), and light rain fell nearly every day during the first week of competition. So if the moon was on the rise, there was little occasion to see it, other than as a smudgy white glow smothered by cloud cover.

While walking in the long shadows of the late afternoon sun along the central axis of Beijing that runs from the Olympic grounds to Tiananmen Square, passing through the Drum and Bell towers, Jingshan Park, and the Forbidden City along the way, it struck me that the feng shui of the lavish Olympic grounds served as an answer to Tiananmen Square, a counterweight of sorts, making it a contender to be the new people's plaza.

The Bird's Nest track-and-field events ran from sunset to midnight. Given the excitement of seeing the fastest men and women on planet earth run around the track, I had forgotten about the moon.

During an interval in the intense competition, I went outside and took a walk around the inspiringly convoluted contours of the new stadium, illuminated largely in red, while admiring the contrast of the adjacent swimming cube, which was glowing a bright blue. As I neared completion of one full circumambulation, going counterclockwise around the stadium, I looked up and abruptly realized I wasn't alone.

A full moon was on the rise in the east, illuminating the new people's plaza with an old familiar glow.

Philip Cunningham
Beijing

About the Author

Philip J Cunningham is a professor of media studies at Doshisha University in Kyoto. A native of New York, he studied Asian history and languages at Cornell and the University of Michigan before moving to Asia, where he has worked ever since. Film and television credits include *The Last Emperor*, *Empire of the Sun*, *Changing China*, *Tragedy at Tiananmen*, and *China Now*. A Nieman Fellow at Harvard University and a Fulbright researcher in Tokyo and Beijing, he writes on politics for the *Japan Times*, *Los Angeles Times*, *International Herald Tribune*, and the *Bangkok Post*. He is working on a new book as a visiting fellow at Cornell University.

ASIAN VOICES
A Subseries of Asian/Pacific/Perspectives
Series Editor: Mark Selden

For more books in this series, go to www.rowman.com/series